SPELLING

DICTION

EFFECTIVE SENTENCES

THE RESEARCH PAPER

A Brief Handbook of English

Third
Edition

A Brief Handbook of English

Third Edition

Hulon Willis
Late of Bakersfield College

Enno Klammer
Eastern Oregon State College

Harcourt Brace Jovanovich, Publishers **HBJ**

San Diego   New York   Chicago   Atlanta   Washington, D.C.
London   Sydney   Toronto

Preface

Significant improvements occur in this Third Edition of *A Brief Handbook of English*, but the original purpose remains intact: to serve as a concise reference guide to usage and grammar for beginning writers. The Third Edition avoids exhaustive analyses and subtle options in various aspects of usage that often serve more to confuse than to enlighten. This textbook concentrates on the writing problems most troublesome to students and gives simple, straightforward statements of acceptable strategies. Its primary goal is to help beginning writers improve the clarity, conciseness, and correctness of their writing.

Although this Third Edition has been thoroughly revised, its format remains essentially unchanged. Chapter 1, a reference book within a reference book, is a brief survey of the basic system of English grammar—brief enough to serve as a review for students who have had previous instruction, yet complete enough for the novice to profit from such study.

The remaining seven chapters of Part One treat writing problems that are closely related to an understanding of grammar. Frequent cross-references to Chapter 1 appear throughout this section as well as in the entire handbook. A list of grammatical terms with page numbers appears on the back cover for fast, convenient reference to Chapter 1.

Part Two answers most of the questions students raise about punctuation and mechanics. Here, too, the directives are clear and forthright as they avoid the complexities of exceptions and variations. For example, the text simply states the rule that a comma is used to separate independent clauses joined by a conjunction. If a student inserts such a comma in one of the rare cases where it is not needed, no error is marked. But a full explanation of such options may simply confuse the student.

By relying more heavily on examples than on complicated explanations, Part Three makes clear some of the more common features of English spelling. Diction (Part Four) and Effective Sentences (Part Five) aim to help students make effective choices in appropriate word choice and style. This Third Edition closes with an elementary and thorough introduction to the library research paper.

Two chapters of the handbook have in particular undergone considerable revision. Chapter 1, "The Basic System of English Grammar," has been completely rewritten to make it more accessible to students, both in its content and in its arrangement. Chapter 27, "The Research Paper," now conforms to the *MLA Handbook for Writers of Research Papers,* Second Edition (1984), and provides a new sample research paper.

Many examples in the text are from students' writing; those that are not are nevertheless typical of problems that appear in student papers. Where students might be confused, examples are clearly labeled *wrong, right, poor style, better style,* and so on.

Two sections of the book may be called glossaries. Section 16g lists homophones—such as *course* and *coarse*—and other words often confused in spelling but not in meaning. Section 22b is composed of words often confused in meaning—such as *infer* and *imply*.

Both instructors and students will profit from use of the charts that appear on the back cover and inside the front and back covers of this textbook. Students can use the charts to troubleshoot their writing; instructors can use the charts to direct students to areas in which their writing needs improvement. Thus, the Third Edition provides an easy guide to solving writing problems. With a minimum of effort, students using the Third Edition can write more clearly and express themselves more concisely.

Contents

6   Subject-Verb Agreement   91

7   Shifts   101

PART TWO
Punctuation and Mechanics

10 The Comma   125

11 The Dash; Parentheses; Brackets; the Colon   138

PART THREE
Spelling

PART FOUR
Diction

PART SIX

The Research Paper

A Brief
Handbook
of English

Third
Edition

PART ONE

GRAMMAR

The Basic System
of English Grammar:
A Brief Introduction

Grammar is like a pattern or blueprint that guides us to an understanding of an entire system. A knowledge of the system of grammar can be as useful to you as is skill in reading a map or in following a diagram. The trail-wise hiker may not need a map to find his way, and the skilled craftsman may not need a diagram to complete his project. Their experience tells them where to go and what to do. In much the same way, experienced writers and speakers often do not consciously think of "grammar" (as it is explained in this chapter) to construct effective sentences. But when they need to talk about their activities and, if necessary, correct certain errors, they all go back to check their plans once more, for grammar is a map or diagram of the structure of language. In that sense grammar is an effective tool to help you construct correct and effective sentences.

You will need to be familiar with the **parts of speech** that form the language of grammar in order to benefit fully from this textbook, so a table with some brief definitions of the parts of speech and a few simple examples has been prepared

Table 1. The Parts of Speech: Form and Function

Form *(what a word looks like)*	Common Functions *(how a word is used in a sentence)*

Content words *(carry the bulk of meaning in our language; open classes)*

noun *(names a person, place, thing, or idea)*	subject *(performs an action)* object *(receives the action)* modifier *(describes or limits)* predicate noun *(renames the subject of a linking verb)*
verb *(an action or state of being)*	main verb -transitive verb *(with direct obj.)* -intransitive verb *(no direct obj.)* -linking verb *(with pred. noun/adj.)* auxiliary verb verbal
adjective *(modifies a noun, adj., or pronoun)*	modifier predicate adjective *(describes the subject of a linking verb)*
adverb *(modifies a verb, adjective, or adverb)*	modifier

Structure words *(provide the framework for sentences; closed classes)*

determiner *(marks a noun)*	determiner
preposition *(relates two words)*	preposition
auxiliary *(part of a verb)*	auxiliary verb
coordinator *(joins equal elements)*	coordinating conjunction
subordinator *(joins unequal elements)*	subordinating conjunction
pronoun *(stands for a noun antecedent)*	subject object modifier
qualifier *(limits an adjective or adverb)*	qualifier

See the back cover for page references for these grammatical terms.

for your convenience. Table 1 will help you grasp the general meaning of terms that may occur in the text before they are discussed in detail.

When we speak or write sentences, we arrange words in order. When we talk about sentences, we give names to those words. The names are assigned according to the **form** of the word (what the word looks like) and according to the **function** of the word (how the word is used in the sentence).

What you see in Table 1 may be quite confusing until you note how each word or group of words combines to express an idea. The sentence in Table 2 illustrates both the form and the function of words as they are used individually and in groups.

By FORM, words are classified as either **content words** (carrying the vast bulk of meaning in our language) or **structure words** (providing the framework within which the content words become meaningful sentences). The content words are called nouns, verbs, adjectives, or adverbs; these four parts of speech are referred to as **open classes** because new words (or new definitions of old words) are constantly appearing to expand the English vocabulary. The structure words are **closed classes** because new words rarely enter the parts of speech that we refer to as determiners, prepositions, auxiliaries, coordinators, subordinators, pronouns, and qualifiers.

By FUNCTION, a word can perform a variety of tasks. For instance, the word *stone* is a noun by its form (because it names a thing), but see how many ways the word functions in the following examples:

NOUN FORM: *stone*

   AS SUBJECT: A rolling *stone* gathers no moss.

   AS MODIFIER: The *stone* fence was mossy and tumbled.

   AS VERB: On Crete, they *stone* witches to death.

   AS OBJECT: Mike used a flat *stone* for the waterfall.

Table 2. Simple Sentence (one subject and one predicate)

			Subject (what you want to talk about)			
				Compound Subject		
FUNCTION:	Det.	Mod.	Subject	Coord. Conj.	Mod.	Subject
FORM:	The	big	house	and	its	yard
	Det.	Adj.	Noun	Coordinator	Poss. Pron.	Noun

Since this text is a reference book, you will not study its chapters in sequence. This introductory chapter contains definitions and examples of all of the basic terms used in this book; you may already know some or all of these terms, but as you review the chapter you will become more familiar with them. To assist you in returning quickly to a topic, the most important terms in Chapter 1 are listed alphabetically on the outside back cover with page references. You may also benefit from referring to the table of terms for brief definitions.

As you review the basics of English grammar in this chapter, you will be preparing yourself to understand the writing problems that are discussed in the rest of this book. This chapter may also be useful to you as you write; it may answer pressing questions or give you insights that will improve the quality of your writing. Think of Chapter 1 as a compact reference book within a larger reference book.

Now that a foundation has been laid, let us move into a detailed discussion of content words. With little effort, you will find that you are able to recognize the characteristics that identify the parts of speech that we call nouns, verbs, adjectives, and adverbs.

Comparing Form and Function of Words

Predicate							
(what you want to say about the subject)							
Future Tense Verb (Intransitive)				Prepositional Phrase			
Aux. Verb	Main Verb	Qualifier	Modifier	Prep.	Modifier	Modifier	Object of Preposition
will	grow	quite	slowly	on	this	construction	schedule.
Verb	Verb	Qualifier	Adverb	Prep.	Pronoun	Noun	Noun

1a   Content Words (parts of speech)

The greatest number of words in the English language are content words. These words are called **nouns, verbs, adjectives,** and **adverbs.** Our language is constantly expanding as new words enter these open classes, or as new definitions of old words are added to common usage. You can often identify content words by their forms, but their functions in the sentence make such identification more nearly certain.

Knowing that parts of speech may be classified by form and by function will help you use other chapters in this book profitably. Further examples of this dual classification appear in section 1f.

1a1   Nouns

A noun is the name of a person, place, thing, or idea. Such names as *student, city, book,* and *politics* are called **common nouns.** Names like *John, Seattle, Bible,* and *Democrat* are called **proper nouns** and begin with a capital letter. When you compare the words *city* and *Seattle,* you can see that the word *city* is a general name for a place and that the word *Seattle* is a specific name for a place. While common nouns are capitalized when they begin a sentence, proper nouns are capitalized wherever they occur in sentences (see Chapter 17).

any **r**iver	BUT	the Grande Ronde **R**iver
a **s**tatue	BUT	the **S**tatue of Liberty
an **o**cean	BUT	the Atlantic **O**cean

As they function in sentences, nouns appear as subjects, direct objects, indirect objects, predicate nouns, objects of prepositions, as well as appearing after determiners (like *the*, *a*, and *an*) as the following examples show.

| | Indirect | |
|Subject| Object | Direct Object |

The **men** gave **Helen** a standing **ovation.**

| After a | Object of | Predicate |
| Determiner | Preposition | Noun |

The   **girl**   in the **convertible** is a **princess.**

a. Plural nouns   Most nouns are singular in their base form (that's the form that you would look up in the dictionary); singular nouns name a single person, place, thing, or idea. The form of almost every noun changes when it becomes plural (names more than one unit) or when it becomes possessive (shows possession or ownership). This can pose a problem for a writer when a noun is both plural and possessive. Some examples of how to handle such form changes will show you how to approach such words.

Singular	Plural
one card	two card<u>s</u>
one string	two string<u>s</u>
one lamp	two lamp<u>s</u>
one woman	two wom<u>e</u>n
one child	two child<u>ren</u>

Some nouns do not change form in the plural, as shown in the following examples.

Singular	Plural
one sheep	two sheep
one fish	two fish
one deer	two deer

b. Possessive nouns   Possessive nouns require an apostrophe (discussed in Chapter 18), which must be placed correctly, as follows:

the girl's hat   [Only one girl had a hat.]
the girls' hats   [*All of the girls* had hats.]

Mr. Chase's car   [a singular possessive]
the Chases' anniversary   [*Both of the Chases* celebrated.]

the child's toy   [a singular possessive]
the children's toy   [*Several children* share the toy.]

c. Determiners   Determiners (subsection 1b1) can signal that a following word is a noun. The indefinite articles *a* and *an,* the definite article *the,* or possessives like *my, your,* or *John's* can introduce the phrase, and the noun is the last word in the phrase, as shown below:

a **light**	the tasty **sausage**
an **orange**	his ragged **jeans**
my **wallet**	your long, difficult **examination**
Fred's **guitar**	Julia's touching **devotion**

Intervening words like *tasty, ragged, long, difficult,* and *touching* should not keep you from understanding how *the, his, your,* and *Julia's* announce the presence of a noun.

d. Noun-forming suffixes   Adding word endings, or suffixes, to other parts of speech creates nouns. (Sometimes suffixes are added to nouns to make new nouns). Note that adding such **noun-forming suffixes** may change the spelling and the pronunciation of the original word. The following typical examples show the suffixes in boldface type:

mile + **age** = mileage
deliver + **ance** = deliverance
assist + **ant** = assistant
dull + **ard** = dullard
refer + **ee** = referee
brother + **hood** = brotherhood
just + **ice** = justice
magic + **ian** = magician
inflect + **ion** = inflection
liberal + **ism** = liberalism

social + **ist** = socialist
labor + **ite** = laborite
equal + **ity** = equality
achieve + **ment** = achievement
kind + **ness** = kindness
counsel + **or** = counselor
hard + **ship** = hardship
young + **ster** = youngster
deliver + **y** = delivery

In the previous list, there are no spelling changes; in the following list, note the spelling changes that occur as the suffix is added.

arrive + **al** = arrival
beg + **ar** = beggar
starve + **ation** = starvation
secret + **cy** = secrecy
wise + **dom** = wisdom
provide + **ence** = providence
reside + **ent** = resident
preside + **ency** = presidency

mine + **er** = miner
judge + **ment** = judgment
brave + **ery** = bravery
China + **ese** = Chinese
dissent + **sion** = dissension
introduce + **tion** = introduction
please + **ure** = pleasure

1a2   Verbs

The verb is the most complicated part of an English sentence; for your convenience, a table of verb terms (Table 3) is included for you to refer to as you familiarize yourself with verbs.

Verbs express action or state of being. Functioning as the main element in the predicate of a sentence, a verb tells what the subject is or does or what condition it is in. A verb can be classified as a **transitive verb,** an **intransitive verb,** or a **linking verb** according to what kind of structure follows the verb in the predicate.

TRANSITIVE VERB:
Howard always **took** a nap after lunch.   [Howard took

what? A nap. The word *nap* is the direct object of the transitive verb *took.*]

INTRANSITIVE VERB:

He **slept** peacefully.   [He slept *how?* Peacefully. The word *peacefully* is a modifying adverb, describing the intransitive verb *slept.*]

LINKING VERB:

His boss **became** somewhat distressed.   [The word *distressed* describes the subject *(boss)* and so it is a predicate adjective, following the linking verb *became.*]

a. Transitive verbs   A transitive verb is an action verb that takes a direct object—that is, the action of the verb is performed on someone or something. (In the following examples, the **verb is boldface** and the *direct object is italics.*)

Jerry **found** a *dollar.*   [Jerry found *what?* A dollar.]

The professor **taught** his *class.*

Mother **baked** *cookies.*

A photographer **took** our *portrait.*

b. Intransitive verbs   An intransitive verb does not have a direct object. It states that an action occurs or a condition exists.

Howard **is sleeping.**

Gloria **reads.**

I **studied.**

While certain words may follow intransitive verbs, such words are not direct objects; they are verb modifiers. The verbs are still intransitive.

Howard **is sleeping** *soundly.*   [Howard is sleeping *how?*]

Gloria **reads** *voraciously.*

I **studied** *hard.*

Table 3. Verb Terms

Verb function categories

1. Transitive verb *(followed by a direct object)*: You **walk** your dog.
2. Intransitive verb *(may be followed by a modifier)*: You **walk** (fast).
3. Linking verb *(followed by a predicate noun or adjective)*: You **are** fast.

Verb forms

1. Nonfinite verb forms *(show no tense)*
   - Infinitive *(base form of verb)*: (to) walk
   - Present Participle *(adds **-ing** to the infinitive)*: walking
   - Past Participle *(adds **-d** or **-ed** to the infinitive)*: walked
     (Regular verbs all form past participle as shown above;
     irregular verbs form past participle in varied ways:
     win, won; teach, taught; lie, lain; lay, laid.)

2. Finite verb forms *(show number, person, voice, mood, and tense)*
   (Finite verbs have subjects; the following examples show appropriate
   pronoun and noun subjects.)

   - Number *(tells how many units are involved)*
     Singular *(only one)*: I, you, he, she, it
     Plural *(more than one)*: we, you, they

   - Person *(identifies the role of each person in a sentence)*
     First *(the person(s) speaking)*: I, me; we, us
     Second *(the person(s) to whom you are speaking)*: you
     Third *(the person(s) about whom you are speaking)*: he, she, it, they,
         and all nouns for which such pronouns may be substituted.

   - Voice:
     Active *(the subject acts)*: He **hit** the ball.
     Passive *(the subject is acted upon)*: The ball **was hit** by him.

   - Mood *(reflects the speaker's feelings about a statement)*
     Indicative *(expresses a fact)*
     Subjunctive *(expresses doubt, obligation, condition contrary to fact)*
     Imperative *(expresses a request or command)*

   - Tense *(establishes the time of action)*

Simple tenses
  Present: it walks
  Past: it walked
  Future: it *will* walk
Perfect tenses *(past part. + **have**)*
  Pres. Perf.: it *has* walked
  Past Perf.: it *had* walked
  Fut. Perf.: it *will have* walked

Progressive tenses *(pres. part. + **be**)*
  Present: it *is* walking
  Past: it *was* walking
  Future: it *will be* walking
  Pres. Perf.: it *has been* walking
  Past Perf.: it *had been* walking
  Fut. Perf.: it *will have been* walking

Sometimes modifiers occur in sentences that have transitive verbs and direct objects, so do not overlook a direct object just because you see a verb modifier in a sentence. You will learn more about verb modifiers, or adverbs, in subsection 1a4.

As you may have already guessed, asking *who?* or *what?* or *how?* after stating both the subject and the verb will help you determine whether a verb is transitive or intransitive. An answer to *who?* or *what?* will identify a direct object, which can follow only a transitive verb. An answer to *how?* will identify a verb modifier, which follows an intransitive verb. Remember, though, that a verb modifier may also occur with a direct object.

> Lucretia drives her car recklessly.   [Lucretia drives what? Her car. The word *car* is the object of the transitive verb *drives.*]

(In the preceding example, you might make a mistake if you posed the question *how?* before you checked for a direct object with the question *what?*; you might decide that the presence of the verb modifier *recklessly* indicated an intransitive verb. Be careful!)

The same word may be a transitive verb in one sentence and an intransitive verb in another sentence. Always ask *who?* or *what?* after you state the subject and the verb. Then, if there is no answer (and no direct object), double-check by asking *how?* to find a modifier and to confirm the verb as intransitive. Compare the following examples:

Transitive	Intransitive
The pilot **flew** the plane. [flew what?]	The bird **flew** slowly. [flew how?]
Andrea **reads** magazines. [reads what?]	Al **reads** to his children. [reads how?]
Henry **smokes** cigars. [smokes what?]	My sister **smokes** heavily. [smokes how?]

c. Linking verbs   A linking verb connects the subject of a sentence with a noun or an adjective in the predicate; the predicate complement follows the verb and completes the sentence. See subsection 1d2.

Jennifer **is** tall.   [The word *tall* is an adjective.]

The cream **turned** sour.   [The word *sour* is an adjective.]

Bruce **became** a cheerleader.   [The word *cheerleader* is a noun.]

Some common linking verbs are listed in Table 4. Linking verbs can cause some special problems in writing.

Be, become, and *seem* are always linking verbs; but the other words in the list may also function as transitive verbs or as intransitive verbs. The following examples illustrate this point:

TRANSITIVE VERBS:

Mother **turned** the sheets on the bed.

The instructor **proved** the theorem.

The bank teller **sounded** the alarm.

INTRANSITIVE VERBS:

The police officer **appeared** suddenly.

Our youngest sister **remained** at home.

Table 4.   Some Common Linking Verbs

be	grow
become	turn
seem	prove
appear	remain
look	feel
sound	taste
smell	weigh

In the following examples, the predicate noun or predicate adjective is underlined:

LINKING VERBS:

> Jennifer **is** <u>his girlfriend.</u>   [predicate noun]
>
> Bruce **became** <u>a cheerleader.</u>   [predicate noun]
>
> The hamburger **weighed** <u>a pound.</u>   [predicate noun]
>
> The cream **turned** <u>sour.</u>   [predicate adjective]
>
> It **tasted** <u>funny.</u>   [predicate adjective]
>
> Harry **remained** <u>loyal.</u>   [predicate adjective]

Do not confuse a predicate noun with a direct object. In the preceding examples of linking verbs, *girlfriend, cheerleader,* and *pound* do indeed answer the question *what* after the subject and verb, but they are predicate nouns nonetheless.

There are two tests to help you distinguish between a transitive verb (that has a direct object) and a linking verb (that has a predicate noun).

1. Substitute the word *is* or *was* in place of the verb. (*Be* is always a linking verb, and so is any verb that *be* can replace.) If the substitution works, then the verb is a linking verb.

2. If you are still not sure what sort of verb you have, turn the sentence around and use a *be* verb to match the tense of the original verb (thereby changing the sentence into the "passive voice" that is discussed later in this section).

> Arnold **wrote** the letter.   [active voice]
>
> The letter **was written** by Arnold.   [passive voice]

Because the subject *(Arnold)* and the object *(letter)* can be reversed successfully and the meaning is still clear, the verb *(wrote)* must be a transitive verb.

Let us test another example.

> Yvonne **became** a cheerleader.

First, we shall try Test #2.

> TEST #2: A cheerleader **was become** by Yvonne.   [Inversion for test #2 does not result in a workable sentence; the non-sentence proves that *became* is not a transitive verb.]

> TEST #1: Yvonne **is** a cheerleader.   [Substituting *is* for the verb works, proving that *became* is a linking verb.]

Some verbs can function as transitive, intransitive, or linking verbs, as shown below.

TRANSITIVE:
> My grandfather **grew** a beard.   [Grew what? A beard. Beard is the direct object of the transitive verb *grew*.]

INTRANSITIVE:
> The rosebushes **grew** slowly.   [Grew what? Nothing; this sentence has no direct object. Grew how? Slowly; the verb modifier *slowly* follows the intransitive verb *grew*.]

LINKING:
> My date **grew** restless. [Grew what? Restless. So, *restless* must be the object? No; apply test #1 and substitute *is* to check for a linking verb, thus identifying *restless* as a predicate adjective (not a direct object).]

In addition to expressing action or state of being, verbs also indicate the time that the action or state of being takes place. Time is indicated in three verb tenses: the past tense (for events that have already occurred), the present tense (for events that are currently occurring), and the future tense (for events that are yet to happen).

PAST TENSE:
> Armand *rode* his bicycle yesterday.

PRESENT TENSE:

> Armand *rides* his bicycle today.

FUTURE TENSE:

> Armand *will ride* his bicycle tomorrow.

When we speak of verb tense, we are speaking of **finite verbs** that show the time of action as they function as the main verbs in well-constructed sentences. They indicate person, number, tense, voice, and mood.

Nonfinite verb forms, on the other hand, do not show tense. The three nonfinite verb forms are the infinitive, the present participle, and the past participle. The **infinitive** is the base form of a verb; it is preceded by the word *to*. The **present participle** is formed by adding *-ing* to the infinitive. The **past participle** is formed by adding *-d* or *-ed* to the infinitive for regular verbs; for irregular verbs, the past participle form may differ considerably from the infinitive form.

We shall return to discuss tense fully; but first you need to understand what is meant by the grammatical terms **number, person, voice,** and **mood.**

d. Number   A **singular** subject names only one person or thing, while a **plural** subject names more than one person or thing. The singular pronouns are *I, you, he, she,* and *it;* the plural pronouns are *we, you,* and *they.* The verb form must agree in number with the subject noun or pronoun.

e. Person   In modern English, the pronoun subject used with a verb identifies the verb form as one of the following persons:

- first person (the person speaking): *I* or *we*
- second person (the person to whom you are speaking): *you*
- third person (the person about whom you are speaking): *he, she, it, they,* and all nouns for which such pronouns may be substituted.

In the present tense, the verb itself changes form only in the third person singular; it adds the ending -s or -es. In the past tense, only the subject of the past tense verb shows the person; the verb form does not change from person to person.

	Present Tense		Past Tense	
Person	Singular	Plural	Singular	Plural
1st	I eat	we eat	I ate	we ate
2nd	you eat	you eat	you ate	you ate
3rd	he eat<u>s</u>	they eat	she ate	they ate
1st	I teach	we teach	I taught	we taught
2nd	you teach	you teach	you taught	you taught
3rd	it teach<u>es</u>	they teach	it taught	they taught

A verb must agree in person and number with the subject of a sentence; this agreement can be clouded if very many words occur between the subject and the verb.

f. Voice   This grammatical term refers to **active voice** (in which the subject acts) and **passive voice** (in which the subject is acted upon). Compare the following examples of active and passive voice, noticing how the passive is formed by the addition of the word *be* in an appropriate tense to match the tense of the active verb. Notice that the verb is then altered to its past participle form.

George **drove** the car.   [active voice]

The car **was driven** by George.   [passive voice]

Shakespeare **may have written** this play.   [active voice]

This play **may have been written** by Shakespeare.   [passive voice]

The monitor **will distribute** some papers.   [active voice]

Some papers **will be distributed** by the monitor.   [passive voice]

g. **Mood**   In grammar, mood refers to the way a speaker or writer regards a statement. There are three moods in modern English: the **indicative mood** (used to express a fact or what is believed to be a fact), the **subjunctive mood** (used to express doubt, potentiality, desirability, obligation, or condition contrary to fact), and the **imperative mood** (used to state a request or a command).

(1) Indicative mood   The indicative mood occurs most frequently, both in statements and in questions.

> The moon **is** bright tonight.
>
> Joe **milked** sixteen cows this morning.
>
> **Did** you **wash** the dishes already?

(2) Subjunctive mood   Except for the verb *be*, which is discussed in section 8d, the subjunctive forms of all verbs look much like those in the indicative mood. The only difference is that the third person singular of the present tense is the same as the infinitive; it does not add *-s* or *-es* as in the indicative mood.

> If the moon **were** bright tonight, we could see Half Dome from here.   [Contrary to fact; the moon is not bright.]
>
> His uncle urged that Joe **milk** sixteen cows each morning.   [Desire or suggestion; **milks** or **milked** would not work, even though *Joe* is the subject.]
>
> Regulations require that all reports **be** in triplicate.   [Obligation; *be* is subjunctive.]
>
> I wish I **were** a millionaire.   [Contrary to fact; I am not a millionaire.]

(3) Imperative mood   The imperative mood usually omits the subject, which is always *you* (either singular or plural). When the subject is retained, the effect is more emphatic.

> Quit doing that.   You quit doing that!
>
> Pass the salt, please.   You pass the salt!

h. **Simple tenses** Now that you understand the grammatical terms *number, person, voice,* and *mood,* we can touch on verb *tense.* At its simplest level, tense is that characteristic of the verb that shows the time when the action occurs; in addition, tense may indicate whether an action is repeated, continuing, or completed. The tense system in English is complicated; but to use this book you need to know only whether a verb form shows one of the present, past, or future tenses.

Consider, for example, the word *ride.* As a noun, *ride* names a thing *(the ride)* but not a time of occurrence; as a verb, *ride* specifies a time of occurrence.

PRESENT TENSE:
> Jack *rides* his bicycle.

FUTURE TENSE:
> Maria *will ride* the train to San Diego.

Notice that a verb may be more than one word: *will ride.*

(1) Verb forms. Both the *-s* on *rides* and the *will* in *will ride* help to identify the word *ride* as a verb by its form. With the exception of the verb *be* (which has eight forms: *be, am, is, are, was, were, being, been*), all verbs have five forms. These five forms are named in the following table, with six examples listed under each form heading.

Infinitive	Present Tense*	Past Tense	Present Participle	Past Participle
(to) ride	rides	rode	riding	ridden
(to) talk	talks	talked	talking	talked
(to) show	shows	showed	showing	shown
(to) laugh	laughs	laughed	laughing	laughed
(to) drive	drives	drove	driving	driven
(to) see	sees	saw	seeing	seen

*3rd person singular: he/she/it rides

The **infinitive** is the base form of a verb. This is the form that is defined in a dictionary, and this is the form that serves as a foundation for the other forms of the verb. As you look at the table of verb forms, you no doubt notice some similarities, as well as some variations, within each column.

The **present tense** is shown in the table in the third-person singular form; this is the form used when the verb is attached to a subject pronoun like *he, she,* or *it* (or when the subject is an expression or a noun that one of those three pronouns could replace). As you can see in the table, the present tense for third-person singular is created by adding **-s** or **-es** to the infinitive.

The **present participle** is formed by adding **-ing** to the infinitive.

When the **past tense** and the **past participle** are formed by adding **-d** or **-ed,** we say that the verb is a **regular verb.**

Many verbs, however, are called **irregular verbs** because their past tense and past participle differ considerably from the infinitive. In the table, notice the past tense and past participle of *ride* (rode, ridden), *drive* (drove, driven), and *see* (saw, seen). These forms differ considerably from the infinitive.

Because the past tense and the past participle of a verb may be irregular or regular, you must learn the three principal parts of each verb so that you can identify any verb as regular or irregular. *The three **principal parts** of a verb are the **infinitive,** the **past tense,** and the **past participle.*** Chapter 8 lists the principal parts of the chief irregular verbs that you ought to learn.

(2) Using participles. Auxiliary verbs are used with present participles and with past participles to create finite verb forms. A form of the auxiliary verb *be* (am, are, is, was, were, been) always precedes a present participle. The past participle uses only a form of the auxiliary verb *have* (has, had). Compare the examples listed here.

be + Present Participle	*have* + Past Participle
she *is* crying	she *has* cried
they *were* talking	they *have* talked
it has *been* raining*	it *had* rained
you *are* reading	you *have* read
Joe *was* seeing	Joe *has* seen
he *is* walking	he *has* walked
I *am* noticing	I *have* noticed
we have *been* hearing*	we *had* heard

i. **Perfect tenses**   As mentioned earlier, tense shows the time when the action occurs. In addition, tense may indicate whether an action is repeated, continuing, or completed.

The simple tenses were introduced earlier—the present, the past, and the future. The perfect tenses (present perfect, past perfect, and future perfect) show that an action was completed or will be completed before another time or action.

In the following table, note that the present and past tenses are single words, the future uses *will* (or sometimes *is going to*) as the auxiliary, and the perfect tenses all use the word *have* as an auxiliary with the past participle.

---

*Don't be misled when the auxiliary verbs *have* and *has* are used with *been*.

	Regular Verb	Irregular Verb
Simple tenses		
Present	He talks	He writes
Past	He talked	He wrote
Future	He will talk	He will write
Perfect tenses		
Present Perfect	He has talked	He has written
Past Perfect	He had talked	He had written
Future Perfect	He will have talked	He will have written

j. Progressive tenses   All verbs also have progressive tenses which indicate continuing action in the time shown. These forms use the auxiliary *be* with the present participle ending in -*ing*. Notice that they also take other auxiliaries in a consistent pattern.

Present	He is talking
Past	He was talking
Future	He will be talking
Present Perfect	He has been talking
Past Perfect	He had been talking
Future Perfect	He will have been talking

Sample sentences can show only a few of the many complicated ideas you can express by choosing tenses appropriately.

PRESENT: I **am telling** you the truth.

Karl often **studies** after midnight.

PAST: He **finished** his paper last night.

Elmer **was eating** pizza at 2:00 A.M.

FUTURE: He **will suffer** indigestion.

He **will be seeing** a doctor soon.

PRESENT PERFECT:

> I **have played** soccer only once.

> Joe **has been playing** since the sixth grade.

PAST PERFECT:

> We **had stopped** before it started to rain.

> We **had been watching** the storm's approach anxiously.

FUTURE PERFECT:

> Andrew **will have finished** his work long before the boss comes.

> By then he **will have been resting** for two hours.

Other sections in this book will help you use verbs appropriately and effectively so that the subject and verb agree with one another (Chapter 6) and so that you do not awkwardly shift from one verb form to another (Chapter 7). Another section (Chapter 8) treats irregular and troublesome verbs in detail.

1a3   Adjectives

An adjective describes or modifies a noun or pronoun by telling something about it: *which one; what kind; how big, small, old,* or *young.* It is the meaning and the use or function in a sentence that identifies an adjective more readily than its form. A convenient test pattern follows (any common noun can be used instead of *person*):

> That _____ person is very _____.

Any word that can fit in both empty slots is an adjective. Thus:

> That **old** man is very **old.**   That **strong** odor is very **strong**

> That **tall** building is very **tall.**   That **loud** noise is very **loud.**

Here is another easy test. In American English any word that follows the verb *seems* is an adjective.

He seems **angry**.   She seems **happy**.   It seems **dead**.
The game seemed **lost** after the first quarter.

Still another position helps to identify an adjective. Commonly such words appear just before the noun or pronoun they modify. Both meaning and position help you recognize such words as adjectives.

the **blue** book   a **serious** student
the **loud** noise   an **ordinary** one

a. Comparatives   Many adjectives can be compared by adding -er and -est, and it is that change in form that helps you recognize certain words as adjectives. (A caution is in order, though; many adverbs can also be compared.) The **positive degree** has no ending; it simply specifies the characteristic which the word names. The **comparative degree** adds -er and states that one item is more or bigger or better than a second item. Use it when you set two things side by side— and only two things. The **superlative degree** ends in -est and suggests that the characteristic exceeds all others in a group of three or more.

Positive	Comparative	Superlative
cloudy	cloudier	cloudiest
great	greater	greatest
happy	happier	happiest
green	greener	greenest

Certain adjectives, usually those with more than two syllables, use the words *more* and *most* to form the comparative and the superlative degrees.

reasonable	more reasonable	most reasonable
beautiful	more beautiful	most beautiful
dramatic	more dramatic	most dramatic

b. Adjective-forming suffixes   Finally, we use a number of suffixes to convert other parts of speech (and occasionally other adjectives) into new adjectives. Here are the most common suffixes (in boldface):

fashion+**able**=fashionable   girl+**ish**=girlish
option+**al**=optional   attract+**ive**=attractive
America+**an**=American   fruit+**less**=fruitless
repent+**ant**=repentant   bird+**like**=birdlike
fortune+**ate**=fortunate   ghost+**ly**=ghostly
conserve+**ative**=conservative   prohibit+**ory**=prohibitory
persist+**ent**=persistent   danger+**ous**=dangerous
joy+**ful**=joyful   quarrel+**some**=quarrelsome
angel+**ic**=angelic   shine+**y**=shiny

These **adjective-forming suffixes** can help you develop a feel for identifying adjectives. Be sure to note that the suffix -*ly* forms only a few adjectives; in most cases that suffix changes an adjective into an adverb.

c. Participles   Two other modifier forms deserve attention. Both come from verbs and both often function like adjectives, though technically they are not true adjectives. They are the present participle (the verb form ending in -*ing*) and the past participle (whose form may be regular—ending in -*d* or -*ed*—or irregular).

an **interesting** idea   [from the verb *interest*]
the **fascinating** play   [from the verb *fascinate*]
the **lost** mittens   [from the verb *lose*]
the **beaten** team   [from the verb *beat*]

You will learn more about such "borrowed" words under Verbals in subsection 1c3.

1a4   Adverbs

Adverbs describe or modify verbs, answering questions like *how, when, where, why,* and *under what circumstances* the action of the verb occurs. (Adverbs also modify many adjectives and some other adverbs.) Its meaning and function identify a word as an adverb, though knowing something about form is also helpful.

Adding the suffix -ly to an adjective changes it to an adverb.

Adjective	Adverb	Adjective	Adverb
open	openly	popular	popularly
selfish	selfishly	rare	rarely
pure	purely		

Caution: Some words that end in -ly are adjectives. The real test to distinguish between an adjective and an adverb is to note what word is modified. These examples show the modified word in italics.

Adjective	Adverb
a **lovely** *lady*	she *replied* **sweetly**
a **friendly** *puppy*	the train *approached* **rapidly**
a **lonely** *soldier*	they **greatly** *admired* it

a. Comparatives   Like adjectives, adverbs can also be compared, most commonly by adding the words *more* and *most.*

Positive	Comparative	Superlative
rashly	more rashly	most rashly
quickly	more quickly	most quickly
frequently	more frequently	most frequently

Some few add -er and -est:

soon	sooner	soonest
late	later	latest
early	earlier	earliest

And some are compared irregularly:

well	better	best
badly	worse	worst

b. **Time and place adverbs** A number of adverbs cannot be compared, but we recognize them as adverbs because they modify verbs by expressing time or place.

never	inside	somewhere
there	now	behind
here	seldom	above
upward	always	

Since so many adverbs express time, place, or manner in regard to the verb, you can often test for adverbs by substituting *then*, *there*, or *thus*, like this:

They'll come **sometime.** = They'll come *then*.

I can't find Harriet **anywhere.** = I can't find Harriet *there*.

Eliot replied **softly.** = Eliot replied *thus*.

In section 1f we will make modification clearer, but understanding the above characteristics of adverbs will give you a feel for identifying them and using them correctly. Some important writing problems depend on the distinction between adjectives and adverbs.

If you remember that adjectives modify or describe nouns and that adverbs describe verbs, you will readily identify these two word classes and use them effectively.

The **huge, old** dog didn't move. [adjectives modifying *dog*]

He lay **quietly.** [adverb modifying *lay*]

His **impatient** mistress shouted at him.
[adjective modifying *mistress*]

He lifted his head **slowly.** [adverb modifying *lifted*]

Here is a little test on content words: Can you tell what part of speech the word *right* is in each sentence?

I have my **rights**! _____

Lincoln **righted** the wrongs done to slaves. _____

Yes, that's the **right** answer. _____

Turn **right** at the next corner. _____

1b Structure Words (parts of speech)

Structure words are fewer in number than are the content words, but contain a greater number of parts of speech. They provide a framework for arranging the content words (nouns, verbs, adjectives, and adverbs) into meaningful sentences. In fact, they help identify the structure of an English sentence when the meanings of the content words are unknown. For example, you probably cannot define *kover, gorfs, glinking, boofly, rilly,* and *marp;* therefore, the following "sentence" is nonsense to you:

The kover gorfs were glinking boofly in the rilly marp.

However, the structure words (*the, were,* and *in*) signal you that it is somehow an English sentence.

The structure words are said to belong to **closed classes** because new words rarely enter these classes. There is some overlapping among the groups (the word *that,* for example, may belong to several groups), and their grammatical behavior is complex. We will mention and briefly define only those of which you need an elementary knowledge in order to use this text as a reference handbook. What follows is only a small part of the total grammar of structure words—the part that will be most useful to you.

1b1 Determiners

Words that signal that a noun is coming are called **determiners;** they determine something about the nature of the noun that follows. Some show that the noun is singular or plural, others that a noun is definite or indefinite, and still others that the noun names something countable or non-countable. Sometimes two determiners precede a noun, and a few single determiners may consist of two or more words. Here are examples of the chief determiners:

a biscuit	**John's** hotrod	**all** students
an apple	**this** lesson	**every** chance
the bottle	**no** exit	**such a** pity
my stereo	**some** person	**all the** excuses

This list shows how parts of speech may be labelled differently as their functions differ. *John* is commonly a noun, but here it functions as a determiner. Any such possessive noun and any pronoun in the possessive case (like *my*) can also be a determiner. *All* and *some* are determiners here, but they can also be pronouns. If you think of any such word as a noun marker, you should have little trouble in recognizing determiners. Of course, other words may come between the determiner and its noun, as in ***a** cute little baby* and ***the** glossy red car.*

1b2   Prepositions

A **preposition** is a structure word that connects the **object of the preposition** (a noun or noun substitute) to another word in the sentence. Many prepositions do have some meaning, but it is their function more than their meaning that helps to identify them.

The preposition and its object form a **prepositional phrase,** and such phrases give some information about the words to which they are connected. (The examples show the preposition in boldface and the prepositional phrase in italics.)

the man **with** *the hoe* (tells which man; connected to noun)
come **into** *the house* (tells where; connected to verb)
good **for** *the country* (tells how good; connected to adjective)
sometime ***in*** *the future* (tells when; connected to adverb)

One teacher has suggested a definition: "A preposition is a little word that tells where a mouse can go." That doesn't take care of all prepositions; there are some that don't fit that description. The only real solution is to familiarize yourself with the list of the most common single-word prepositions.

about	behind	during	on	to
above	below	except	onto	toward(s)
across	beneath	for	out	under
after	beside	from	outside	underneath
against	besides	in	over	until
along	between	inside	past	up
among	beyond	into	save	upon
around	but	like	since	with
as	by	near	through	within
at	despite	of	till	without
before	down	off		

In addition, some groups of two or three words function as **compound** or **phrasal prepositions.**

according to	by way of	in spite of
along with	contrary to	inside of
ahead of	due to	instead of
apart from	except for	on account of
as for	for the sake of	out of
as well as	in addition to	owing to
aside from	in back of	rather than
away from	in case of	together with
because of	in front of	with regard to
by means of	in place of	

Some of these compound prepositions—as in the contruction *in addition to the money*—may appear to form two prepositional phrases rather than one phrase with a compound preposition. You will learn more about how and when to use prepositional phrases effectively as you study subsection 1c2.

1b3   Verb auxiliaries and verb phrases

Because they help to specify the tense, mood, and voice of verbs, the **auxiliaries** are often called simply "helping verbs." Such auxiliaries may be one word or more than one. They always appear in front of a form of the main verb. (These examples show the auxiliaries in boldface.)

I **did** go	It **will be** gone
She **has** gone	We **should have been** going
They **may** go	He **is** going

The number of possible combinations of auxiliaries in the English verb system is enormous. Fortunately, to use this text you need only *recognize* the auxiliaries, not understand their complex grammar fully.

The simple present and past tenses of verbs have their individual forms, as in she *walks,* we *saw,* they *jumped.* When auxiliaries appear with the verb, certain regular patterns of the main verb occur.

a.   **be**   When *be* is the auxiliary used with an active verb, that main verb always ends in *-ing,* the form we call the present participle (but when you studied the passive voice on page 18, you saw how *be* also takes the past participle in that case).

He **is** sleep**ing.**

Joe may have **been** tell**ing** lies.

Al **was** shoot**ing** tin cans with his BB gun.

b.   **have**   When *have* is the auxiliary, the next word must be in the past participle form, even if that next word is another auxiliary.

She **has** se**en** the movie twice.

We **had** walk**ed** four miles by sundown.

They may **have** be**en** kidding us.

c. **do** When *do* is an auxiliary, the following verb appears in the infinitive or base form (the one with no ending).

I **did do** my assignment.

Marcia **does respect** her parents.

Each of the three auxiliaries *be, have,* and *do* can also function as a main verb in the sentence. When each does, it has meanings different from its meaning as an auxiliary.

I **have** a new stereo. (*have* has the meaning of *possess*)

I **have** bought a new stereo. (*have* is an auxiliary that forms the present perfect tense of *bring*)

d. Modal auxiliaries A small group of words is called modal auxiliaries. Although they are used with the main verb, they carry important meanings of their own, expressing such notions as *intent, necessity, obligation, permission,* and *possibility.* A list of modal auxiliaries follows:

may	can	shall	will	must
might	could	should	would	ought to

None of these words takes the ending *-s* in the third person singular. When used, they always appear before any other auxiliaries and the main verb, and whatever word follows such a modal appears in its infinitive or base form.

I **might** leave early.

You **ought to** help the committee.

John **may** have given his report already.

Mary **can** sing beautifully.

e. Semi-modals Another group of words functions much like the modal auxiliaries. The group is easy to recognize; it is that large number of expressions that end in *to: seem to, dare to, have to, be supposed to, used to, be about to, be going to.* Although they are not among the true modals, their position in the verb phrase and their meaning or function is to indicate possibility, probability, or necessity. As was the case with the true modals, the semi-modals also take a verb in the infinitive.

I **am going to** buy that car.

He **is supposed to** finish washing the wall.

Sheila **dared to** wear her bikini to the party.

Mike **has to** go home every weekend.

All of these verb-like words together (all the auxiliaries plus the main verb) comprise a **verb phrase.** As you see, such verb phrases can express a large number of complex ideas. You should note certain conditions and certain regular patterns. The following comments will help you use verbs and verb phrases correctly and effectively.

You can have no more than one modal or semi-modal in any verb phrase (*he ought to have could* just won't work); when a modal, a semi-modal, or the word *do* is the auxiliary, the next word must be the infinitive form of the verb; you may use a combination of a modal, the word *have*, and the word *be* (all three) as auxiliaries, but you must use them in that order; a past participle always follows the word *have;* and a word ending in *-ing* follows the auxiliary *be* (except in the passive voice).

1b4   Coordinating connectives

A coordinating connective joins two constructions of equal grammatical rank into compound structures; these may be any two words, two prepositional phrases, or two independent clauses. The two units must be of the same kind; you cannot, for example, join a noun and a verb, nor can you join a phrase and a clause. Many of the chapters in this text refer to such compound structures. You need to know two classes of these connectives.

a.   **Coordinating conjunctions**   Coordinating conjunctions (with several exceptions) join many kinds of constructions, from single words to independent clauses. (Clauses will be discussed later in this chapter in section 1d.) The coordinating conjunctions are the following:

and	for	both . . . and
or	so	not only . . . but (also)
nor	yet	either . . . or
but		neither . . . nor

For and *so* join only independent clauses. The two-part conjunctions are called correlatives.

b. Conjunctive adverbs   Conjunctive adverbs can join only independent clauses. Here are some conjunctive adverbs:

accordingly	earlier	moreover	then
afterward(s)	furthermore	nevertheless	therefore
also	hence	nonetheless	thus
besides	however	otherwise	yet
consequently	later	still	

Both kinds of coordinating connectives express such relationships as **contrast, cause-and-effect, accumulation, conditions,** and **time.** When a coordinating connective joins two independent clauses, each *could* stand by itself as a full, complete sentence, for a sentence may begin with a coordinating connective. The coordinating connectives technically belong to neither clause; they are merely connectives: Punctuating such constructions requires attention to certain regular patterns (see sections 3b and 12b, and Chapter 10). The examples show boldface coordinating connectives.

man **and** wife   [two nouns]

a boy **and** his dog   [two phrases]

We ran **and** swam.   [two verbs]

inside the house **and** on the roof   [two prepositional phrases]

Al read, **but** Sam slept quietly.   [two independent clauses]

Eloise practiced diligently; **consequently,** she almost became a concert pianist.   [two independent clauses with a conjunctive adverb as the connective]

1b5   Subordinating conjunctions

Another class of connectives joins two ideas that are not of equal rank; that is, one of the ideas could stand alone as a complete sentence, but the idea introduced by the subordinating conjunction cannot. Subordinating conjunctions can join only whole clauses (not single words or phrases) to some other word or construction. Such clauses are called subordinate or dependent clauses (treated more fully in subsection 1d4 and section 1i). For reference, see the list of subordinating conjunctions.

after	even though	no matter how	though
although	if	now that	till
as	in case (that)	once	unless
as . . . as	in order that	provided (that)	until
as if	in that	since	when
as long as	inasmuch as	so long as	whenever
as soon as	less than	so (that)	where
as though	like	than	wherever
because	more than	that	while
before			

Notice that some such subordinating conjunctions are more than one word, and a number of such words can be prepositions or other connectives in other constructions. These important words express such adverbial relationships as **cause-and-effect, contrast, condition, manner, method, purpose, time,** and **place.** Just a few examples at this point will help you see their uses (with the subordinate clauses italicized):

> *After John got home,* he checked the fire *before he went to bed.*
>
> *Now that you are here,* we can begin the meeting.
>
> Helen had loved Jeffrey *as long as she had known him.*
>
> We'll have to wait *until the caterer delivers the snacks.*

None of the italicized subordinate clauses can stand alone as a complete sentence, for the subordinating conjunction is an important part of the clause it introduces (it *does* belong to its clause). Section 10c explains when and where (and why) to use commas in such complex sentences.

1b6 Pronouns

A word that takes the place of a noun or a noun substitute is a **pronoun,** and the word or structure it replaces or refers to is its **antecedent.** The complex English pronoun system causes so many problems in writing that it will be dealt with in several other chapters in this book, notably Chapters 5, 6, and 24. This beginning chapter will identify only five kinds of pronouns: personal, relative, interrogative, demonstrative, and indefinite. Learn their forms, and note also a few of their functions here.

a. **Personal pronouns**   The personal pronouns identify the person speaking (first person: *I* and *we*), the person spoken to (second person: *you*), and the person or thing spoken about (third person: *he, she, it,* and *they*).

The personal pronouns have **case,** which means that they change their form according to their use in the sentence. The three cases in English are the **subjective,** the **objective,** and the **possessive.** Notice that no pronoun in the possessive case has an apostrophe. When and how to use the different cases of pronouns will appear in Chapters 5, 6, and 24.

Number	Person	Subjective Case	Objective Case	Possessive Case
Singular	1st	I	me	my, mine
	2nd	you	you	your, yours
	3rd	he	him	his
		she	her	her, hers
		it	it	its
Plural	1st	we	us	our, ours
	2nd	you	you	your, yours
	3rd	they	them	their, theirs

The personal pronouns also have **reflexive** forms, as follows (See also section 5h):

myself	himself	[not *hisself*]
ourselves	herself	
yourself	itself	
yourselves	themselves	[not *theirselves*]

b. Relative pronouns   The chief relative pronouns are *who* (subjective case), *whom* (objective case), *whose* (possessive case), *which*, and *that* (these last two do not have case). A relative pronoun connects or relates a particular kind of dependent clause to a noun in another part of the sentence. Such a clause follows as close as possible after the noun it refers to. The example shows the relative clause in italics:

That's the lawyer ***who*** *called me yesterday.*

The antecedent of *who* is *lawyer.* *Who* introduces the dependent clause and relates it to the preceding noun. Such dependent clauses that begin with a relative pronoun are called **relative clauses** (see subsection 1d4). Since they describe something about the noun (as adjectives do), they are also known as **adjective clauses.** They modify nouns and pronouns by telling *which one* or *what kind.*

The camera ***that*** *I bought yesterday* takes good pictures.

The word *that* refers to its antecedent *camera.* Notice also that the main clause (The camera takes good pictures) may be broken apart and the relative clause inserted in the middle immediately after the noun to which it refers.

Sometimes a relative pronoun is not stated but is understood in the sentence. The preceding sentence could just as well read like this:

The camera *I bought yesterday* takes good pictures.

The relative pronoun *that* (still with *camera* as its antecedent) is understood before *I*.

Clauses, including relative clauses, are more thoroughly explained in section 1d.

c. Interrogative pronouns *Who, whose,* and *whom* (with *what* and *which*) are also interrogative pronouns. They form questions. Distinguish between *who* as a relative pronoun and *who* as an interrogative.

> That's the lady **who** left me this big tip. (relative pronoun)
>
> **Who** left me this big tip? (interrogative pronoun)

Choosing between *who* and *whom* often poses a problem in writing. Section 5c will clarify the puzzle.

d. Demonstrative pronouns The demonstrative pronouns are *this* and *that* (both singular) and *these* and *those* (both plural). They point to something that is nearer or more distant and can be used alone or with a following noun.

> **This** is your mitt, but **that** is mine.
>
> **These** flowers have wilted, but **those** are still fresh.

Sometimes the demonstrative pronouns refer in a general way to whole ideas.

> I was afraid the battery in my car would die, and **that** is exactly what happened.
>
> "You've been late to work for the last three days. **This** has got to stop," said the boss.

In the two examples **this** and **that** have whole ideas as their antecedents.

e. Indefinite pronouns A sizable number of words in English known as indefinite pronouns function as singular pronouns but make indefinite reference to people or things. Some of these words are listed on the next page.

one	each	either, neither
someone	somebody	something
anyone	anybody	anything
everyone	everybody	everything
no one (two words)	nobody	nothing

A verb following such an **indefinite pronoun** should be singular, and a later pronoun referring to the indefinite pronoun should also be singular.

In Europe **one eats** with the fork in the left hand.

Of the two possibilities, **either is** acceptable.

Has anyone here **lost his** billfold?

Everyone at the Ladies Auxiliary **had prepaid her** registration.

1b7   Qualifiers

A small group of words either increases or decreases the intensity of a following adjective or adverb. These **qualifiers** limit in some way or qualify the meaning of the words they modify. Some colloquial qualifiers discussed in section 20b generally should not appear in semiformal writing (the kind of writing most college classes call for). The following list names most of the qualifiers used in semiformal writing.

very	rather	somewhat	wholly
quite	fairly	especially	a little

Examples of qualifiers used with adjectives and adverbs:

Prof. Bailey was **somewhat** displeased with our test results.   [modifies an adjective]

He wasn't **very** happy at all.   [modifies an adjective]

He was **quite** surely going to flunk us.   [modifies an adverb]

He suggested that we were living **rather** dangerously.
[modifies an adverb]

Those are the parts of speech. The rest of Chapter 1 explains how we put the parts of speech together to form phrases, clauses, and sentences. As an example, consider the opening sentence in this paragraph:

Demonstrative Pronoun	Linking Verb	Determiner	Noun	Preposition	Noun
Those	are	the	parts	of	speech.

1c Phrases

A phrase is a group of words that functions as a unit but that does not have a subject and a predicate. You need to understand three kinds of phrases in order to use this book.

1c1 Noun phrases

A noun phrase consists of a noun as the headword or most important word plus its determiners and modifiers.

> **an apple**   [determiner plus noun]
>
> **a large basket**   [determiner, adjective, and noun]
>
> **the lightning rod on the roof**   [determiner, adjective, noun, and modifying prepositional phrase]
>
> **A list of members serving on the committee** was posted on **the bulletin board in the hallway.**

In the last two examples you see how noun phrases may also appear as parts of larger constructions: *the roof, a list, the committee, the bulletin board,* and *the hallway* are themselves noun phrases. Note also that noun phrases can appear wherever a single noun could function.

1c2 Prepositional phrases

A prepositional phrase begins with a preposition (see the list in subsection 1b2) and closes with the object of the preposition, usually a noun or a pronoun. If the object of the preposition is a pronoun, remember to use the objective case. These examples show each prepositional phrase underlined:

The man in the grey-flannel suit was sitting on the bench in the park across the street from his hotel.

Prepositional phrases are modifiers. When they describe a noun by telling *what kind* or *which one*, they function like adjectives.

The picture **on my wall** depicts a scene **in Spain.** [*On my wall* modifies the noun *picture; in Spain* modifies the noun *scene.*]

This book **of poetry** recounts tales **of love.** [*Of poetry* tells which book and thus modifies the noun; *of love* tells what kind of tales and thus modifies the noun.]

Prepositional phrases also modify verbs and adjectives and thus act much as single-word adverbs do.

We slept **on the beach, in tents, under the trees,** and **in our cars.** [Each prepositional phrase answers the question *where* in regard to the verb; thus, it acts like an adverb.]

This old razor must still be good **for something.**
[*For something* modifies the adjective *good.*]

Section 1f treats such modifiers in greater detail.

1c3 Verbals and verbal phrases

The most complicated among the three kinds of phrases are those in which a verb form is the headword. To begin with, you must distinguish between a simple **verb phrase** as described in subsection 1a2 (the main verb in the predicate together with its auxiliaries) and the **verbals** and **verbal phrases** we now introduce.

A **verbal** is a nonfinite verb form that functions as a noun or an adjective. The three *forms* that can so function are the infinitive (the base form of the verb preceded by *to),* the present participle (ending in -ing), and the past participle (the form usually following the auxiliary *have*).

Infinitive	Present Participle	Past Participle
to eat	eating	eaten
to catch	catching	caught
to beat	beating	beaten
to swim	swimming	swum
to walk	walking	walked

None of the finite verb forms (those that show tense) can be a verbal; only these three forms can be used as nouns or adjectives. Note the following:

The **act** requires energy.   [*Act* is a noun.]

To swim requires energy.   [*To swim* is the infinitive used as a noun to name an action; it is a verbal.]

Swimming requires energy.   [*Swimming* is the present participle used as a noun; again, it names an action and thus it is a verbal.]

All three verbals can also act like adjectives; that is, they can modify nouns.

Art had a strong desire **to travel.**   [*To travel,* the infinitive, modifies the noun *desire* by telling which one.]

Our **swimming** instructor told us to rest a while.   [As a present participle, *swimming* modifies the noun *instructor*; she was the one who coached swimming, not volleyball.]

The **beaten** team dragged its way into the locker room. [*Beaten* is a past participle used as an adjective to modify the noun *team.*]

When such nonfinite verbs are single words, we call them **verbals.** Since they are indeed verbs, they can also take "subjects" and "objects" to form **verbal phrases** (they are not sentences, however; they are only phrases).

To swim the English Channel is an amazing feat.   [The entire phrase *to swim the English Channel* is the verbal phrase, and *the English Channel* is the object of *to swim*.]

His eating three whole pizzas was disgusting.   [The entire unit in boldface is a verbal phrase. *Eating* is the present participle and has a subject *his;* but note that in this kind of construction it is in the possessive case. *Three whole pizzas* is the object of *eating*. The entire unit acts like a noun and is the subject of the sentence.]

The infinitive can even be used as an adverb, as in "John waited **to see Sue.**" Here *to see Sue* answers the question *why* after the verb *waited*. Past participles can be used only as adjectives.

Your instructor may choose to use certain technical terms to identify these verbal phrases. The infinitive is simply the **infinitive;** when the present participle serves as a noun (as in "Swimming can be fun"), it is called a **gerund;** when either participle is used as an adjective, it ordinarily gets the name **participle** or **participial phrase.**

Verbal phrases are discussed in sections 5e and 26a.

1d   Clauses

A **clause** is a construction that has both a subject and a predicate. Clauses are either independent or dependent.

1d1   Subjects

The **subject** names the person, thing, or concept about which the rest of the clause makes a statement. Such a subject may be a single word noun, a pronoun, or a noun phrase.

Hal sweeps the garage after work.   [a single noun as subject]

He feels good about his job.   [a pronoun as subject]

His uncle on his mother's side got him the job.
[a noun phrase]

His hobby after work is nobody's business but his own.
[a noun phrase]

For him to keep it a secret required ingenuity.
[an infinitive phrase]

If the verb is in the active voice, the subject performs the action. If the verb is passive, the subject receives the action. If the verb is a linking verb, the subject is in the state of being that the verb expresses (see subsection 1a2).

Hal really takes pictures as a hobby.   [The subject acts.]

Some of his pictures have been published already.
[The subject, *pictures*, is acted upon; that is,
they *have been published*.]

Hal is happy about that.   [*Is* as a linking verb merely joins the describing adjective *happy* to the subject *Hal*.]

A simple test for determining the subject is to ask *who* or *what* about the verb.

Hal won a prize last year.   [active verb]

Who won the prize? Hal did. *Hal* is the subject.

A prize was won by Hal last year.   [passive verb]

What was won? *A prize* is the subject.

His mother seemed delighted.   [*Seemed* is a linking verb.]

Who seemed? *His mother*, which is the subject.

A noun phrase with determiners and modifiers is called the **complete subject.**

All the people at his house that day congratulated him.

Who congratulated him? *All the people at his house that day,* which is the complete subject. The central noun or headword in a long subject is known as the **simple subject.** The word *people* is the simple subject. Another example:

A representative from the National Association of Amateur Photographers presented the prize.

The complete subject is in boldface, but the simple subject is the one word *representative*.

In the majority of English sentences, the subject precedes the verb. However, when sentences begin with *there* or *it* as **expletives** (fillers without meaning), the verb precedes the subject. In the examples, the complete subject is bold.

There is **no way to measure Hal's joy.**

It is clear **that he will try again.**

In both sentences the entire boldface constructions are the subjects. In the first sentence *no way* is the simple subject. There is no single expression that serves as the simple subject in the second example.

Some writers do at times use other kinds of inverted word order to create a certain stylistic effect; however, you can find the subject by asking *who* or *what* about the verb.

1d2 Predicates

The predicate in a sentence is the verb with its auxiliaries, its complement (if it has one), plus any modifiers (see section 1f). The examples show the predicates in boldface.

The hunter **shot an elk.**

Six deer **were browsing nearby.**

Two of them **merely gazed at the hunter.**

The remaining four **must have been startled by the noise.**

a. Verbs The headword in the predicate is always the verb (which may be one or more words). The verb must be a **finite** verb; that is, it must be a form that shows time of action.

They **were** soon **running** away from the source of danger.

The nimrod **ignored** all six deer.

He **was** not **allowed to hunt** them during elk season anyway.

The nonfinite verb forms do not show tense. They are the infinitive (often beginning with *to)*, the present participle (always ending in -ing), and the past participle (often ending in -d, -ed, or -en). The following groups of words are not sentences:

>He **known** the laws quite thoroughly.

>He **been studying** them before the hunt.

Adding auxiliaries that show tense would make these verbs finite and make correct sentences:

>He **had known** the laws quite thoroughly.

>He **must have been studying** them before the hunt.

A review of subsection 1a2 and Chapter 8 will give you additional help in understanding the verb and its uses.

b. Complements   Many predicates have complements of the verbs—those words or constructions that complete a meaning initiated in the verb. To use this book effectively, you need understand only four kinds of complements: **direct objects, indirect objects, predicate nouns,** and **predicate adjectives.** Any other words or phrases in the predicate will be modifiers of one kind of another.

(1) Direct objects   A direct object is the person or thing that receives the action of a transitive verb (intransitive verbs and linking verbs do not take objects).

>Gus lit **the cigar.**

>The transcriber omitted **an expletive.**

>The actor recited **his lines** listlessly.

A simple test for finding the direct object is to ask *who* or *what* after you have stated both the subject and the verb. Gus lit what? The *cigar* is the direct object. The actor recited what? *His lines* is the direct object (*listlessly* is an adverb modifying the verb).

(2) Indirect objects Some sentences with transitive verbs name also an indirect object. It specifies for whose benefit the action of the verb was performed. An indirect object never appears unless the sentence also has a direct object.

Father bought **Mother** a fur coat.

She gave **him** a big kiss.

First find the direct objects; *coat* and *kiss* answer the questions. What did Father buy? (He certainly did not buy Mother) and what did she give? The indirect objects are *Mother* and *him*, for they tell for whose benefit the actions were performed. Indirect objects can always be converted into prepositional phrases beginning with *to* or *for*, but then they are simply modifiers and no longer indirect objects.

Father bought a fur coat **for Mother.**

She gave a big kiss **to him.**

(3) Predicate nouns A predicate noun is a noun that follows a linking verb like *be, become,* and so on. It renames the subject in a different way.

Roger remained **a student.**

The young lady became **a debutante.**

Roger and *student* are the same being; *young lady* and *debutante* name the same person. A direct object after a transitive verb rarely names the same thing as the subject; a predicate noun after a linking verb *always* names the same person or thing as the subject. The difference lies in the kind of verb each sentence has.

(4) Predicate adjectives A predicate adjective is an adjective that follows a linking verb and describes the subject.

The wind is **cold** tonight.

Arnold became **bitter** later on.

Cold describes the wind, and *bitter* describes Arnold. You can test for predicate adjectives (those that follow the linking verb) by mentally placing them in front of the subject, like this: *cold wind, bitter Arnold.*

The complements plus the verbs and modifiers form the sentence predicates.

1d3   Independent clauses

Clauses are either independent or dependent. An **independent clause** (also called a **main clause**) is in effect a simple sentence. It is a clause that can stand alone as a complete sentence beginning with a capital letter and ending with a period or a question mark. Each example above is both a simple sentence and an independent clause. Even when it appears in a complex or compound sentence (subsections 1e2 and 1e3), such a clause that *could* stand alone is still called an independent clause.

> **Heidi couldn't start her car** because the battery was dead.

> **She had to buy a new one;** consequently, **she delayed the start of her trip.**

> When she finally arrived, **she was exhausted.**

Each boldface construction is an independent clause; it could stand alone as a complete sentence. *Because the battery was dead* and *when she finally arrived* are indeed clauses, but they cannot stand alone as separate sentence; they are dependent clauses.

1d4   Dependent clauses

Like the independent clauses treated above, **dependent clauses** (also called **subordinate clauses**) are indeed clauses; they have both a subject and a predicate containing a finite verb that shows tense or time of action. They differ from independent clauses in that they begin with a subordinating connective (pp. 36 and 38), which keeps them from standing alone as complete sentences. Grammatically, a dependent clause depends on the rest of the sentence. The dependent clause functions in much the same way that a single-word part of speech would—as an adjective, an adverb, or a noun.

a. **Adjective clauses** Adjective clauses generally begin with one of these relative pronouns, which serve as subordinating connectives: *who, whose, whom, which,* and *that.* (For that reason adjective clauses are often called **relative clauses.**) Like simple adjectives, such relative clauses usually modify a noun or a pronoun by telling *which one* or *what kind.* The noun or pronoun that is being modified is the **antecedent.** The antecedent is italicized in these examples.

> *The guest* **who arrives last** will receive a booby prize.
>
> *A man* **whose wife is beautiful** is always worried.
>
> We elected *Sneedby,* **who paid two dollars a vote.**
>
> I voted for *Scraggs,* **to whom I owed a debt.**

The relative pronoun always stands first in its own clause (unless a preposition belongs to the pronoun). To see the relationship between the relative clause and its antecedent, think of two sentences in which the same noun is repeated:

> **The guest** will receive a booby prize.
>
> **The guest** arrives late.

Then change the noun in the second sentence to a relative pronoun (be sure to use the right case of the pronoun) and insert the whole clause into the first sentence immediately after the noun it modifies. *The guest* in the second sentence becomes *who,* and the entire clause is inserted appropriately into the first sentence.

Which form of *who* to use depends on the form of the noun it replaces in its own clause. In *A man whose wife is beautiful,* the pronoun *whose* is correct because the sentence from which it came originally read *The man's* (possessive case) *wife is beautiful.* (See also section 5c.)

Note also the word order here: *I voted for Scraggs, to whom I owed a debt.* When the relative pronoun functions as some other element in its own clause, it must nevertheless move to the front of the clause. *Whom* is the object of the preposition *to.* Reconstructing the sentence from which the relative clause was derived shows the original relationship: *I owed a debt to Scraggs* becomes *to whom I owed a debt.*

Occasionally an adjective clause can modify the whole idea of a sentence or word group to which it is attached, in which case it must begin with *which* and be set off by a comma. In this example, the adjective clause (in boldface) modifies the whole idea of the independent clause:

> The catcher on our team batted .406 this year, **which set a new local record.**

An understanding of adjective clauses is especially important in knowing how to punctuate correctly (see section 10f).

b. Adverb clauses   Adverb clauses begin with one of the subordinating conjunctions listed in subsection 1b5. The subordinating conjunction expresses a relationship between the adverb clause to which it belongs and some word or whole idea in the rest of the sentence. Like simple adverbs, many such clauses modify the verb in another clause by specifying such matters as the **time, place, manner, frequency,** or **reason** for the action of the verb.

> **Since you don't answer my calls,** I have decided to write.
>
> Margie came to see me **after I had already gone to bed.**
>
> She was excited **because Oscar had proposed to her.**
>
> **Though he isn't the handsomest man in the world,** she accepted **because she loves him.**

The simple subjects and predicate verbs of the preceding adverb clauses are listed on the next page.

```
  you / answer
    I / had gone
Oscar / had proposed
   he / isn't
  she / loves
```

Thus, they are indeed clauses, but the conjunctions *since*, *after*, and *though* make them dependent clauses and keep them from standing alone. If you tried to use such dependent clauses as complete sentences, you would have written fragments (see Chapter 2).

c. Noun clauses   Noun clauses begin with *that* (a meaningless subordinating connective), with *what, whatever, whoever, whichever*, with a relative pronoun, or with a subordinating conjunction. (Only a few of the subordinating conjunctions can begin a noun clause.) The distinctive characteristic of noun clauses is that they function as nouns in sentences—usually as subjects or direct objects. The best way to test for a noun clause is to see if you can substitute *someone* or *something* for it.

I know **that you love me**.   [I know something.]

What you do is your business.   [Something is your business.]

Whatever I say doesn't matter.   [Something doesn't matter.]

She distributed the tickets to **whoever showed up.**   [Here the noun clause functions as the object *to*; she distributed the tickets to someone.]

That, what, whatever, and *whoever* prevent the clauses from standing as complete sentences. They are clauses, however, since each has a subject and a predicate:

```
    you / love me
    you / do
      I / say
whoever / showed up
```

Note that noun clauses are *not* set off by commas any more than single-word nouns are. A number of the following chapters, especially those on punctuation, will deal with dependent clauses.

1e Sentences

The parts of speech defined in sections 1a and 1b, the phrases defined in section 1c, and the clauses defined in section 1d are variously arranged to form sentences. Every sentence has at least one independent clause, and every independent clause *could* be a sentence in its own right (subsections 1d1 and 1d2). How clauses are used separately or in combination determines the kind of sentence an utterance is. For simplicity, we will identify four types.

1e1 Simple sentences

A simple sentence consists of one independent clause only; it has no dependent clauses (see section 1d for a description of clauses). Even though various kinds of phrases carrying additional ideas may be in such a sentence, it is still called a simple sentence.

My thermos bottle leaks profusely.

To begin with, its plastic cap, screwed in tightly, never seems to fit precisely.

The simple subjects and predicates are *bottle/leaks* and *cap/ seems to fit*; all the other words and phrases are modifiers.

Regardless of its length, a simple sentence has only one subject and one predicate, though either the subject or the predicate or both may contain more than one element (see section 6d).

COMPOUND SUBJECT:

Joe and **Ellen** / came to my house last night.

COMPOUND PREDICATE:

We / **drank beer** and **ate pizza**.

COMPOUND SUBJECT AND COMPOUND PREDICATE:

> **May and Joan** / also **dropped by** and **stayed for an hour.**

1e2 Compound sentences

A compound sentence joins two or more independent clauses but no dependent clauses into one sentence. The connective may be one of the coordinating conjunctions or a conjunctive adverb (subsection 1b4); sometimes a semicolon alone joins the independent clauses. Examples, with the independent clauses in boldface:

> **We didn't care about breaking the speed limit,** for **Sheila was about to have her baby.**

> **The sun and moon appear to be about the same size;** however, **the one is really vastly larger than the other.**

> **We need a new car; our old jalopy doesn't start easily.**

Punctuating compound sentences is not difficult if you follow the rules in Chapter 3, in section 10b, and in Chapter 12.

1e3 Complex sentences

A complex sentence has one independent clause (and *only* one) plus one or more dependent clauses. Such dependent clauses may be adjective (or relative) clauses, adverb clauses, or noun clauses, and these may appear in any appropriate position in the sentence. To recognize a complex sentence, identify all the clauses individually; then determine which one is independent and which are dependent. The examples show the dependent or subordinate clauses in boldface.

> The horse **that I bet on** came in last.   [adjective clause]

> **While Ruthie kept guard,** I climbed through the transom. [adverb clause]

> **If it rains,** we'll call off the race, **since the track will be too slick for our tires.**   [Both dependent clauses are adverb clauses.]

That you are a jerk is obvious.   [The noun clause is the subject of the independent clause.]

What I want to know is **why you are angry.**   [Both dependent clauses are noun clauses; substituting *something* for each clause reveals the structure of the main idea: *Something is something.* It is a complex sentence.]

1e4   Compound-complex sentences

A compound-complex sentence contains at least two independent clauses and at least one dependent clause. The examples show the dependent clauses in boldface and the independent clauses in italics.

If the weather is fair, *we will go on our camping trip,* and *I expect to have a great time.*

Since I could see his hat on the table, *I knew of the intruder's presence,* but *I made no move* **in case he had a pistol.**

The traditional four-fold classification of sentences does not tell the whole truth about the great variety of structures in English sentences, but it is a useful starting point. (Can you tell what kind of sentence this last sentence is?)

1f   Modifiers

A **modifier** is a word or word group that describes, limits, or adds to another word or word group. For example, if to the phrase *a shirt* we add the modifier *blue* to get *a blue shirt,* we have (1) described the shirt to a degree; (2) limited the shirt, since all non-blue shirts are now excluded; and (3) in a sense, added to the shirt, since we have told something about it that formerly we did not know. This all seems simple, but actually modification is one of the complex features of language. You need to know some of the aspects of modification in order to deal with many writing problems treated in the following chapters.

There are three general kinds of modifiers: those that affect nouns, those that affect verbs, and those that relate to whole sentences. In discussing them, we return to the fact that parts of speech are classified by form and function. Thus, some words may function as adjectives and adverbs though they are classified as other parts of speech according to their form. Units larger than a single word may also serve as modifiers. In addition to single-word adjectives and adverbs (sections 1a3 and 1a4) we note the three kinds of modifiers: **adjectivals, adverbials,** and **sentence modifiers.**

1f1 Adjectivals

Any word or word group that modifies a noun or pronoun is by function an **adjectival** (the ending -al means *like an adjective*). They may be single words (adjectives, nouns, verbals, and adverbs), phrases (prepositional phrases and verbal phrases), and clauses (both relative clauses and adverb clauses). The following examples illustrate various kinds of single-word adjectivals, with the adjectival itself in boldface and the noun it modifies in italics.

> the **biggest** *bonus*   [adjective]
> This *soup* tastes **salty.**   [adjective]
> the **table** *lamp*   [noun]
> the **riding** *instructor*   [verbal]
> the *apartment* **below**   [adverb]

Prepositional phrases are also commonly used as adjectivals modifying nouns; in much the same way, verbal phrases also have that function.

> the *dancer* **on stage**   [prepositional phrase]
> the *bee* **in her bonnet**   [prepositional phrase
> the *girl* **wearing the bikini**   [verbal phrase]
> **Being exhausted,** *Joe* took a nap.   [verbal phrase]
> the *team* **beaten by 17 points**   [verbal phrase]

Clauses, notably relative clauses, serve as adjectivals. Sometimes adverb clauses also modify nouns.

> the *plays* **which Shakespeare wrote**   [adjective clause]
> a *time* **when all the chickens are asleep**   [adverb clause]
> the *building* **where I live**   [adverb clause]

Although most of the constructions in boldface are not adjectives, they are adjectivals by function because they modify nouns. Note also the various positions such adjectivals may take relative to the nouns they modify. More information about modifiers appears in Chapters 4 and 23.

1f2   Adverbials

Any word or word group that modifies a verb, an adjective, or another adverb is an **adverbial** by function (again, note the spelling with the *-ial* ending that means *like an adverb*). Most adverbials answer questions like *where, when, how,* and *why* in regard to the verb. They may be single words (adverbs themselves function as adverbials, adjectives, and verbals), phrases (prepositional phrases and verbal phrases), and clauses. What differentiates adverbials from adjectivals is their function—what adverbials modify is not the noun or pronoun but a verb (and sometimes an adjective or another adverb). The examples show the adverbials in boldface and the words they modify are in italics.

> to *sing* **loudly**   [a single-word adverb]
> *arrived* **yesterday**   [a noun functioning as an adverbial]
> If you *study* **long,** you *study* **wrong.**   [both are adjectives]
> the cherries *eaten* **by the robins**   [a prepositional phrase]
> to *watch* **sitting in the bleachers**   [a verbal phrase]
> I *studied* hard **to improve my grades**   [an infinitive phrase]
> *smoking* **where it is forbidden**   [an adverb clause]

All of the constructions in boldface are adverbials because they modify verbs. Single-word adverbs and adverb clauses may occupy various positions in the sentence; most other adverbials follow the words they modify. Chapter 4 and Chapter 23 give additional information about adverbials.

1f3 Sentence modifiers

In some sentences an expression modifies a whole idea rather than a single word. Then it is a **sentence modifier,** usually set off from the rest of the sentence by a comma. Here are examples of sentence modifiers, in boldface:

Clearly, he did not explain the situation. [*Clearly* is an adverb modifying the whole sentence. Note how different in meaning the sentence is from "He did not explain the situation clearly," in which *clearly* is an adverbial modifying only the one word *explain.*]

Yes, you may have a snack. [*Yes* responds to the whole idea which follows, not to any single word.]

Strictly speaking, the purchase of a new car is not an investment. [The verbal phrase modifies the whole idea.]

We played the slot machines at Tahoe, **which is a good way to go broke fast.** [The dependent clause refers to the entire idea stated in the first clause, not just to one word.]

In determining what a word or word group modifies, the best approach is to ask *what goes with what.* Sentence modifiers, you see, do not pinpoint only one word; rather, they refer to a whole idea. In subsections 1f1 and 1f2 you can readily see that the boldface constructions modify what is italicized.

1g Appositives

Basically, an **appositive** is a noun repeater; that is, it renames in different words the noun that it is in apposition to. It gives more information about that noun as it specifies more exactly what is meant. An appositive may be a single word, a phrase, or a clause. The examples show the appositive in boldface; the noun it renames is in italics:

My uncle, **a retired sea-captain,** told stories of intrigue and adventure. [The appositive is a noun phrase.]

My sister **Pat** hates to do the dishes. [A single noun is the appositive.]

The belief **that he is guilty** requires proof. [*That he is guilty* is a noun clause that expands and specifies the word *belief* as it renames it.]

Her first love, **eating wild mushrooms,** was her last act. [A verbal phrase used as a noun is in apposition to the noun *love.*]

Sometimes an appositive is in apposition to a whole idea, as in the following example:

He conceded the election, **a gesture his backers disapproved of.**

The appositive in boldface is in apposition to the italicized sentence. Occasionally appositives are introduced by connectives like *that is, such as, for example,* and *in other words.*

Vibrissae, or **whiskers,** grow on the faces of all species of cats and seals.

Kangaroos are *marsupials,* that is, **mammals that carry their young in pouches.**

Appositives often serve to define unfamiliar words by substituting specific and better known expressions. In the examples, you may have noted that some appositives are set off by commas while others are not. Section 10f explains such punctuation more fully.

1h Coordination

Coordination means the joining of two or more sentence parts or independent clauses so that they are equal in rank. This grammatical function, which involves problems in punctuation and sentence structure, usually calls for one of the coordinating connectives discussed in section 1b4 or particular punctuation marks. When two parts are coordinated, they are said to be **compounded;** when three or more parts are coordinated, we speak of them as **items in a series.** They may be single words, phrases of all kinds, or whole clauses.

COMPOUNDS:

> **Jim** and **Buck** sit in the front row.   [two nouns]
>
> They **laugh** and **chatter** continually.   [two verbs]
>
> They didn't show up **for the quiz** or **for the final.**   [two phrases]
>
> **Both failed,** but **they can re-enroll.**   [two clauses]

ITEMS IN A SERIES:

> **Updike, Faulkner,** and **Hemingway** are American authors.
>
> **Riding horses, drinking whiskey,** and **writing novels** were Faulkner's favorite pastimes.

1i Subordination

Subordination means that one sentence part is unequal in rank to another part. Prepositional phrases and verbal phrases are always subordinate to the words or ideas they modify. Subordinate clauses are usually introduced by one of the subordinating conjunctions (subsection 1b5), by a relative pronoun (subsections 1b6 and 1d4), or by *that* or *what*. Sentence modifiers (subsection 1f3) are also subordinate constructions. The example shows the subordinate element in boldface.

> Vodka is intoxicating, **though it is free of fusel oils.**

The word *though* produces the subordination. If it is changed to *but*, coordination results and the two clauses are equal in rank.

> Vodka is intoxicating, but it is free of fusel oils.

Coordination and subordination are involved in various aspects of sentence structure and punctuation. An understanding of both is important for expressing meaning precisely.

1j Ambiguity

An important term in grammar is ambiguity. This means that a sentence has two possible meanings, often with no clue to show the reader which meaning is intended.

> John discussed his problem with the teacher. [Did he try to get an answer from the teacher about a particular problem that puzzled him? Or was the teacher John's problem?]

> Todd is a poor mechanic. [Is he poverty-stricken? Or is he just not able to repair machinery well?]

Can you detect the ambiguity in the following examples?

> How would you like to see a model home?

> Bathing beauties can be fun.

> I will lose no time in reading your paper.

> The students are revolting.

Ambiguities can be entertaining, but usually ambiguity is a grave weakness in writing.

The foregoing brief explanations of the basics of English grammar pertain to writing problems discussed in the rest of this handbook. You will benefit most from this course if you refer to Chapter 1 first for answers to your grammar questions, then refer to later chapters as indicated. Consider Chapter 1 as a compact reference guide within the text; use the list of terms on the back cover to find the topics on which you have questions. The more familiar you are with Chapter 1, the more valuable a tool this textbook will prove; the more your writing reflects the fundamental points of good grammar, the more effectively you will communicate your thoughts with those around you. Effective communication is perhaps one of the most important factors in a successful life. It is in your hands now.

2

Sentence Fragments

A sentence is a group of words containing a subject and a predicate and expressing a complete thought. Every sentence must have at least one independent clause. In addition to a well-formed subject and a well-formed predicate, many sentences also have various phrases and subordinate clauses as modifiers.

One of the most common problems among beginning writers who have not developed their "sentence sense" is that they write in sentence fragments, or non-sentences. The "sentences" may well begin with a capital letter and end with a period or a question mark, and the structures may indeed contain a subject and a predicate; nevertheless, the thought is in some way incomplete and it should not stand alone as if it were a complete sentence.

In conversation people often speak in fragments because they are responding to ideas in previous sentences. In semiformal writing (the kind your college classes call for), fragments are serious errors.

To recognize fragments (and to avoid them or correct them in your own writing) you need to recognize two kinds of meaning: one is the meaning that the words themselves express; the other is the grammatical meaning of the words in combination within the sentence. It is the grammatical meaning that fulfills the notion that the structure is complete and independent. Consider the following example:

FRAGMENT:
> While the mechanic described how a carburetor works.

Every content word in that construction has its own full meaning without reference to a preceding sentence; yet the construction is not a complete sentence. It is not *grammatically* complete.

On the other hand, here is a sentence that is grammatically complete.

> He showed it to them.

None of the words except *showed* has much meaning unless you know what an earlier sentence said. Yet the structure is a complete sentence; *he* is the subject, and *showed it to them* is the predicate.

Sentence sense lets you recognize the following characteristics of a sentence.

1. Pronoun reference to a preceding sentence does not prevent a construction from being a sentence.

   SENTENCE:
   > We saw them there.

2. Reference of a verb auxiliary to a preceding sentence does not prevent a construction from being a sentence.

   SENTENCE:
   > I haven't, but neither has he, nor could she.

The auxiliaries *haven't*, *has*, and *could* must draw

their meaning from verbs in a preceding sentence. In spite of its lack of content, this example is a sentence.

3. The reference of *so, thus, then,* and *there* to a preceding sentence does not prevent a construction from being a sentence.

SENTENCE:
   So did the two of them.

Not only *so* in this sentence but also *did, two,* and *them* get their meaning from a preceding sentence. Grammatically, however, the construction is a complete sentence.

4. A construction may begin with a coordinating connective or a transitional phrase and still stand alone as a complete sentence.

SENTENCES:
   But the house on the corner was vacant.

   In addition, we found the garage empty, too.

Coordinating connectives like *but* and transitional phrases like *in addition* often serve to begin a sentence when the relationship to the preceding sentence is clear.

On the other hand, sentence sense lets us recognize the following flaws in "sentences."

1. A clause beginning with a subordinating connective (subordinating conjunctions, relative pronouns, and a few connectives such as *that* and *what*—see subsection 1b4) is a fragment; it is not a sentence.

FRAGMENTS:
   Because I've sent Aunt Martha a card each birthday.

   As long as I can remember.

   That she shouldn't be so negative.

Each of these is a clause, but the subordinating connectives *because, as long as,* and *that* keep them from being complete sentences capable of standing alone.

2. A construction without a subject and a predicate is not a grammatical sentence.

FRAGMENTS:

To sleep. Perchance to dream.

If not today, then tomorrow.

Claiming to be a messenger from outer space.

Though these constructions deliver more meaning than, say, *I will if you can,* they are not grammatical sentences because they do not have subject-predicate combinations.

You should study sections 1c and 1e (and perhaps all of Chapter 1) if you need to refer to Chapters 2 and 3 often.

2a Detached Clauses as Sentence Fragments

Write in complete sentences; do not let a detached clause stand as a sentence.

A common kind of sentence fragment is a **detached dependent clause.** A dependent clause cannot stand by itself with a beginning capital letter and end punctuation. This sort of error usually occurs through oversight rather than because of ignorance. Attach dependent clauses to the preceding sentence, sometimes with (and sometimes without) a comma separating them. The following examples show the fragments in *italics.*

WRONG: People's failure to voice complaints often results from embarrassment. *Because they don't want to make a scene.*

RIGHT: People's failure to voice complaints often results from embarrassment because they don't want to make a scene.

WRONG: Strangely, the dean asked us if we would accept the new assignments. *After he had already circulated the announcement.*

RIGHT: Strangely, the dean asked us if we would accept the new assignments after he had already circulated the announcement.

WRONG: The moon was bright that night. *Which allowed us to find our way back to the cabin.*

RIGHT: The moon was bright that night, which allowed us to find our way back to the cabin.

Subordinating connectives such as *because, after,* and *which* prevent detached dependent clauses from standing as sentences. For such connectives see subsection 1b5.

Another effective way to correct such fragments resulting from detached clauses is to eliminate the subordinating connectives and make each clause an independent sentence. Notice how the preceding wrong examples have been corrected by this method.

RIGHT: People's failure to voice complaints often results from embarrassment. They don't want to make a scene.

RIGHT: Strangely, the dean asked us if we would accept the new assignments. He had already circulated the announcement.

RIGHT: The moon was bright that night. It allowed us to find our way back to the cabin.

2b   Detached Phrases as Sentence Fragments

Write in complete sentences; do not let a phrase stand alone as a sentence.

A phrase is a construction without a subject-predicate combination. Such phrases have various functions in sentences, often as noun substitutes or noun or verb modifiers. However, the very fact that they have neither a subject nor a predicate prevents them from standing alone as sentences. Make a **detached phrase** part of a sentence either by attaching it to a preceding sentence or by supplying a subject and a predicate. The following examples show the detached phrases in italics.

WRONG: To play sandlot baseball you need only a few items. *A bat, a ball, four bases, and a few players.*

RIGHT: To play sandlot baseball you need only a few items: a bat, a ball, four bases, and a few players.

WRONG: What a day we had! *Beaten by the team from Cove!*

RIGHT: What a day we had! Of all things, we were beaten by the team from Cove!

WRONG: Grandma gave each of us a basket and told us to look for eggs. *In the barn, under the bushes, and behind the toolshed.*

RIGHT: Grandma gave each of us a basket and told us to look for eggs in the barn, under the bushes, and behind the toolshed.

Noun phrases, prepositional phrases, and the various kinds of verbal phrases frequently are detached from sentences they belong to. Thus, they become fragments. (See *Phrases* in section 1c.)

2c Sentence Fragments due to Confused Structures

Write in complete and well-formed sentences; avoid jumbled structures.

A third kind of sentence fragment is one in which a necessary part of a sentence has been omitted or in which the sentence structure is jumbled rather than complete and grammatically consistent (see also section 23a).

> WRONG: Most homeowners who buy woodstoves to save on fuel costs, which is the main reason for making such purchases.
>
> RIGHT: Most homeowners who buy woodstoves to save on fuel costs, which is the main reason for making such purchases, do not recover their investment for several years.

The writer forgot to compose a predicate to go with the subject *homeowners*. Neither the relative clause beginning with *who* nor the clause beginning with *which* serves that function. In the following example the reader is frustrated because an entire independent clause is missing—the one that completes the idea begun in *When I fish*.

> WRONG: When I fish, especially in cold weather, which is one reason I can't tie the knots easily.
>
> RIGHT: When I fish, especially in cold weather, which is one reason I can't tie the knots easily, it takes me a long time to get started.
>
> RIGHT: When I fish, especially in cold weather, I can't tie the knots easily.

2d Fragments with Nonfinite Verb Forms

Write in complete sentences; do not let a construction with a nonfinite verb form stand as a sentence.

A fourth type of sentence fragment is a construction with a nonfinite verb rather than a finite or sentence-forming verb (see section 1c2). Such fragments can be corrected by making the verb finite, by adding an auxiliary verb, or by using the verbal in one of its acceptable functions (see section 1c3). In the following examples the nonfinite verb forms are in italics.

> WRONG: I cut my finger while whittling and then *going* to the doctor to have my wound stitched.

RIGHT: I cut my finger while whittling and then went to the doctor to have my wound stitched.

WRONG: *Swimming* in the river at our annual church picnic.

RIGHT: We went swimming in the river at our annual church picnic.

WRONG: *To milk* the cows every morning and evening.

RIGHT: Elmer's job was to milk the cows every morning and evening. (The infinitive phrase is now a predicate noun.)

RIGHT: To milk the cows every morning and evening was an odious task. (The infinitive phrase functions as the subject.)

Many, perhaps most, such fragments are due to carelessness, but some may result from the writer's lack of sentence sense.

3

Comma Splices and
Run-Together Sentences

Two independent clauses may be joined to one another to form a compound sentence. If one or more dependent clauses are added to such a compound sentence, the construction is a compound-complex sentence (subsection 1e4). Such constructions require specific kinds of connectives and punctuation.

Independent clauses are in effect simple sentences, and they may, of course, be punctuated as separate items.

SIMPLE SENTENCES:

Tom plays the sousaphone. He isn't really very proficient at it.

Suzanne didn't have a date for the dance. She stayed home all Saturday night.

When two such sentences are closely related in thought, they may be joined to form compound sentences. One method is to add a comma plus an appropriate coordinating conjunction (section 10b).

COMPOUND SENTENCES:

> Tom plays the sousaphone, **but** he isn't really very proficient at it.

> Suzanne didn't have a date for the dance, **so** she stayed home all Saturday night.

Another method of joining independent clauses into a compound sentence is to use a semicolon without a coordinating connective. Such a semicolon has the same force as a period; it is normally used only when the independent clauses are especially closely related (see also section 12a).

COMPOUND SENTENCE:

> The jet was hardly above tree-top level; its roar frightened all the animals in the neighborhood.

When a conjunctive adverb (section 1b4) joins two independent clauses, a semicolon must appear before and a comma must follow the conjunctive adverb (see section 12b).

COMPOUND SENTENCE:

> Jo hadn't paid her tuition yet; **nevertheless,** she attended classes regularly.

These are correct methods of dealing with two independent clauses. What follows illustrates common errors and explains how to correct them.

3a Comma Splices without Connective Words

Do not use a comma alone to separate two independent clauses that are not joined by a coordinating conjunction.

A comma alone, with no connective, incorrectly "splices" the sentence and produces a **comma splice.** In such cases, the second sentence usually begins with a word like *this, another, there,* or *it* that leads the reader to believe that the sentence is continuing when actually a new sentence has begun. Either a period, a semicolon, or the addition of a coordinating conjunction after the comma corrects such a comma splice.

WRONG: Many times a homeowner installs another electrical outlet in a room, this will give him an additional spot to plug in a lamp or a fan.

RIGHT: Many times a homeowner installs another electrical outlet in a room, **for** this will give him an additional spot to plug in a lamp or a fan.   [Adding the conjunction *for* corrects the error.]

RIGHT: Many times a homeowner installs another electrical outlet in a room; this will give him an additional spot to plug in a lamp or a fan.   [A period could serve as well as the semicolon after *room*.]

WRONG: Stringing the wires to the fuse box is not too hard, making the final connections is equally as easy.

RIGHT: Stringing the wires to the fuse box is not too hard, **and** making the final connection is equally as easy.   [The combination of a comma plus the coordinating conjunction correctly joins the two clauses.]

RIGHT: Stringing the wires to the fuse box is not too hard; making the final connection is equally as easy.

In the last example, a period instead of a semicolon would also be correct. A semicolon calls for the same duration of voice pause that a period does. Thus where a period is correct, a semicolon normally cannot be called wrong. However, in some sentences it may produce awkward style.

3b Comma Splices with Conjunctive Adverbs

Conjunctive adverbs like *however, therefore,* and *nevertheless* frequently join sentences (or independent clauses), but they are not coordinating conjunctions (for a list of conjunctive adverbs see section 1b4). A comma instead of a period or semicolon produces a comma splice.

WRONG: The ordinary homeowner can probably do the job,

however, he must have it checked by a licensed electrician.

RIGHT: The ordinary homeowner can probably do the job**;** **however,** he must have it checked by a licensed electrician.

Note several points here: (1) With a comma before and after *however*, the rapid reader might not at first know which clause the *however* goes with; quite often sentences end with a conjunctive adverb. (2) A period after *job* would also be correct. And (3), the *however* could be shifted to the interior or the end of the second clause—after *must* or after *electrician*, for example. Such a shift provides you with a test; if the connective can be shifted, a period or a semicolon must come after the first clause.

WRONG: Building codes vary from one city to the next, accordingly, a wise person will check them before he begins.

RIGHT: Building codes vary from one city to the next**;** **accordingly,** a wise person will check them before he begins.

A period after *next* would not be wrong. Apply the test: *Accordingly* could be shifted, as in, *A wise person, accordingly, will check them before he begins.*

WRONG: Plugging in the lamp caused a fuse to blow instantly, then I decided to start over again.

RIGHT: Plugging in the lamp caused a fuse to blow instantly**;** then I decided to start over again.

In this sentence *then* is a conjunctive adverb; thus either a period or a semicolon must come after *instantly*. (Note in the preceding example and in the first sentence in this paragraph that some conjunctive adverbs like *then* and *thus* need not be followed by a comma.)

3c   Run-Together Sentences

Do not run two sentences together without adding some punctuation between them.

A **run-together sentence** (sometimes called a **run-on sentence**) occurs when two sentences run on with no punctuation mark at all and no coordinating connective between them. The fact that the second sentence does not begin with a capital letter may indicate that the writer has merely been careless. Usually, however, it suggests that the writer has not developed the skill called *sentence sense*. The cure is simple: Use a period or a semicolon.

WRONG: The decision to start over prompted me to check the manual that is what I should have done in the first place.

RIGHT: The decision to start over prompted me to check the manual. That is what I should have done in the first place.

WRONG: The second attempt worked perfectly this is what I had wanted all along.

RIGHT: The second attempt worked perfectly; this is what I had wanted all along.

When to write separate sentences, when to use a comma plus a coordinating conjunction, and when to use a conjunctive adverb with its correct punctuation depends on how close the relationship is between the independent clauses.

If you find that you must refer to this chapter or to section 12b frequently, you may need to study sections 1c and 1d carefully and perhaps all of Chapter 1.

4

Misused Modifiers

A modifier is a word or a word group that describes, limits, or adds to another word or word group. Adjectives and adjectivals answer questions like *which one* and *what kind* about a noun (subsection 1a3 and section 1f). Adverbs and adverbials answer questions like *when, where, why, how, how often,* and *under what circumstances* about the verb (subsection 1a4 and section 1f).

The common misuses of modifiers are the incorrect use of an adjective for an adverb to modify a verb, and the incorrect use of an adverb as a predicate adjective (subsection 1d2).

4a   Misused Adjective Forms

An adjective form cannot be used to modify an intransitive or a transitive verb.

Correct writing requires that an adverb modify a verb. To determine whether a word is modifying a verb, ask *What goes with what?*

Joseph attends the symphony concert very seldom.

Ask "What does *seldom* go with?" The answer should be *seldom attends;* the adverb *seldom* modifies (goes with) the verb of the sentence and is correctly used.

Often an adjective is misused as a verb modifier, especially when the adjective follows the verb at some distance. Here are examples of adjectives misused as adverbs, with the modified verb underlined:

WRONG: Because of interference in my ham radio, I had <u>to speak</u> each word *slow* and *separate.*

RIGHT: Because of interference in my ham radio, I had <u>to speak</u> each word **slowly** and **separately.**

WRONG: Alton <u>played</u> his guitar so *lovely* that I just closed my eyes and drifted into dreamland.

RIGHT: Alton <u>played</u> his guitar **in such a lovely manner** that I just closed my eyes and drifted into dreamland.

Again, ask "What goes with what?" In the first example you must write *to speak slowly and separately;* both adverbs end in *-ly.* In the second example *lovely* is one of a few adjectives (*heavenly, friendly,* and others) that end in *-ly;* you cannot use it to modify the verb *played.* Because *lovelily* would sound awkward, use the prepositional phrase *in a lovely manner* instead.

WRONG: My calculator <u>extracts</u> the square root of a number real *easy.*

RIGHT: My calculator <u>extracts</u> the square root of a number quite **easily.**

WRONG: Ernie <u>had to weave</u> in and out among the speeding cars real *careful.*

RIGHT: Ernie <u>had to weave</u> in and out among the speeding cars rather **carefully.**

The adverbs *easily* and *carefully* correctly go with or modify the verbs *extracts* and *had to weave*. Notice also that the overused qualifier *real* in both examples changes to another word in the corrected sentences.

a. **well / good** A particularly sticky writing problem involves *well* and *good*. *Well* can be either an adjective (He is a *well* man now that he has been cured) or an adverb (Helen rides her horse *well*). *Good* is only an adjective. A writer should always use *well* to modify a verb. The verbs are underlined in the following examples.

> WRONG: Van Cliburn certainly <u>plays</u> the piano *good*, but he can hardly get a clear note out of the violin.

> RIGHT: Van Cliburn certainly <u>plays</u> the piano **well,** but he can hardly get a clear note out of the violin.

> WRONG: Art claims he <u>did</u> *good* on the final, but he still got only a C for the course.

> RIGHT: Art claims he <u>did</u> **well** on the final, but he still got only a C for the course.

Remember that you *do well, write well, play well, argue well, dress well, behave well,* and *work well.*

b. **nearly** Another adjective often misused for an adverb is *near* for *nearly.*

> WRONG: Brunhilda isn't *near* as pretty as she thinks she is.

> RIGHT: Brunhilda isn't **nearly** as pretty as she thinks she is.

> WRONG: Even though Lisa came in so late Sunday morning, Dad didn't scold her *near* as harshly as Mother did.

> RIGHT: Even though Lisa came in so late Sunday morning, Dad didn't scold her **nearly** as harshly as Mother did.

c.   **fun**   A related problem is the misuse of the noun *fun* as an adjective.

WRONG: We had a *fun* time at the dance.

RIGHT: We had a **good** time at the dance.

RIGHT: We had **fun** at the dance.   [Now *fun* is correctly used as a noun, not as an adjective modifying *time*.]

4b   Misused Adverb Forms

Do not use an adverb as a predicate adjective after a linking verb.

After a linking verb, the correct modifier is not an adverb, but an adjective which describes the subject. The chief linking verbs are *be, get, feel, seem, sound, taste, look, remain, become,* and *appear.* Sometimes verbs that are normally linking—such as *to feel* and *to taste*—are used as intransitive or transitive verbs.

When she lost her wedding ring, Mother **felt** terrible. [linking]

When she wanted to make a new blouse, Mother **felt** the material first.   [transitive]

After a hard day in the woods, bean and bacon soup **tastes** good.   [linking]

Before dinner was served, Dad always **tasted** the soup. [transitive]

Occasionally certain intransitive or transitive verbs may function as linking verbs. The clue is that the linking verb is followed by an adjective that modifies the subject or by a predicate noun that renames the subject (see subsection 1a2). Thus such verbs as *go, turn, marry, die,* and *retire* are normally intransitive or transitive but occasionally function as linking, being followed by predicate adjectives that describe the subjects.

Mother **went** to the store.   [intransitive]

Within sight of the water, the thirsty animals **went** *crazy*.   [linking]

The cook **turned** the pancakes.   [transitive]

George **turned** *belligerent*.   [linking]

Heidi **married** David.   [transitive]

Louise **married** *young*.   [linking]

Our dog Missy **died** yesterday.   [intransitive]

Pablo Casals **died** *old*.   [linking]

Mr. Kearns **retired** recently.   [intransitive]

Mr. Bailey **retired** *happy*.   [linking]

Since the meanings of each second example are *crazy animals, belligerent George, young Louise, old Pablo Casals,* and *happy Mr. Bailey,* the verbs are linking verbs, and adjectives must follow them.

badly   The most commonly misused adverb form is *badly* after the linking verb *feel*.

WRONG: After I was caught plagiarizing, I felt *badly*.

RIGHT: After I was caught plagiarizing, I felt **bad.**

WRONG: Rich said he felt *badly* about dropping that pass in the last seconds of the game.

RIGHT: Rich said he felt **bad** about dropping that pass in the last seconds of the game.

WRONG: I still feel *badly* every time I remember how I forgot my lines on opening night.

RIGHT: I still feel **bad** every time I remember how I forgot my lines on opening night.

Because *feel* and *felt* are linking verbs, the adjective *bad* is needed as the predicate adjective. You would be very unlikely to say either of the following sentences:

WRONG: I felt *sadly* about your divorce.

WRONG: I feel *gladly* that you were chosen homecoming queen.

Sad and *glad* are the correct predicate adjectives. In the same way *feel bad* is the correct form.

Occasionally a writer will use other adverb forms incorrectly after linking verbs.

WRONG: Without a tent, the campers all felt *miserably* as they slept in the rain.

RIGHT: Without a tent, the campers all felt **miserable** as they slept in the rain.

WRONG: I remember how *angrily* Katherine sounded after I read her love letters at the dinner table.

RIGHT: I remember how **angry** Katherine sounded after I read her love letters at the dinner table.

After the linking verbs *felt* and *sounded* you need predicate adjectives to produce *the miserable campers* and *angry Katherine*. Here is another test. Since *be* is a linking verb, substitute *is* or *was* (or another form) in place of the verb.

RIGHT: The campers *were miserable*.   [You would hardly say *The campers were miserably*.]

RIGHT: Katherine *was angry*.   [You would not say *Katherine was angrily*.]

4c   Double Negatives

Do not use a double negative.

Words that say or imply "no" are just as surely modifiers as are other adjectives and adverbs. A **double negative** is a construction in which two words expressing negation are used to make one negative statement. Such errors in writing often occur after an abbreviated form such as *don't, didn't, hasn't,* and *isn't.* In usage, such double negative constructions are considered as unacceptable as *ain't.* The two negatives are italicized in the incorrect examples.

WRONG: For the first week of her visit, my cousin *didn't* know *nobody* at all.

RIGHT: For the first week of her visit, my cousin **didn't know anybody** at all.

WRONG: It *didn't* seem to make *no* difference to her; she soon had lots of friends.

RIGHT: It **didn't** seem to make **any** difference to her; she soon had lots of friends.

The correct constructions are *not . . . anybody, not . . . anything, not . . . any, don't (doesn't) . . . any.*

hardly / scarcely Another double negative involves the words *hardly* and *scarcely.* Both are negatives. Using another negative in the same construction produces an incorrect double negative. The double negatives are italicized in the incorrect examples.

WRONG: Mrs. Rich constantly complains to her husband that she *doesn't* have *hardly* any clothes to wear.

RIGHT: Mrs. Rich constantly complains to her husband that she **has hardly** any (or: **doesn't have many**) clothes to wear.

WRONG: He *hadn't scarcely* finished his breakfast when Harry came to pick him up.

RIGHT: He **had scarcely** finished his breakfast when Harry came to pick him up.

Remember never to use *no* or *not* in a construction with *hardly* or *scarcely.*

5

Pronoun Case Form

Pronouns may appear in a sentence in any one of three case forms.

- The **subjective case** forms are I, we; you; he, she, it, and they. Subjective pronouns serve as subjects and as predicate nouns (or, more exactly, as predicate pronouns) after linking verbs.

- The **objective case** forms are me, us; you; him, her, it, and them. Objective pronouns serve as objects or indirect objects of a verb and as objects of prepositions.

- Some of the **possessive case** forms function as determiners for the nouns that they precede as they indicate possession; these forms are my, our; your; his, her, its and their. Other possessive pronouns are used without a noun; these forms are mine, ours; yours; his, hers, its, and theirs. You can avoid making one of the most common errors in writing if you learn now that possessive pronouns never use an apostrophe; never ever.

5a Compound Constructions

Use subjective case forms as subjects in compound constructions; use objective case forms as objects in compound constructions.

Writers and speakers rarely use a wrong pronoun case form when a single pronoun is a subject or an object. For example, you could wait for years and probably not hear constructions such as these:

WRONG: *Her* didn't get an invitation to Sybil's wedding.

WRONG: The letter was addressed to *I*.

5a1 Pronoun subjects

When two pronouns—or a noun and a pronoun together—occur in compound constructions, a faulty pronoun case form may occur. These examples show the faulty pronoun forms italicized.

WRONG: *Him* and *me* decided to go surfing.

RIGHT: **He** and **I** decided to go surfing.

WRONG: Dad and *him* began to set up the tent.

RIGHT: Dad and **he** began to set up the tent.

Since all the pronouns above function as subjects in their sentences, the subjective case form must be used. When in doubt, you can test such constructions by omitting one part of such a compound construction. You would not, for example, say *Him decided to go surfing*, nor would you say *Me decided to go surfing; he and I* are the correct forms, whether used together or singly.

5a2   Pronoun objects

Do not use the subjective case form of a pronoun that functions as an object.

WRONG: George sent both my sister and I separate gifts.

RIGHT: George sent both my sister and **me** separate gifts.   [*My sister* and *me* are indirect objects.]

WRONG: Mrs. Banks, the manager, warned Arlene and *she* about their repeated tardiness.

RIGHT: Mrs. Banks, the manager, warned Arlene and **her** about their repeated tardiness.   [*Arlene* and *her* are both direct objects of *warned.*]

WRONG: Between Harold and I, we thought it was a good way to make money.

RIGHT: Between Harold and **me,** we thought it was a good way to make money.   [Harold and *me* are both objects of the preposition *between.*]

The simple test of omitting one part of the compound construction works every time. You would not write *George sent I a gift, Mrs. Banks warned she,* or *Between I. . . .*

5b   After Linking Verbs

Use subjective pronoun forms after forms of the linking verb **be** and after all linking verbs.

A predicate noun (see subsection 1d2) renames the subject after linking verbs like *be* (in all of its forms: *am, are, is; was, were*). Choosing the correct form of a noun in the predicate poses no problem—nouns have neither a subjective nor an objective case form. For pronouns, however, the general rule states that you should use the subjective case form in the predicate, especially in formal or semiformal writing.

SEMIFORMAL:

> It is **I.**
>
> The guilty ones were **they.**
>
> I'm sure it was **he.**
>
> It might have been **she.**

Many people find such expressions awkward. But when the predicate pronoun is used in conjunction with other constructions, much of the awkwardness disappears.

SEMIFORMAL:

> It is **I** whom you are looking for.
>
> The guilty ones were **they** and the residents of the third floor.
>
> I'm sure it was **he** who borrowed your blow drier.
>
> It might have been **she** who knocked on our door.

In informal use nowadays, especially in speech, many people habitually use objective pronoun forms after the linking verb *be.*

INFORMAL:

> It's **me!**
>
> I'm sure it was **her** we saw in the plaza.
>
> Could that have been **him** driving the Ferrari?

Even in informal conversation many people still prefer the subjective case forms in such constructions. In semiformal writing (what your college class assignments call for) you are well advised to follow the general rule for using subjective pronouns after linking verbs.

5c When to Use **who** and **whom**

Use **who** (**whoever**) in subject positions and **whom** (**whomever**) in object positions.

In semiformal or formal writing you should distinguish between *who* and *whom.*

I explained the problem to the clerk **whom** I was talking to.   [object of the preposition *to*]

Whom did you contact at the embassy?   [object of the verb *contact*]

The secretary referred me to Mr. Fisk, **who,** she said, would correct the error.   [subject of the verb *would correct*]

After the accident I was ready to turn to **whoever** could help me.   [subject of *could help*; not the object of the preposition *to*]

A test for who and whom   A convenient two-part test helps you choose between *who* and *whom*:

1. Turn a question into a simple declarative sentence or express the part containing a form of *who* as a simple sentence.

2. Substitute the pronouns *he* or *him* into the *who* slot in your simple sentence. If *he* fits, use *who*; if *him* fits, use *whom*.

(*Who* or *Whom*?) _____ were you looking for?
    TEST: You were looking for *him*.   [object of *for*]
    RIGHT: **Whom** were you looking for?

(*Who* or *Whom*?) _____ did you say won the marathon?
    TEST: You did say *he* won the marathon.   [subject of the verb *won*]
    RIGHT: **Who** did you say won the marathon?

(*Who* or *Whom*?) _____ did you meet at the top of Half Dome?
    TEST: You did meet *him*. . . .   [object of the verb *meet*]
    RIGHT: **Whom** did you meet at the top of Half Dome?

We usually avoid someone _____ (*who* or *whom*?) we owe money to.
    TEST: We owe money to *him*.   [object of the preposition *to*]
    RIGHT: We usually avoid someone **whom** we owe money to. [Use *whom* even though it is removed from *to*.]

Jim is one of those people _____ (*who* or *whom*?), it seems, is everybody's friend.

> TEST: *He* is everybody's friend. [Don't let the parenthetical *it seems* throw you off; *he* is the subject.]
>
> RIGHT: Jim is one of those people **who,** it seems, is everybody's friend.

The test is simple and reliable. Even though in casual conversation many people use the subjective case form *who* almost exclusively, in semiformal writing you should choose *who* or *whom* to fit appropriately into the grammatical construction.

5d Comparative Constructions with **as** and **than**

After the comparative words **as** and **than**, use the pronoun case form that the understood part of the clause calls for.

When two clauses compare an action, speakers and writers often omit a part of the second clause in order to avoid undue repetition. Such omission frequently leads to confusion. For example, the following sentence may have different meanings, depending on the choice of pronoun.

> AMBIGUOUS: **I gave more to charity than** *(he* or *him?).*

Testing such a sentence by mentally supplying the understood part of the second clause will tell you which meaning is intended.

> CLEAR: I gave more to charity than **he** (gave to charity).

> CLEAR: I gave more to charity than (I gave to) **him.**

In some cases there is only one choice; in others, the choice you make determines the meaning. The examples show the understood parts in parentheses.

> My sister was married earlier than **I** (was married).

> Since we were so close in age, our parents always gave Marty the same Christmas presents as (they gave) **me.**

The coach gave the other team members as much credit as (he gave) **me.**   [But notice the change in meaning in the next example.]

The coach gave the other team members as much credit as **I** (gave them).

5e Verbal Phrases

Use the possessive form of a pronoun (or noun) to modify an **-ing** verbal phrase when the phrase refers to just one aspect of a person and not to the person as a whole.

Remembering two ideas will help you avoid choosing a wrong pronoun case form to use with verbal phrases. First, all possessive forms may function as determiners or noun markers (subsection 1b1). Second, verbal phrases beginning with a present participle (the -*ing* form of the verb) may function as nouns as they name an action (subsection 1c3).

A common error is to use the objective case form of a pronoun before an -*ing* phrase.

> WRONG: The crowd was disappointed at *him* missing the field goal.

Him is incorrect, for the crowd was not disappointed at him as a person; rather, it was the act (missing the field goal) that disappointed them. Use the possessive case form as the determiner.

> The crowd was disappointed at **his** missing the field goal.

The same rule applies if the determiner before a verbal -*ing* phrase is a noun: use the possessive case form.

> **Kathy's** singing the national anthem was a proud moment for her parents.

> What delayed the concert was the **drummer's** arriving late.

In the preceding example, it was not the drummer as a person that delayed the concert; it was his *act* that did it. (In fact, if you substitute the word *act* or *action* or *event* in place of the verbal phrase, you will readily see that the possessive case form is necessary: *What delayed the concert was the* **drummer's** *action.*)

5f   The **we-students** / **us-students** Construction

Use **we** or **us** in conjunction with a noun according to whether the noun functions as a subject or an object.

If the noun is a subject, use *we*; if it is an object, use *us*. A very simple test will guide you correctly. Mentally omit the noun and substitute the pronoun form that sounds natural. The examples show the omitted noun in parentheses.

After failing to convince the dean, **we** (freshmen) took our case directly to the president.

The president treated **us** (students) with patience and dignity.

The public often looks on all of **us** (motorcyclists) as roughnecks.

Grandpa often told **us** (children) stories about his war experiences.

Since no one would write constructions such as *us took* or *looks on all of we*, this test is thoroughly reliable.

5g   Demonstrative Pronouns

Never use **them** as a demonstrative ("pointing") pronoun in place of **these** or **those**.

The pronoun *them* is a complete object; it does not function as a demonstrative modifier of a noun.

WRONG: I want to wear *them* socks to school today.

RIGHT: I want to wear **those** socks to school today.

WRONG: Give me three of *them*!   [Pointing and speaking with emphasis]

RIGHT: Give me three of **those** (or **these**)!

When there is no pointing action, *them* is correct, as in the following sentences:

Marilyn was the first to recognize **them.**

We spoke with **them** about the terms of the agreement.

5h Reflexive Pronouns

Do not use a reflexive pronoun as a subject or predicate.

The reflexive pronouns are frequently used in error in compound subjects and objects. Guard against this by simplifying the sentence.

WRONG: Ken and *myself* were able to catch the bus just before it left the station.   *[myself* was able; not natural]

RIGHT: Ken and **I** were able to catch the bus just before it left the station.   *[I* was able; sounds better]

WRONG: I'm sorry we didn't let Ellen and *yourself* know in time.   [we let *yourself* know; not right]

RIGHT: I'm sorry we didn't let Ellen and **you** know in time.   [we let *you* know; sounds better]

Use the reflexive pronoun as an object only when it refers to the same person as the subject, as in *Most men shave **themselves.*** Note also the correct spellings of the reflexive pronouns.

Correct		Incorrect
himself	NOT	hisself
itself	NOT	its self
themselves	NOT	theirselves

6

Subject-Verb Agreement

The grammatical term **number** indicates how many units are involved. The two numbers in our grammar are the **singular** (only one) and the **plural** (more than one), and such numbers apply to both subjects and verbs. For writing to be correct, verbs must agree in number with their subjects; that is, if the subject is singular, the verb must also be singular.

Subjects can be nouns or noun substitutes such as pronouns or noun phrases. Most (but not all) nouns and pronouns show singular and plural number by a change in form (subsection 1a1).

Singular	Plural	Singular	Plural
book	books	sheep	sheep
lamp	lamps	I	we
church	churches	you	you
woman	women	he, she, it	they
child	children		

All English verbs (except one—*to be*) show a distinct number only in the present tense, and then only in the third person singular. When *he, she,* or *it* (or an expression that can replace these pronouns) is the subject, **-s** or **-es** is added to the stem of the verb (subsection 1a2). In the following examples, note the changes in the forms of the verbs themselves.

I see	we see	I touch	we touch
you see	you see	you touch	you touch
he see**s**	they see	it touch**es**	they touch
I kiss	we kiss	I have	we have
you kiss	you kiss	you have	you have
she kiss**es**	they kiss	he ha**s**	they have

No change in the form of the verb itself occurs once you have established the past tense.

I saw	we saw	I touched	we touched
you saw	you saw	you touched	you touched
he saw	they saw	it touched	they touched
I kissed	we kissed	I had	we had
you kissed	you kissed	you had	you had
she kissed	they kissed	he had	they had

The irregular verb *to be* shows number in both the present and the past tenses.

Present Tense		Past Tense	
I **am**	we **are**	I **was**	we **were**
you **are**	you **are**	you **were**	you **were**
he **is**	they **are**	he **was**	they **were**

Modal auxiliaries (subsection 1b3) do not change at all. The same form is used whether the subject is singular or plural.

I (we) **can** run	I (we) **must** hurry
you **can** run	you **must** hurry
he (they) **can** run	he (they) **must** hurry

Generally, errors in subject-verb agreement occur only in the third person singular of the present tense or when a form of *to be* is the main verb or an auxiliary. Although such problem areas are limited, we will cover a number of trouble spots in the following sections.

6a Noun Phrases as Subjects

The verb of a sentence should agree in number with the head-word of a noun-phrase subject.

Subject-verb agreement is rarely a problem when the subject is a pronoun or a single noun (such as a person's name) or a common noun with its determiner. The examples show boldface subjects and italic verbs.

The **memorandum** *refers* to Christmas vacation.

Dean Hottois *recommends* an early dismissal.

My **colleagues** *agree* wholeheartedly.

But often a more complicated noun phrase functions as a subject. The whole noun phrase is the **complete subject,** and the **headword** of the noun phrase is the **simple subject.** The headword is that noun (or noun substitute, such as *many*) that governs the entire phrase; all other words or word groups in the noun phrase either modify the headword or they modify other words in the phrase. The simple subject, or headword of the noun phrase, governs the verb. Thus singular headwords call for singular verbs and plural headwords call for plural verbs. The examples show boldface headwords, or simple subjects, and italic verbs.

A **specialist** from the Twin Cities *visits* our clinic regularly.

The **trailer** with both its wheels missing *was* our secret hide-out.

Do not let the plural words *Twin Cities* and *wheels* mislead you. The singular headwords (simple subjects) *specialist* and *trailer* require the singular verbs *visits* and *was*. In the following example, the headword *coeds* calls for the plural verb *were;* do not let the intervening words confuse you.

Several **coeds** with no brains but lots of money *were* very popular in Las Vegas.

When the headword is followed by a prepositional phrase with the compound prepositions *as well as* or *together with,* the object of the prepositional phrase does not affect the verb. Often such a prepositional phrase is set off by commas.

WRONG: The coach, as well as the veteran players, were trying to help us beginners learn the fundamentals.

RIGHT: The **coach,** as well as the veteran players, *was* trying to help us beginners learn the fundamentals.

WRONG: The mother, together with her three children, were hurrying through the toy department.

RIGHT: The **mother,** together with her three children, *was* hurrying through the toy department.

6b   Indefinite Pronouns as Subjects

Indefinite pronouns are singular and require singular verbs.

To remember that indefinite pronouns are singular (subsection 1b6), you may mentally supply the words *any* or *one* or *single,* like this: *everybody* becomes *every (single) body; nobody* becomes *not (any) body; nothing* becomes *not (one) thing; each* becomes *each (one);* and so on.

WRONG: Either of those cookbooks explain how to bake bread.

RIGHT: **Either** of those cookbooks **explains** how to bake bread.

WRONG: Each describe ethnic varieties.

RIGHT: **Each describes** ethnic varieties.

WRONG: Neither omit step-by-step instructions.

RIGHT: **Neither omits** step-by-step instructions.

RIGHT: Only **one** of the books **contains** historical notes.

Certain adjectives functioning as indefinite pronouns may be either singular or plural in meaning.

Many of those recipes in my mother's collection **forget** to mention how long you should bake the bread.

All are at least one hundred years old.

None of you **is** (or **are**) to blame.

Any of the voters **is** (or **are**) entitled to challenge the candidates.

6c Relative Pronouns as Subjects

When a relative pronoun is the subject of its own clause, its verb agrees in number with the pronoun's antecedent.

The rule states that *who, which,* and *that* are either singular or plural according to the nouns they refer to (see Adjective Clauses, subsection 1d4). The examples show the relative pronoun and its antecedent in boldface.

I have a **cat that** frequently *climbs* the curtains.

The **pets which** *live* at our neighbor's house are better behaved.

The **man who** *owns* them has apparently trained them well.

A special subject-verb agreement problem involving relative pronouns appears in sentences with the construction *one of those . . . who* (or *which* or *that*).

Garfinkle is one of those **cats who** *are* often in trouble. [*Is* would be wrong.]

The point is that *cats,* and not *Garfinkle,* is the antecedent of *who,* which means that a plural verb is required. When in doubt, use a simple test to choose the verb. See if the sentence will undergo this sort of a transformation:

> Of those cats who *are* often in trouble, Garfinkle is one.

The test clearly shows the verb form you need.

6d   Compound Subjects

Compound subjects consist of two or more coordinated constituents (or unified parts of a sentence).

6d1   The coordinating conjunction **and**

When two (or more) subjects are joined by **and** to form a plural subject, they take a plural verb.

In the following examples, the word *and* links two equal subjects to make a plural subject. The correlative *both . . . and* makes a compound subject also.

> Lisa and James **are** the parents of Joel
>
> Gretchen and Morris **have** no children yet.
>
> What you do and where you go **are** nobody's business but your own.
>
> Both peaches and cream **are** on sale today.

When two nouns or constructions are joined by *and* to form a single unit, that single subject takes a singular verb.

> **Peaches and cream** *is* my favorite dessert.
>
> When Mother cooks for guests, **bacon and eggs** *is* her first choice for breakfast.

Peaches and cream is considered a single dish, and the combination of *bacon and eggs* is treated as a single unit.

6d2   Connectives: **either . . . or** and **but not**

When compound subjects are joined by correlatives or by **but not**, the verb agrees in number with that part of the subject that is closer to the verb.

The correlatives are the two-part connectives *(either) . . . or, (neither) . . . nor, not only . . . but (also),* and *not . . . but.*

The examples show the verb in italics with the noun that governs the verb in boldface.

Neither the down payment nor the monthly **installments** *were* excessive.

Neither the monthly installments nor the **down payment** *was* excessive.

Not only Harry but also his **sisters** *sing* in the choir.

Not only his sisters but also **Harry** *sings* in the choir.

Sometimes the *either* of *either . . . or*, the *neither* of *neither . . . nor*, and the *also* of *not only . . . but also* are omitted, but the rule for subject-verb agreement stays the same.

Two tablets or **one spoonful** *is* recommended.

One spoonful or **two tablets** *are* recommended.

When the connective *but not* joins two subjects, the verb agrees in number with the part of the subject closer to the verb.

All the wives but not **a single husband** *was* willing to attend the bazaar.

Mrs. Gooding but not her **neighbors** *were* anxious to see the show.

6e Special Nouns as Subjects

Three special kinds of nouns sometimes cause problems in subject-verb agreement: collective nouns, singular nouns that are plural in form, and nouns of weight, measure, time, and money.

6e1 Collective nouns

Collective nouns (describing a group) take singular verbs *unless* a collective noun is used to describe the separate individuals of that group.

a. **Singular verb** Collective nouns are singular in form but plural in meaning; they specify many individuals. Some of the most common collective nouns are *family, team, crew, series, jury, flock, student body, faculty, staff, pride* (of lions), *gaggle* (of geese), and *collection.*

When such a group acts as a unit, it takes a singular verb.

The **team** *is scheduled* to practice at 4:00.

The **student body** *meets* monthly.

The **series** of lectures beginning tomorrow *deals* with wine-making.

b. **Plural verb** However, when a collective noun is used so that it *must* be thought of as meaning separate individuals, it takes a plural verb.

My **family** *are* individualists.

c. **Either singular or plural verb** The collective nouns *number, crowd, group* pose a different problem. When one of these singular nouns is followed by a prepositional phrase with a plural noun object, the verb may be plural. Although some writers prefer singular verbs in such sentences, the plural verb must also be considered correct when individuals are clearly the subject. The examples show boldface simple subjects and italicized verbs.

A **number** of demonstrators *were* arrested.

A **crowd** of spectators *were* turned away.

A **group** of children *were* ushered into the concert hall.

6e2 Singular nouns that are plural in form

Nouns that are plural in form but singular in meaning take singular verbs.

The list includes such common nouns as *athletics, eco-*

nomics, *physics, mathematics, politics, statistics, checkers, means, measles, mumps,* and *molasses.*

Athletics *was* Marty's best subject in high school.

Mumps sometimes *affects* grown men adversely.

Statistics *is* a required course in my program   [Here, *statistics* refers to an organized body of knowledge.]

Statistics *prove* him wrong.   [Here, *statistics* is a plural form of the noun *statistic* (meaning fact) and it takes a plural verb.]

6e3   Nouns of weight, measure, time, and money

A plural noun that establishes a weight, a measure, a period of time, or an amount of money takes a singular verb.

Thirty-six inches *equals* a yard.

Two hundred fifty miles *is* a short trip for a DC-10.

Ten days *was* the length of our last vacation.

Five hundred dollars *is* the best I can offer for that used car.

6f   Subjects in Inverted Sentence Order

When a subject follows its verb, the verb must still agree in number with the subject.

The examples show italic verbs with boldface subjects.

Sitting by his side *were* both **his wife and his daughters.**

At his feet *was* also **his Great Dane.**

Note that the nouns *side* and *feet* have no effect on the verbs. The subjects are *his wife and daughters* and *his Great Dane.* When the word *there* is an adverb meaning *at that place,* no problem is likely to occur in subject-verb agreement.

There Elisa sits, rummaging through her desk.

There she keeps her most important papers.

The subject-verb combinations are *Elisa sits* and *she keeps.*

However, when *there* begins a sentence as an expletive (a filler with no meaning), the real subject follows the verb. Such inverted sentence order often leads to problems in subject-verb agreement. To find the real subject, re-arrange the sentence by asking *who* or *what* of the verb.

WRONG: There has been a few good programs on television lately. [THINK: A few good programs have been . . .]

RIGHT: There *have been* a few good **programs** on television lately.

WRONG: There seems to be several inconsistencies in the report. [THINK: Several inconsistencies seem . . .]

RIGHT: There *seem* to be several **inconsistencies** in the report.

A related problem occurs when the linking verb *is* or *was* functions as the main verb in the sentence and the predicate noun (what follows the linking verb as a complement) is plural. Do not let the subject complement govern the number of the verb. The rule still holds true: The verb must agree in number *with its subject.*

WRONG: His problem are frequent mistakes in spelling. [*Mistakes* is the complement, not the subject.]

RIGHT: His **problem** *is* frequent mistakes in spelling. [The subject *problem* takes the singular verb *is.*]

WRONG: Elsa's sole support are her two part-time jobs.

RIGHT: Elsa's sole **support** *is* her two part-time jobs.

7

Shifts

A **faulty shift in grammatical constructions** occurs when a writer begins with one kind of construction and then shifts to a different kind of construction.

INCONSISTENT:

> *Every client* should ask *their* lawyer to explain the terms of a contract clearly.

The writer began with the singular *every client,* thus committing himself or herself to talk about the client in the singular, which is perfectly acceptable. But the writer then shifted to the plural *their.* To provide for consistency, the writer should either make both terms singular or both plural. Maintaining complete grammatical consistency is not an easy task even for accomplished writers. This chapter will deal briefly with six kinds of shifts that produce most inconsistencies. They are shifts in **number, person, tense, voice, mood,** and **point of view.**

7a   Number

Do not shift from the singular to the plural or from the plural to the singular within a sentence.

A common kind of faulty shift in number is from a singular noun to a plural pronoun.

> A *person* may at times feel that *they* have been mistreated, but often *they* merely imagine such conditions. [Inconsistent: *A person . . . they*]

> People may at times feel that **they** have been mistreated, but often **they** merely imagine such conditions. [Consistent: *People . . . they*]

> When *a company* offers *a special bargain* on TV, *they* often tell you to wait six or eight weeks for *them* to arrive. [Inconsistent]

> When **companies** offer special bargains on TV, **they** often tell you to wait six or eight weeks for such bargains to arrive. [Consistently plural]

Sometimes the shift is from the plural to the singular.

> What *they* believe in *their* hearts governs a *person's* behavior— or ought to. [Inconsistent]

> What **an individual** believes in **his** or **her heart** governs **his** or **her** behavior—or ought to. [Consistent]

To avoid the awkwardness of "his or her" combinations, it is usually better to make all the terms plural.

> What **people** believe in **their hearts** governs **their** behavior—or ought to. [Consistently plural]

7b   Person

Do not shift from the third person to the second or from the second to the third.

There are three **persons** in English grammar (subsection 1a2): the **first person** refers to the person(s) speaking (*I, me,* *we, us*); the **second person** is the person spoken to (*you*); the **third person,** is that person or thing spoken about (*he, him, she, her, it, they, them,* and all nouns and indefinite pronouns like *one, everyone, anyone*). English also uses the **indefinite second person** pronoun *you* to refer to people in general—a legitimate construction.

> **You** learn to crawl before **you** learn to walk.
> [Consistent: second person]

> **Children** learn to crawl before **they** learn to walk.
> [Consistent: third person]

It is improper to begin a passage in the third person and then shift to the indefinite *you*.

INCONSISTENT:
> *A person* learns to crawl before *you* learn to walk.
> [third person and second person]

CONSISTENT:
> **A person** learns to crawl before **he** learns to walk.
> [third person]

INCONSISTENT:
> *Everyone* needs to know that *you* are loved.
> [third person and second person]

CONSISTENT:
> **People** need to know that **they** are loved.

CONSISTENT:
> **You** need to know that **you** are loved.

CONSISTENT:
> **One** needs to know that **one** is loved.

The last correction above maintains consistency, but some would consider it too formal to be good style. The first correction (with both the noun and pronoun in the third person) and the second correction (with *you . . . you*) are better.

7c Tense

In summarizing fiction or history, do not shift from the past to the present tense or from the present to the past tense.

The English verb expresses the time of an action by means of various tenses (section 1a2). In summarizing events, a writer may use the past tenses throughout (as if looking back in time) or the **historical present tenses** throughout (as if reporting the actions at the time they occur). Shifting from one tense to another is careless writing.

INCONSISTENT:

> In this movie two patrolmen *walked* into the cafe for their morning break. They *sit* down at the counter and *have* a cup of coffee and a doughnut. When they *come* out again, their squad car *is* missing.

CONSISTENT:

> In this movie two patrolmen **walk** into the cafe for their morning break. They **sit** down at the counter and **have** a cup of coffee and a doughnut. When they **come** out again, their squad car **is** missing.

INCONSISTENT:

> We *were* strolling quietly along the boulevard when suddenly a convertible *comes* racing down the street, *jumps* the curb, almost *hits* us, and *crashes* into a tree.

CONSISTENT:

> We **were** strolling quietly along the boulevard when suddenly a convertible **came** racing down the street, **jumped** the curb, almost **hit** us, and **crashed** into a tree.

In each of the preceding examples, the writer began in the past tense but then shifted to the historical present. The first correction has restored consistency by changing the past tense (*walked*) to the present (*walk*) so that all verbs are in the present tense. To correct the second example, we changed all present tense verbs to the past (*came, jumped, hit,* and *crashed*). The point is to be consistent.

7d Voice

Do not shift from the active to the passive voice.

In the active voice, the subject performs the action; in the passive voice the subject is acted upon (subsection 1a2). Mature writers find the active voice more forceful, but there are on occasion good reasons for using passive constructions. However, once you have started describing a sequence of actions in the active voice, do not shift to the passive.

INCONSISTENT:

After I *had put* the washer and the bearings on the axle, I *lifted* the wheel into place. Next, the second set of bearings *was inserted*, another washer *was added*, and a cotter pin *was placed* into its hole and crimped. Finally, I *attached* the hub cap to complete my go-kart.

CONSISTENT:

After I **had put** the washer and the bearings on the axle, I **lifted** the wheel into place. Next, I **inserted** the second set of bearings, **added** another washer, and **placed** a cotter pin into its hole and **crimped** it. Finally, I **attached** the hub cap to complete my go-kart.

In the inconsistent passage, the first and third sentences are in the active voice, but the middle sentence shifts to the passive voice. Since the writer is performing all the actions—including those in the second sentence—there is no reason to report them vaguely in the passive.

7e Mood

Do not shift from the imperative mood to the subjunctive mood.

The three moods of the English verb show the writer's

attitude toward the statements he or she makes (subsection 1a2). Few problems occur when the verb is in the **indicative mood,** which suggests that a statement is true or is believed to be true. It is the **imperative** and **subjunctive** moods that give rise to inconsistent writing. The imperative mood gives a command, makes a request, or explains directions, as in the following:

> First **go** to . . . , then **take** a left turn . . . , and **turn** left again at the first stop light.

The boldface verbs are in the imperative mood. One form of the subjunctive mood uses *should* or *ought to* so that the writer suggests but does not directly command or order. One common problem occurs when writers shift from the imperative mood to the subjunctive mood with *should.*

INCONSISTENT:

> When you begin to work on that batch of cookies, first *gather* all your bowls and measuring cups and *make* sure you have all the ingredients. Then *you should follow* each step of the recipe. *You should take* your time and *measure* everything carefully. When you have finished mixing the batter, *drop* the cookie dough by spoonfuls onto the baking sheet and *bake* each batch at 350° for ten minutes.

CONSISTENT:

> (Simply remove the *you should*'s from sentences two and three.)

7f   Point of View

Do not shift the point of view when discussing or explaining someone's opinion.

Point of view identifies whose idea an opinion or a statement is. Your writing should make clear whether an idea is yours or that of a person you are discussing. Compose your sentences so that you do not shift the point of view.

INCONSISTENT:

> Everybody nowadays thinks slavery is a wholly inhumane and unacceptable institution, but Aristotle thought it was rooted in human nature and thus acceptable. Some people are born to be leaders and some to be followers or servants. Human nature can't be changed, and thus the slave class remains the slave class. Slavery is fixed in human nature.

CONSISTENT:

> Everybody nowadays thinks slavery is a wholly inhumane and unacceptable institution, but Aristotle thought that it was rooted in human nature and thus acceptable. **He claimed** that some people are born to be leaders and some to be followers or servants. **He maintained** that human nature can't be changed and that that is why the slave class remains the slave class. Slavery, **he argued,** is fixed in human nature.

In the inconsistent passage it is clear that the first sentence is the writer's opinion; the second sentence introduces some notions held by Aristotle. But who is it that believes what the remainder of the paragraph states, the writer or Aristotle? Adding *he claimed, he maintained,* and *he argued* clearly shows that these last sentences reflect Aristotle's opinions.

7g   Direct and Indirect Discourse

Do not shift from direct to indirect discourse.

In **direct discourse** you report, in quotation marks, the exact words of a speaker or writer. In **indirect discourse** you use your own words to report, without quotation marks, the substance of what someone has said or asked.

DIRECT: He said, "I'm hungry."

INDIRECT:

> He said that he was hungry.

DIRECT: She asked, "Can you come to my party?"

INDIRECT:

>She asked whether we could come to her party.

Note that indirect discourse uses words like *that, if,* and *whether* and that changes occur in the subjects, verbs, pronouns, and word order.

If you begin by quoting directly (with quotation marks) and shift to indirect discourse, your writing is inconsistent.

INCONSISTENT:

>Tom asked if we had fixed the carburetor and is anything else wrong with the motor.

Even though no quotation marks enclose the expression *is anything else wrong with the motor,* they are clearly Tom's actual words. To be consistent, both parts of the report must be in indirect discourse (or both must be in direct discourse).

CONSISTENT:

>Tom asked if we had fixed the carburetor and **whether anything else was wrong with the motor.**

CONSISTENT:

>Tom asked, "Did you fix the carburetor, and is anything else wrong with the motor?"

INCONSISTENT:

>The report concluded: "Protecting our wilderness areas is vital to our water supply" and that we had better begin to take steps now.

CONSISTENT:

>The report concluded that protecting our wilderness areas was vital to our water supply and that we had better begin to take steps now.

CONSISTENT:

>The report concluded: "Protecting our wilderness areas is vital to our water supply. We had better begin to take steps now."

8

Verb Forms

Incorrect subject-verb agreement (Chapter 6) perhaps accounts for most verb problems in writing. However, occasionally wrong verb forms are used, chiefly because English has both regular and irregular verbs that sometimes cause confusion.

All English verbs (with slight exceptions for *be*) have five forms.

Infinitive	Present Tense (third-person singular)	Past Tense	Present Participle	Past Participle
(to) talk	talks	talked	talking	talked
(to) freeze	freezes	froze	freezing	frozen
(to) bring	brings	brought	bringing	brought

- The present tense (except for the third person) is always the infinitive without the *to*.

Two of the remaining forms are always regular.

- The third-person singular present tense always ends in -*s* or -*es*.
- The present participle of all verbs ends in -*ing*.

8a   Irregular Verbs

Irregularities or differences appear in only two verb forms: the past tense and the past participle. Verbs that end in -*ed* in both the past tense and the past participle are called regular verbs; others are called irregular verbs. Sometimes the past tense and past participle forms of a verb are different from each other (as with *freeze*) and sometimes identical (as with *bring* and *keep*).

For your reference, Table 5 lists the principal parts of the chief irregular verbs in English. A dictionary lists the principal parts of all irregular verbs; if no principal parts are listed, the verb is regular. In the table, the stem is the infinitive without the word *to* and is the present-tense form of the verb.

8b   Past-Tense Forms

Unless the two forms are identical, do not use the past participle of an irregular verb as the past tense form.

WRONG: Beth *run* the car without enough water until she *seen* steam pouring out.

RIGHT: Beth **ran** the car without enough water until she **saw** steam pouring out.

WRONG: After we *come* to the beach, we *swum* in the surf.

RIGHT: After we **came** to the beach, we **swam** in the surf.

WRONG: Helen *begun* to cheer when the team *run* onto the floor.

RIGHT: Helen **began** to cheer when the team **ran** onto the floor.

8c   Past-Participle Forms

Unless the two forms are identical, do not use the past-tense form of an irregular verb as the past participle.

The past participle is always used with an auxiliary, often *have, has,* or *had* (and in the passive voice with a form of *to be*). Be particularly cautious when a form of *have* is contracted, as in *I've, he's, they've.*

> WRONG: Mark had *arose* before six, but he still missed the chuckwagon breakfast.

> RIGHT: Mark had **arisen** before six, but he still missed the chuckwagon breakfast.

> WRONG: I have *bore* all the insults I will take.

> RIGHT: I have **borne** all the insults I will take.

> WRONG: We've *went* 600 miles since this morning, and Harry has *drove* almost all the way.

> RIGHT: We've **gone** 600 miles since this morning, and Harry has **driven** almost all the way.

Be careful not to handle an irregular verb form as if it were a regular verb, by adding *-d* or *-ed* to form the past tense.

> WRONG: We *blowed* the dirt out of the bearings and put new grease in.

> RIGHT: We **blew** the dirt out of the bearings and put new grease in.

> WRONG: Harvey claimed he *catched* thirteen trout out of one little riffle in the creek.

> RIGHT: Harvey claimed he **caught** thirteen trout out of one little riffle in the creek.

Table 5.   Irregular Verbs

Stem	Past Tense	Past Participle
arise	arose	has arisen
bear	bore	has borne, was born
begin	began	has begun
bind	bound	has bound
bite	bit	has bitten
blow	blew	has blown
break	broke	has broken
bring	brought	has brought
buy	bought	has bought
catch	caught	has caught
choose	chose	has chosen
come	came	has come
creep	crept	has crept
cut	cut	has cut
deal	dealt	has dealt
dive	dove	has dived
do	did	has done
draw	drew	has drawn
dream	dreamed, dreamt	has dreamed, dreamt
drink	drank	has drunk
eat	ate	has eaten
fall	fell	has fallen
find	found	has found
flee	fled	has fled
fly	flew	has flown [as a bird]
fly	flied	has flied [as in baseball]
forbid	forbad, forbade	has forbidden
forget	forgot	has forgotten
freeze	froze	has frozen
give	gave	has given
go	went	has gone
grow	grew	has grown
hang	hung	has hung [clothes]
hang	hanged	has hanged [execution]
know	knew	has known
lay	laid	has laid
lead	led	has led

Table 5. (continued)

Stem	Past Tense	Past Participle
lie	lay	has lain
lose	lost	has lost
mean	meant	has meant
pay	paid	has paid
ride	rode	has ridden
ring	rang	has rung
rise	rose	has risen
run	ran	has run
say	said	has said
see	saw	has seen
seek	sought	has sought
send	sent	has sent
sit	sat	has sat
shake	shook	has shaken
shine	shone, shined	has shone, shined
sing	sang	has sung
sink	sank	has sunk
sleep	slept	has slept
slide	slid	has slid
speak	spoke	has spoken
spin	spun	has spun
spit	spit, spat	has spit, spat
spread	spread	has spread
steal	stole	has stolen
stink	stank	has stunk
swear	swore	has sworn
swim	swam	has swum
swing	swung	has swung
take	took	has taken
teach	taught	has taught
tear	tore	has torn
thrive	thrived, throve	has thrived, thriven
throw	threw	has thrown
wear	wore	has worn
weep	wept	has wept
write	write	has written

Caution: Never use the word *of* when you intend to use the contraction of *have*.

WRONG: You *should of* asked me earlier.

RIGHT: You **should have** asked me earlier.
[*Should have* may be contracted to *should've*.]

8d Confusing Verbs

Do not confuse **lie** and **sit** with **lay** and **set**.

The key to understanding these verbs, and to using them with confidence, is found when you classify the verb as either transitive (with a direct object) or intransitive (without a direct object). In other words, today you and I can *lie* down or *sit* up straight (both are intransitive verbs, having no direct object) while we *lay* a book on a table and *set* a glass beside it (*book* and *glass* are direct objects, thus both verbs are transitive). Yesterday, you and I *lay* down or *sat* up straight while we *laid* a book on a table and *set* a glass beside it.

Here are the principal parts of these verbs.

	Infinitive	Past Tense	Past Participle
Intransitive verbs			
lie (tell untruth)	lie	lied	lied
lie (recline)	lie	lay	lain
sit (be seated)	sit	sat	sat
Transitive verbs			
lay (put or place)	lay	laid	laid
set (put or place)	set	set	set

8d1 **lay** and **lie**

a. **lay** *Lay* is a transitive verb; it always has a direct object. The examples show the direct objects in italics.

Hens **lay** *eggs*.

A good carpenter always **lays** his *plane* on its side.

So that the champagne would ferment properly, Antonio **laid** the *bottles* on their sides.

Fred's uncle **has been laying** *bricks* all his life.

Professionals have always **laid** our *carpets* for us.

b. **lie**   *Lie* is an intransitive verb; it has no direct object.

Mother always **lies** down when she has a headache.

Fido **lay** on the floor all evening after supper yesterday.

Last Saturday I **had lain** in bed until 10.00 A.M.

My bike was rusty after it **had been lying** in the snow all winter.

c. Common errors   Errors occur when forms of *lay* are used instead of forms of *lie*. In the following examples, *here*, *in the corner*, and *in bed* are not objects; they are adverbial modifiers. Hence, the intransitive verb *lie* is the correct verb to use.

WRONG: Let's *lay* here quietly and watch the sunset.

RIGHT: Let's **lie** here quietly and watch the sunset.

WRONG: That old blanket *has been laying* in the corner for months.

RIGHT: The old blanket **has been lying** in the corner for months.

WRONG: Dad *laid* in bed for ten days after his operation.

RIGHT: Dad **lay** in bed for ten days after his operation.

8d2   **set** and **sit**

a. **set**   *Set* is a transitive verb with a direct object. The examples show the direct objects in italics.

Yvonne, will you **set** the *glasses* in the cupboard?

"I **set** *them* on the sideboard already," she replied.

Where **have** you **set** the *silverware*?

I **was setting** *it* to the left of the plates until Judy corrected me.

b.   **sit**   *Sit* is an intransitive verb; it never takes a direct object.

RIGHT: We have an antique clock that **sits** on the mantel.

RIGHT: Next to it **sat** an old six-shooter of my Dad's.

RIGHT: It **had sat** there for six years before Mother moved it.

RIGHT: Now it **is sitting** on Dad's desk in the den.

c.   Common errors   Errors occur when forms of *set* are used instead of forms of *sit*.

WRONG: You'll be able to go on after you *set* awhile.

RIGHT: You'll be able to go on after you **sit** awhile.

WRONG: Emily *set* quietly in the corner while Homer drove.

RIGHT: Emily **sat** quietly in the corner while Homer drove.

WRONG: We could have *set* all night and listened to the songs.

RIGHT: We could have **sat** all night and listened to the songs.

WRONG: While we were *setting* there, the alarm sounded.

RIGHT: While we were **sitting** there, the alarm sounded.

8d3   **bear**

The verb *bear* also needs mentioning.

a. **bear/borne**   In active-voice sentences, *borne* is the past participle of the verb *bear* when it means to carry or to give birth to. Notice also that *bear* is a transitive verb (with a direct object) in these examples.

> Is it true that your mother **has borne** ten *children*?

> Hamlet said that Yorick **had borne** *him* on his back a thousand times.

b. **bear/born**   In the passive voice, *born* is the past participle of *bear* in the meaning of coming into the world.

> Solomon Grundy **was born** on Monday.

> My brother **was born** in April.

8e   Subjunctive Verb Forms

Use the subjunctive form of a verb to express a wish or a condition contrary to fact.

While the indicative mood states a fact or what is thought to be a fact, the subjunctive mood (1) expresses a wish or (2) states a condition contrary to fact or (3) appears in a *that*-clause of resolution, recommendation, or demand.

The subjunctive forms of all verbs (except *be*) differ from the indicative in only one way: there is no -*s* on the third-person singular present tense.

> WRONG: It is necessary that each participant *registers.*

> RIGHT: It is necessary that each participant **register.**

> WRONG: The chaperone insisted that Renee *stays* in the ballroom.

> RIGHT: The chaperone insisted that Renee **stay** in the ballroom.

The verb *be* has distinct subjunctive forms in both tenses.

Present Tense

(if) I be	(if) we be
(if) you be	(if) you be
(if) he/she/it be	(if) they be

Past Tense

(if) I were	(if) we were
(if) you were	(if) you were
(if) he/she/it were	(if) they were

WRONG: I wish Reid *was* my doctor.

RIGHT: I wish Reid **were** my doctor.

WRONG: If she *was* to study harder, her grades would improve.

RIGHT: If she **were** to study harder, her grades would improve.

WRONG: Lois moves that the report *is* adopted.

RIGHT: Lois moves that the report **be** adopted.

PART TWO

PUNCTUATION
AND
MECHANICS

119

9

End Punctuation

. ? !

End punctuation occurs at the end of sentences and at the end of some constructions that are not sentences.

9a The Period .

Use a period to end a normal sentence that is not a question and is not especially emphatic.

Declarative and imperative sentences end with periods.

a. **Declarative sentences** Statements that declare or state something are called declarative sentences.

The secretary consulted the engagement calendar.

She was so preoccupied she did not hear the door open.

b. **Imperative sentences** Requests or commands or directions are called imperative sentences. The examples show the imperative verbs italicized.

> *Be* careful at this point; *let* the juice simmer slowly for exactly three minutes.

> *Watch out* for cars entering from Fourth Street.

c. **Indirect questions**   There are two kinds of indirect questions, and both end with periods.

(1)   Some simply state that someone asked something.

> Jody asked whether the invitations had been sent already.

(2)   Some ask for an answer but are not phrased in question form.

> Carl wonders if he should warn them about the steering wheel.

Note: If you quote the *exact* words of a question, enclose them—and the question mark—within quotation marks.

> Helen asked me, "Do you have a towel to lend me?"

If you report the preceding question as an indirect question, note that you must rephrase the original and end with a period. Use no quotation marks.

> WRONG: Helen asked me did I have a towel to lend her?

> RIGHT: Helen asked if I had a towel to lend her.

d. **Courtesy questions**   In a courtesy question, the words *will you* are equivalent to *please.* Because no response is expected, these sentences normally are closed with periods rather than question marks, though a question mark at the end of such a sentence is not wrong.

> Will you let me know what time you hope to arrive.

> Will you let me know what time you hope to arrive?

(Periods used with abbreviations are illustrated in Chapter 14.)

9b The Question Mark ?

Use a question mark to close a question.

A question mark is a signal that a response is expected from the person being spoken to.

Where can I find information about space wars?

Was that telephone call for me?

When the exact words of a question are quoted, the question mark comes at the end of the quotation no matter where the introductory expression appears. In the following examples the expressions *Father repeated, my roommate continued,* and *Capt. Hunt asked Col. Hicks* come at the beginning, in the middle, and at the end of the quoted questions. Observe the correct placement of the question mark in each case (See also section 13e, Rule 8).

Father repeated, "Why didn't you call us?"

"Were you ever," my roommate continued, "afraid of the dark?"

"Should I move my men into position now?" Capt. Hunt asked Col. Hicks. [Note that only the quotation is a direct question, but that the introductory expression *Capt. Hunt asked Col. Hicks* is a declarative statement and therefore ends with a period.]

A question mark also is used in parentheses to indicate that the immediately preceding information is not certain or is questionable.

The altruism (?) of some tycoons makes them richer.

Information enclosed in parentheses is followed by a question mark when the information is uncertain.

George Chapman (1559?–1634) translated Homer's works into English.

9c   The Exclamation Point !

Use an exclamation point after an interjection to show the strong emotion of an emphatic statement or command.

Exclamation points are especially effective to show emotion after short expressions; in longer expressions, a careful choice of words will serve to express feelings more effectively.

"Attention!" shouted the irate drill sergeant.

Well! I have never been so insulted in all my life!
[The second exclamation point is not really needed to convey the meaning.]

Our first week's sales (25,000 copies!) exceeded even our most optimistic predictions.

Use the exclamation point sparingly. Overuse weakens its effectiveness. In a short time no reader will believe in the force of exclamation points if they are used without judgment.

10

The Comma

,

The comma is the most commonly used mark of punctuation. It serves as a signal to the reader when it **separates elements of equal value** (such as independent clauses and items in a series) and when it **sets off elements of unequal value** (such as subordinate clauses and parenthetical words or phrases). Using commas to surround a minor element within a sentence, *like this element*, has the same effect on the reader as a change in inflection does; when you speak, you alter your voice—speaking more softly to de-emphasize some words and speaking louder to make a point.

In Chapter 10, we will touch on the basic rules for using commas effectively. When you have mastered these basic rules, you may wish to exercise the options that exist; but we shall not elaborate on the exceptions in this textbook.

10a Commas Separate Words, Phrases, and Clauses of Equal Importance

10a1 Series

Rule 1 Use commas to separate three or more words, phrases, or clauses in a series.

Observe that a comma is used between the last and the next-to-last item of the preceding rule, even though the word *or* is used.

For breakfast I had juice, coffee, and toast.

Last summer we drove through Glacier National Park, across northern Montana, into North Dakota, and to the Twin Cities in Minnesota.

When Marty will arrive, how long he will stay, and whether he has made arrangements for his return trip puzzled us.

If *two* elements in a series are not joined by a coordinating conjunction, they should be separated by a comma.

I learned to live without working, to consume without sharing.

10a2 Compound sentences

Rule 2 Use a comma to separate independent clauses that are joined by a coordinating conjunction to form one sentence.

The coordinating conjunctions are *and, but, yet, or, nor, for,* and *so.* The examples show the coordinating conjunctions in boldface.

George wrote three poems for *The Torch,* **but** only one appeared in print.

The Circle K Club ran the prettiest candidate for homecoming queen, **yet** she received the fewest votes.

The association started a fund-raising campaign, **for** its treasury was almost empty.

However, be sure to distinguish between compound sentences (as above) and those constructions that may have either a compound subject or a compound predicate (see subsection 1d1). Do not use a comma between two elements if only the subject or only the predicate is compounded.

WRONG: Neither the initial cost, nor the monthly payments kept him from buying the motorcycle.

RIGHT: Neither the initial cost nor the monthly payments kept him from buying the motorcycle.

WRONG: Mary entered the ten-kilometer run, and came in second.

RIGHT: Mary entered the ten-kilometer run and came in second.

10a3 Coordinate adjectives

Rule 3 Use a comma to separate coordinate adjectives that come in front of a noun and that are not joined by **and.**

The best definition of coordinate adjectives is that they are two adjectives that would sound natural if joined by *and*. If two modifiers in front of a noun will not sound natural when joined by *and*, they are not coordinate. The examples show the adjectival modifiers italicized.

SOUNDS UNNATURAL:
 the *fuzzy* and *pink* sweater

SOUNDS UNNATURAL:
 the *clear* and *blue* sky

SOUNDS UNNATURAL:
 the *bright* and *red* paint

Since the adjectives do not sound natural with *and* joining them, they are not coordinate. With the *and* removed they would not be separated by commas.

the fuzzy pink sweater
the clear blue sky
the bright red paint

Here are some examples of adjectives that do sound natural joined by *and*:

SOUNDS NATURAL:
>a *long* and *hot* summer

SOUNDS NATURAL:
>a *dry* and *dusty* trail

SOUNDS NATURAL:
>a *cute* and *cuddly* puppy

These adjectives are coordinate and thus the normal and correct punctuation would be as follows:

>a long, hot summer
>a dry, dusty trail
>a cute, cuddly puppy

Of course more than two coordinate adjectives can occur in front of a noun, in which case all of them would be separated by commas, as in the following phrase:

>a long, difficult, tedious, exhausting march

But in actuality writers do not often use more than two coordinate adjectives in front of a noun.

10a4 Dates and addresses

Rule 4 In full dates use a comma to separate the name of a day from the month, and to separate the date of the month from the year, as well as to follow the number of the year.

>On Sunday, April 7, 1985, many people celebrated Easter.

>Tuesday, June 15, 1982, marked the thirtieth wedding anniversary of our parents.

When only a month and year are given, no punctuation is necessary.

>I can find the proof I want in the June 1974 issue of *Scientific American.*

Rule 5 In addresses use commas to separate the name of a person or establishment from the street address, the street address from the city, and the city from the state.

> You can rent sickroom supplies at the Red Cross Drug Store, 1302 Adams Avenue, Greenville, Wisconsin.

> The landscaping at 1400 Blair Street, St. Paul, Minnesota, recreates a desert scene.

10b Commas Set Off Words, Phrases, and Clauses of Unequal Importance

When something is *set off* in a sentence, it must be surrounded by commas; the commas *before* and *after* serve to separate it from the main sentence. (The exceptions are those words, phrases, and clauses that occur at the very beginning or at the end of a sentence; these obviously cannot have a comma before *and* after them, yet they are separated from the main sentence by a single comma.)

The most common error occurs when one comma is left off. Frequently, the second comma is forgotten because there are other commas within the phrase or clause. These other commas are functioning between items of equal importance (like a series) and may confuse you if you do not remember to check for comma pairs around words, phrases, and clauses of unequal importance.

10b1 Introductory words, phrases, and clauses

Rule 6 Use a comma to set off an introductory word, phrase, or clause whose meaning exhibits some separation from the sentence subject.

Most sentences open with their subjects, but many open with a word, phrase, or clause that is not a part of the full subject. Such introductory words, phrases, and clauses should normally be set off by commas.

Frankly, we thought the project had not been planned well.

To tell the truth, we didn't trust Agnes.

Having seen her in action earlier, we knew she would forget at least one important element.

When the plans were completed, we checked them thoroughly once more.

Noting our concern, Agnes withdrew from the project in a huff.

Introductory adverb clauses (subsection 1d4) and verbal phrases (subsection 1c3) are almost always set off with commas as in the last two examples, since they are usually followed by a voice pause.

10b2 Terminal words, phrases, and clauses

Rule 7 Use a comma to set off a terminal word, phrase, or clause (often expressing a contrast at the end of a sentence) that is preceded by a distinct voice pause.

Ken is just eccentric, not crazy.

We play poker for fun, not money.

Getting on Turner's basketball team takes skill, not pull.

(Sometimes terminal words, phrases, and clauses are set off by dashes, as is explained in Chapter 11.)

10b3 Parenthetical words, phrases, and clauses

Rule 8 Use commas to set off parenthetical words, phrases, and clauses within a sentence.

A parenthetical expression is a kind of aside. It is an expression that is not a part of the main sentence but that contains a comment or information that the writer wants to insert within the sentence. Some examples are *on the other hand*, *from what I hear*, *in the first place*, and *as you note*. Also, conjunctive adverbs and transitional phrases that come within an independent clause are considered parenthetical; they are words and phrases such as *however, moreover, for example,* and *in fact.*

> The highest football score ever, according to the *Guinness Book of Records,* was 222 to 0.

> In recent years, however, they stop the game when one team is more than fifty points ahead.

> Hockey games, of course, never reach such high scores.

> The way to a man's heart, an old adage claims, is through his stomach.

> My mother, for example, admits that she caught Dad by that means.

10b4 Modifiers and appositives

Rule 9 Use commas to set off nonessential words, phrases, and clauses.

a. Nonessential/nonrestrictive modifiers Often a noun is followed by a modifying adjective clause or a phrase derived from such a clause, or by an appositive that renames the noun.

> Elizabeth, *who used to be so shy,* surprised us all by her success in business.   [adjective clause]

> Peter, *educated as an electrical engineer,* went to work the day after graduation.   [adjective phrase]

> Georgine, *my aunt,* used to produce amateur plays for us.   [appositive]

Since *Elizabeth, Peter,* and *Georgine* are proper nouns and thus are clearly identified, the expressions in italics are not necessary to establish which particular persons are meant. In that sense, the expressions are nonessential or nonrestrictive and are set off by commas.

b. **Essential/restrictive modifiers**   If an adjective clause or phrase is necessary to identify which one of several is meant, the absence of commas shows that the modifier is essential or restrictive and should not be set off.

Consider this sentence:

West Point cadets *who break the honor code* are expelled.

If the italicized adjective clause were removed, the sentence would mean that all West Point cadets are expelled. The clause is needed to identify *which* cadets are meant—only those who break the honor code. Thus no commas are called for. Now consider the following sentence:

The commander of West Point, *who personally investigated the cheating scandal,* urged leniency.

Since there is only one Commander of West Point, the term is already clearly identified. The adjective clause is nonessential and is therefore set off by commas.

The presence or absence of commas can alter meaning. Note what happens to two versions of the same sentence, one with commas and one without.

The computer, which I learned to program last year, has helped me in my research.

The computer which I learned to program last year has helped me in my research.

In the first sentence the commas indicate that the writer refers to the computer as a tool and does not mean any particular computer. The absence of commas in the second sentence makes the clause essential: "this particular computer—the one I learned to program last year."

Here are further examples, with explanations. The essential and nonessential clauses are italicized.

WRONG: Howard's wife *who presented him with three children in five years* had to postpone her own career.

RIGHT: Howard's wife, *who presented him with three children in five years,* had to postpone her own career.

The first sentence (without commas) makes the unlikely suggestion that Howard had more than one wife and that it was the particular wife who had presented him with three children who had had to postpone her own career. The second sentence (with commas) recognizes that Howard had only one wife. The adjective clause is not essential to identify her; rather, it gives additional information.

Some sentences may be correctly punctuated with or without commas, depending on the meaning you wish to convey.

> The students *who did most of the work building the float* were intensely pro-fraternity.

Only those students who did most of the work are meant. However, if *students* has been fully identified in a previous sentence, the adjective clause is nonessential and thus set off.

> We were surrounded by a group of students who were regaling us with odd stories about college homecomings. The students, *who did most of the work building the float*, were intensely pro-fraternity.

More examples, with adjective phrases italicized:

ESSENTIAL:
> A person *driven by excessive ambition* may later regret that he neglected his family.

NON-ESSENTIAL:
> Oscar, *driven by ambition*, soon had his own company.

c. **The test** To determine whether commas are needed in a sentence, remove the modifying element or appositive. If that removal changes the meaning of the sentence, then the modifier is essential and should *not* be set off by commas. In the first sentence, only the kind of person who is driven by excessive ambition is meant. In the second sentence, Oscar is identified by name, and the modifying phrase merely gives additional information.

The general rule can be summed up as follows:

> essential = without commas
> nonessential = with commas

More examples, with appositives italicized:

WRONG: We elected Donna's husband *John* to serve on the school board.

RIGHT: We elected Donna's husband, *John,* to serve on the school board.

In the wrong sentence, *John* is made essential, thus identifying which of Donna's husbands is being mentioned. But since (presumably) Donna has only one husband, the expression *Donna's husband* already identifies him, and his name is nonessential information.

WRONG: The American novelist, Sinclair Lewis, depicted small-town life unfavorably

RIGHT: The American novelist Sinclair Lewis depicted small-town life unfavorably.

Since America has more than one novelist, the name is essential to identify which one is under discussion.

RIGHT (if Morley has written only one novel):
Richard Morley's novel, *Rotten in Denmark,* has sold only two hundred copies.

RIGHT (if Morley has written more than one novel):
Richard Morley's novel *Rotten in Denmark* has sold only two hundred copies.

Some examples of incorrectly punctuated sentences from student writing:

WRONG: Emily Dickinson wrote mostly about nature *which she felt had God-like qualities.*

WRONG: I took the case to my counselor *who backed the teacher and gave me no help at all.*

WRONG: We owe many duties to our parents *who nourish and care for us from birth until we can be self-supporting.*

WRONG: We came to the conclusion, *that it takes money to make money.*

Nature, my counselor, and *our parents* are fully identified without the italicized adjective clauses; the clauses, therefore, are nonessential and must be set off with commas. In the last sentence, the italicized clause is essential to identify *conclusion* and thus the comma should *not* precede it.

Nonessential words, phrases, and clauses may also be set off with dashes (see Chapter 11).

10b5 Adverb clauses

Rule 10 Use commas to set off internal or terminal adverb clauses when separated from the rest of the sentence by a distinct voice pause.

Introductory adverb clauses are normally set off by commas, as Rule 6 in section 10b directs. However, since adverb clauses, which are introduced by subordinating conjunctions, cannot be clearly classified as essential or nonessential (except in the case of *when* and *where* clauses), no rule more definitive than that above can be given for punctuating them. Quite often an internal adverb clause will need to be set off because it requires distinct voice pauses.

The rebels, once they had crossed the Potomac into Virginia, were safe for a while.

Lincoln, because he was disappointed with Mead's performance, soon appointed a new general.

A terminal adverb clause may or may not have a voice pause preceding it. In this aspect of punctuation, writers are mostly on their own with no precise rules to guide them.

He made the decision on his own initiative, since his cabinet members could not agree with one another.

(But change the *since* to *because* and many professional writers would feel no need for a comma. The subtleties of this aspect of punctuation are too great to be covered in this brief discussion.)

10c Common Comma Errors to Watch Out For in Your Writing

Do NOT enter an obstructive comma into any part of a sentence.

10c1 Between subject and verb

Rule 11   Do not separate a subject from its verb with a single comma.

>WRONG: What bothered Ellen, was her roommate's lack of promptness.

>RIGHT: What bothered Ellen was her roommate's lack of promptness.

>WRONG: Two of the pictures I had submitted, were chosen for the travelling exhibit.

>RIGHT: Two of the pictures I had submitted were chosen for the travelling exhibit.

Of course a parenthetical or nonessential word, phrase, or clause that is set off by commas on both sides may come between a subject and its verb.

10c2 Between verb and complement

Rule 12   Do not separate a verb from its complement (like a direct object or a predicate noun) with a single comma.

>WRONG: The problem we encountered was, that we had forgotten to plug in the cord.

>RIGHT: The problem we encountered was that we had forgotten to plug in the cord.

Of course a word, phrase, or clause that is set off on both sides by commas can come between a verb and its complement.

> The problem we encountered was, believe it or not, that we had forgotten to plug in the cord.

10c3 Between noncoordinate adjectives

Rule 13 Do not separate noncoordinate adjectives with a comma.

> WRONG: Vera had saved one, antique vase from her grandmother's estate.
>
> RIGHT: Vera had saved one antique vase from her grandmother's estate.

> WRONG: A fine, old house served as a faculty and alumni club.
>
> RIGHT: A fine old house served as a faculty and alumni club.

One and antique and *fine and old* would not sound natural, and thus in each instance the two modifiers are not coordinate and should not be separated with commas.

10c4 Between two equal elements joined by a coordinating conjunction

Rule 14 Do not separate two words or phrases that are joined by a coordinating conjunction.

> WRONG: He insisted that we couldn't have our cake, and eat it too.
>
> RIGHT: He insisted that we couldn't have our cake and eat it too.

11

The Dash; Parentheses; Brackets; the Colon
— ( ) [ ] :

11a Uses of the Dash ▬

On the typewriter a dash is made with two hyphens (--); a handwritten dash is twice as long as a single hyphen. Do not leave a space before or after the dash in a sentence.

As a mark of punctuation, the dash has uses similar to some uses of the comma. Generally it is used when, for emphasis, the writer wants a pause slightly longer than a comma calls for or when other commas in the sentence make dashes necessary for clarity.

Rule 1 Use dashes to set off a parenthetical comment that is very long or that is a complete sentence itself.

You may say many wise things——you who have lived past your allotted three score years and ten——but we young will continue to listen to our own inner voices. [Commas would also be correct here, but dashes provide more emphasis.]

I wrote these words——I was completely isolated at the time—— when my pessimism had reached its greatest depth.

Parentheses instead of dashes would be wrong because the writers want the interpolated comments to stand out boldly rather than being an aside.

Rule 2 Use a dash or dashes to set off nonessential words, phrases, and clauses that are especially emphatic or that already contain commas.

> On my first day as a Little League coach I benched——of all people!——the sponsor's son.

> How would you respond if someone like Genghis Khan——that monster——suddenly appeared?

In the preceding examples the writers wanted to add emphasis to the nonessential phrases and thus used dashes instead of commas to set them off.

Dashes provide clarity. Since the following example's nonessential appositive has commas of its own, using commas to set it off would cause confusion.

> Our three dogs——a Pekingese, a Dachshund, and a German Shepherd——all bark loudly when a stranger approaches.

Rule 3 Use a dash to give emphasis to a word, phrase, or clause that would not normally be set off.

> Those corrupt politicians deserve credit for giving Americans an overdue——and much-needed——civics lesson.

And much-needed need not be set off at all, but the writer set it off with dashes in order to emphasize it. Commas would provide some emphasis but not as much as dashes.

Rule 4 Use a dash to set off a terminal word, phrase, or clause that is an explanation of a preceding item or that is a very distinct afterthought.

> After all his legitimate attempts had failed, he resorted to his only remaining hope——flattery. [A colon after *hope* would also be correct, but more formal.]

> One thing to do if you are lost in a blizzard is to dig a cave in the snow——or pray for a St. Bernard to find you.

In the second example, only a dash will produce the delayed-afterthought effect the writer wanted.

Rule 5   Use a dash to set off an initial series of words, phrases, or clauses that are summarized by a noun or pronoun that serves as the sentence subject.

> Tone, rhythm, melody, harmony——all contributed to the success of Mager's symphony.

The pronoun *all* is used to summarize the four preceding words in order to emphasize them.

Caution: Do not use other punctuation marks in combination with dashes.

WRONG: Before World War I,——but not since 1918,——Austria-Hungary was one nation.

RIGHT: Before World War I——but not since 1918——Austria-Hungary was one nation.

WRONG: There's a simple explanation for the rash of recent burglaries——inside jobs——.

RIGHT: There's a simple explanation for the rash of recent burglaries——inside jobs.

11b   Uses of Parentheses **( )**

The word *parentheses* is plural, meaning both of the curved marks that go by that name (*parenthesis* is the singular). A space is used outside a parenthesis unless another mark of punctuation follows it, but no space is used on the inside of a parenthesis. If an entire sentence following a mark of end punctuation is enclosed in parentheses, the period to close the sentence goes inside the final parenthesis. If only the terminal part of a sentence is enclosed in parentheses, the period closing the sentence goes outside the parenthesis.

<u>Rule 6</u> Use parentheses to enclose any kind of parenthetical or nonessential word, phrase, or clause—even a sentence or group of sentences—to show isolation from the main sentence.

> We continued to frolic with carefree abandon (later we would learn that we had troubles).

The writer does not intend to discuss the troubles at this point; hence the parenthetic comment is in parentheses, which isolate it more than a dash would. Note that the period closing the whole sentence goes outside the parenthesis because the nonenclosed sentence does not have end punctuation. Another correct way of punctuating this construction is this (note where the final period is now placed):

> We continued to frolic with carefree abandon. (Later we would learn that we had troubles.)

> In 1933 Norris Baxter (later to become a movie star) attracted much attention with his theory of orgones.

Parentheses rather than dashes or commas set off this construction because it has a tone of isolation or is somewhat of an afterthought or an aside.

> Both Turner and Avinger were refusing to sign contracts. (Grady and Towle had signed as early as February, but they were hardly star players. Tooey had signed, too, but he alone could not constitute a pitching staff.) Not only were they asking for huge salary increases but also for other concessions. . . .
> [The enclosed two sentences are an aside, not directly a part of the discussion of Turner and Avinger.]

Note that the *they* of the last sentence refers to Turner and Avinger, not to the names within the parentheses. Also note that the period goes inside the parentheses because complete sentences are enclosed.

<u>Rule 7</u>   Use parentheses to enclose numerals used to number items in a series.

> Writing a compelling essay includes **(1)** choosing and limiting a subject, **(2)** determining the thesis, **(3)** organizing the material, **(4)** writing the first draft, **(5)** editing and revising, and **(6)** proofreading after preparing the final manuscript.

Note that the conjunction *and* precedes the parentheses that enclose the last item.

<u>Rule 8</u>   Use parentheses to enclose cross-references and bits of information that are not to be a part of the grammatical structure of the sentence.

> One of the leaders of Pre-Raphaelitism **(**see also "The Fleshly School"**)** was Dante Gabriel Rossetti **(**1828-1882**)**.

The first enclosure is a cross-reference. The second enclosure is information—birth and death dates—that the writer wanted to insert without composing another sentence.

11c   Uses of Brackets   [ ]

Square brackets [like the ones enclosing this phrase] should not be confused with parentheses.

<u>Rule 9</u>   Use brackets to enclose nonquoted material inserted into a direct quotation for the purpose of clarification.

> Malcom continues: "That great document **[**The Monroe Doctrine, 1823**]** has protected and preserved the Western Hemisphere for a century and a half."

The writer uses a direct quotation, but the readers would not have known the reference *document*. Therefore the reference is given in brackets for clarification.

Rule 10 Use brackets to enclose comments inserted into direct quotations.

Such insertions may be information included to make a quotation intelligible or to add your personal comments.

> His answer read as follows: "Sourcasim [sic] is no less a form of irony than invective, though the latter is stronger in intent."

The word *sic* means *thus* and is used by the writer to indicate that the error was in the original quotation.

Sometimes a writer wants to insert a personal comment at the appropriate place rather than to delay the comment until the quotation is ended.

> "Bailey insists [as he naturally would] that the committee will stay clear of politics."

11d   Uses of the Colon   :

The colon is a mark of punctuation used to introduce various kinds of constituents or longer passages of discourse. Do not confuse the colon with the semicolon.

Rule 11 Use a colon after the salutation in a formal letter (an informal letter uses a comma).

FORMAL:
>   Dear Professor Burnsides:

INFORMAL:
>   Dear Millie,

Rule 12 Use a colon after an introductory label.

INCORRECT:
>   Peel them potatoes.

CORRECT:
>   Peel those potatoes.

Rule 13   Use a colon to introduce a series that is prepared for in the main clause of a sentence.

> The directions for the standardized test included the following items: be in your seat five minutes prior to the beginning of the test; bring at least two well-sharpened pencils, scratch paper, and erasers; and check all personal items with the monitor.

Rule 14   A colon may be used after a sentence that introduces a direct quotation.

> It was William James who said: "To *know* is one thing, and to know for certain *that* we know is another. One may hold to the first being possible without the second."

Rule 15   A colon may be used to introduce a terminal word, phrase, or clause that is an explanation.

> After that long and difficult winter there is only one thing I need: a vacation.

A dash after *need* would also be correct, though more informal.

Rule 16   Use a colon to separate subtitle and titles, to indicate time, and to cite Biblical sources.

> *Writing: Readings and Advice*
> *Literature: Structure, Sound, and Sense*
> 1:45 A.M.   12:14 P.M.
> John 3:16   Titus 3:4-8

Rule 17   Do not use a colon directly after the verbs **are** and **were**.

Are and *were* are linking verbs (subsection 1a2). As such, they must be followed by predicate nouns or predicate adjectives as complements. Either use no punctuation after *are* and *were* (thus the following list becomes the complement), or use words like *these* or *the following* to complete the introductory expression.

WRONG: The steps we took were: dig a trench, pour the footings, build the framework, pour the walls for the basement, and construct the subfloor.

RIGHT: The steps we took were *the following*: dig a trench, pour the footings, build the framework, pour the walls for the basement, and construct the subfloor.

WRONG: The first three planets in order from the sun are: Mercury, Venus, and Earth.

RIGHT: The first three planets in order from the sun are *these*: Mercury, Venus, and Earth.

RIGHT: The first three planets in order from the sun are Mercury, Venus, and Earth.

WRONG: The examples Joann listed in her paper were: her child had kicked the doctor in the stomach, she had poured sugar in the gas tank, and she had insulted Grandma by calling her fat.

RIGHT: The examples Joann listed in her paper were *the following*: her child had kicked the doctor in the stomach, she had poured sugar in the gas tank, and she had insulted Grandma by calling her fat.

12

The Semicolon

;

A general rule is that semicolons are used to separate only coordinate, not noncoordinate, constituents. The semicolon calls for a voice pause as long as that of a period, but it is used only as internal punctuation.

12a Compound Sentences without Connectives

<u>Rule 1</u> Use a semicolon to separate two independent clauses that form a compound sentence but that do not have a connective word between them.

The storm continued all night; by morning our tent was soaked.

Underground fires in mines are hard to put out; some have burned for decades.

Writers use compound sentences because they do not want to separate closely related clauses into separate sentences. Note particularly that semicolons are required between the clauses; commas would produce comma splices (see Chapter 3).

12b Compound Sentences with Connectives

Rule 2 Use a semicolon to separate two independent clauses that are joined by a connective other than a coordinating conjunction.

When independent clauses are joined by a coordinating conjunction (subsection 1b4), they usually need only a comma between them. When they are connected by a conjunctive adverb (subsection 1b4) or a transitional phrase, they must be separated by a semicolon. Even when the conjunctive adverb or transitional phrase is shifted to the interior of the second clause, the semicolon is necessary. (Note also that a comma follows the conjunctive adverb that introduces the second clause.)

> The ordeal in the dentist's chair was finally over; *however*, Becky's discomfort continued.

> Marcy and Ellen had taken a wrong turn; they would, *therefore*, have to retrace their steps before proceeding.

The semicolons in these examples are necessary, unless each example were punctuated as two sentences. Commas in place of the semicolons would produce comma splices (see Chapter 3).

In summary: Closely related independent clauses can be punctuated in five ways: (1) Leave them as separate sentences; (2) join them with a comma plus a coordinating conjunction; (3) join them with a semicolon and no connective; (4) join them with a semicolon and a conjunctive adverb followed by a comma; and (5) join them with a semicolon when a conjunctive adverb or a transitional phrase is shifted to the interior of the second clause. Failure to use one of these methods results in a comma splice or a run-together sentence (Chapter 3).

12c Phrases or Clauses in a Series

<u>Rule 3</u> Use semicolons to separate phrases or clauses in a series when the phrases or clauses have internal punctuation or when they are especially long.

> The participants divided themselves into three groups: (1) philosophers, theologians, and linguists; (2) poets, novelists, and dramatists; and (3) historians, economists, and geographers.

Since each of the three parts of the series has commas of its own, semicolons clarify the structure. Note that the semicolons still separate coordinate phrases. (Also note that this example illustrates one use of the colon and one use of parentheses.)

> Professor Means's study showed that American Indians from reservations made lower average scores on standardized tests than Indians living off reservations; that Indians who live in a stable community scored higher than those who are migrant; and that Indians tested in their own languages scored higher on I.Q. tests than Indians tested in English.

Because the clauses in a series in this example are so long, the semicolons make the sentence structure more clear than commas would, although commas would be acceptable.

12d Misused Semicolons

<u>Rule 4</u> Do not use a semicolon between non-coordinate words, phrases, or clauses.

> WRONG: The horse races had been the most exciting part of our holiday; especially the photo finish in the sixth.
>
> RIGHT: The horse races had been the most exciting part of our holiday, especially the photo finish in the sixth.

A comma is correct because the second clause is not an independent clause and thus is not coordinate with the independent clause that begins the sentence.

Rule 5 Do not use a semicolon before or after the connective **such as.**

WRONG: I dislike several foods that are supposed to be good for me; such as broccoli, spinach, and green peppers.

WRONG: I dislike several foods that are supposed to be good for me, such as; broccoli, spinach, and green peppers.

RIGHT: I dislike several foods that are supposed to be good for me, such as broccoli, spinach, and green peppers.

Rule 6 Do not use a semicolon in place of a dash or colon.

WRONG: Just one thing kept me from carrying out my plan; lack of money.

RIGHT: Just one thing kept me from carrying out my plan— lack of money.

WRONG: Neapolitan sherbet usually comes in three flavors; vanilla, orange, and strawberry.

RIGHT: Neapolitan sherbet usually comes in three flavors: vanilla, orange, and strawberry.

13

Quotation Marks

" "

13a Direct Quotations " "

Rule 1 Enclose direct quotations in quotation marks.

Phil told Arlene, "If we hurry, we can get to the second show yet."

"I don't think we have enough time to make it," Arlene responded.

These are straightforward examples of the *exact* words each speaker used. *Phil told Arlene* and *Arlene responded* are both called introductory expressions, even though one appears at the beginning and the other at the end of the sentences. Note that a direct quotation begins with a capital letter, and that the period (in the first sentence) and the comma (in the second) come before the closing quotation marks.

Feuer maintained that "a minority of students are turning to shallow faculties on the outskirts of the universities where a variety of [charlatans] . . . offer courses in which they provide answers as well as questions."

This is the kind of direct quotation that might appear in a term paper. Since the quotation forms an integral part of the sentence structure, no comma follows *Feuer maintained that.* (Note that square brackets enclose material not in the direct quotation but interjected by the writer for clarification. Also note that three spaced periods indicate **ellipsis,** or omission of part of the quotation.)

> He maintained that children are "credulous" and "unresistant to indoctrination."

When such a connective as *and* joins two quoted units, as in the above example, each quoted unit is enclosed in quotation marks but the unquoted connective word is not.

> Roger announced, "All of you must report to the captain."
>
> "All of us?" asked George.
>
> "Yes," Roger responded. "You'll get your assignments from him."

This is an example of direct quotations as they are used in dialogue in fiction. The words of each new speaker appear in a separate paragraph.

13b Quotations within Quotations " " ' "

<u>Rule 2</u> When a direct quotation is used within a direct quotation, enclose the internal quotation in single quotation marks and enclose the whole quotation in double quotation marks.

> The commencement speaker said: "In Ecclesiastes we read that 'in much wisdom is much grief, and he who increaseth knowledge increaseth sorrow,' but we must still pursue knowledge for the fulfillment of God's will."

If they appear within a direct quotation, the words and phrases covered in Rules 3, 4, 5, and 6 (in sections 13c and 13d) should be enclosed in single quotation marks.

13c Titles

Rule 3 Use quotation marks to indicate titles of short stories, short poems, one-act plays, individual radio and television episodes, essays, chapters, and other short literary works (less than book or three-act-play length).

Faulkner's "Barn Burning" is often anthologized.

In her short poem "The Golf Links" Sarah Cleghorn points out an ironic social condition.

Lady Gregory produced a masterpiece of humor in her one-act play "The Workhouse Ward."

The second chapter of Evelyn Waugh's *A Handful of Dust* is titled "English Gothic." [Note that the book title is in italics.]

"By Friday you should have read Steinbeck's 'The Chrysanthemums,' " Ms. Ewing announced.

Note the single quotation marks enclosing the title in the last example.

Titles of book-length literary works (*A Handful of Dust* in the fourth example) are underlined in longhand and italicized in print (see section 14b). No title should ever be both underlined and enclosed in quotation marks.

Rule 4 Do not put quotation marks around a title used as the heading of a theme or essay.

Of course if a quoted unit is included in the title, that unit is enclosed in quotation marks.

TITLE AS HEADING:
    The Care of Infants

TITLE AS HEADING:
    The Plea for Reason in Milton's "Areopagitica"

If the second title appeared in a paragraph, the whole title would be in regular quotation marks and the title of the story would be in single quotation marks.

13d Special Words

<u>Rule 5</u> A word used as a word and not for its meaning may be enclosed in quotation marks.

When Paul said "physician" he meant to say "physicist."

Jambura's proposal was marked by numerous "if's" and "however's."

Americans overuse the word "very" almost as much as the British employ "rather" excessively.

Such words used as words may instead be underlined in longhand and italicized in print (see section 14b), but never are they both underlined and put in quotation marks.

<u>Rule 6</u> Use quotation marks to enclose a word or phrase used in a special or ironical sense.

Joel's "prophecy" came right out of the pages of his economics textbook.

Margo always claimed she lived in a "palace"; in reality, it was a one-bedroom bungalow.

Bob's rusty muffler on a pedestal, which he called "art," was still just a rusty muffler to me.

The writer does not believe as Joel does that his pronouncements are prophetic; instead, they were quite ordinary. Nor does the writer believe that Margo's home was palatial.

You should avoid enclosing slang terms in quotation marks as an apology for their use. If a slang term is worth using, do so without apology.

POOR USAGE:

Claudette thought the rich boys who tried to date her were "nerds."

BETTER: Claudette thought the rich boys who tried to date her were nerds.

13e   With Other Marks of Punctuation

Rule 7   Always put periods and commas inside (rather than outside) quotation marks, regardless of whether the period or comma belongs to the quoted unit.

I entitled my paper "Existentialism in *Moby Dick*."

Although our preacher says "The way of the transgressor is hard," I notice that our local crooks have an easy time of it.

Neither the period in the first example nor the comma in the second belongs to the quoted unit, but each is correctly placed within the quotation marks.

Rule 8   Marks of punctuation other than the period and the comma are placed inside quotation marks when they are a part of the quoted unit and outside the quotation marks when they are not a part of the quoted unit.

Did Professor Gallegos say "to chapter ten" or "through chapter ten"?

Since the question mark does not belong to the quoted unit, it is placed outside the quotation marks.

Ann Landers was heard to utter, "Why am I so lonely?"

Since the question mark belongs to the quoted unit, it is placed inside the quotation marks. Note also that no additional period is used even though the whole sentence is a statement and not a question.

Franklin said, "He who hesitates is lost"; he also said, "Look before you leap."

The semicolon is not a part of the quoted unit and thus is placed outside the quotation marks.

14

Mechanics

14a   Manuscript Form

14a1   Handwritten papers

Observe the following directions in preparing handwritten papers:

1. Use blue or black ink, if possible. Never use colored inks or perfumed inks.

2. Write on lined 8½ × 11 notebook paper. Cut off edges of paper torn from a spiral notebook.

3. To allow for corrections and comments, many instructors require that you skip every other line—especially for out-of-class assignments. Avoid narrow-spaced paper, if possible.

4. Write on one side of the paper only.

5. Compose a title (not just a statement of the topic) for your paper. Skip a line between the title and the first line of your paper.

6. Do *not* enclose the title in quotation marks, do *not* underline it, and do *not* use a period (titles do not ordinarily have end punctuation). A unit within the title, such as the title of a short story or a word used in a special sense (see section 13d), should be enclosed in quotation marks. The title of a book within your paper's title should be underlined.

7. Do not write outside the left-hand margin line (usually in red, if there is one), except to put numbers of questions if you are writing a test.

8. Leave at least a one-inch margin on the right-hand side of your notebook paper and at the bottom; do not crowd the right-hand side nor write down the right-hand margin. However, do not leave an excessively wide right-hand margin.

9. Use a hyphen to divide a word at the end of a line and divide *only* between syllables. Do *not* divide a one-syllable word, such as *twel-ve* or *walk-ed*. Do *not* divide a word so that a single letter is set apart, such as *a-bove* or *pun-y*. Consult a dictionary, if necessary, for syllabification.

10. Never let a mark of end punctuation, a comma, a semicolon, or a colon begin a line of your paper. Never end a line with the first of a set of quotation marks, parentheses, or brackets.

11. Indent each paragraph about one inch.

12. It is acceptable to draw a single line through an error and to write the correction neatly above it. Recopy a page that contains more than two errors. Try to make every physical aspect of your paper neat. Proofread carefully.

13. Follow your instructor's directions for folding your paper and entering your name and other information on it.

14a2 Typewritten papers

Observe the following directions in preparing typewritten papers:

1. Use unruled 8½ × 11 bond paper, if possible. Do not use onionskin paper or erasable paper.

2. Use a black ribbon and type on one side of the paper only.

3. For your title, follow directions 5 and 6 in section 14a1.

4. Double-space between the lines of your paper.

5. Double-space horizontally (that is, use two typewriter spaces instead of one) after all marks of end punctuation and colons.

6. Single-space after commas, semicolons, parentheses, and brackets.

7. Make a dash with two hyphens (--) and leave no space before or after a dash.

8. When underlining to show italics, underline the spaces between words too, unless your instructor gives you different instructions.

9. To make the numeral 1, use the small letter *l* on the keyboard, *not* the capital *i*.

10. Do not number page one; place page numbers in the upper right-hand corners of succeeding pages. Use Arabic numerals (2, 3, 4) to number pages, rather than Roman numerals (II, III, IV).

11. Follow direction 9 in subsection 14a1 for dividing words at the end of a line.

12. Maintain a 1½-inch margin on the left-hand side of each page and about a one-inch margin on the other three sides. Of course the right-hand ends of lines in typewriting will be uneven.

Figure 1 illustrates an acceptable setup for the first page of a manuscript.

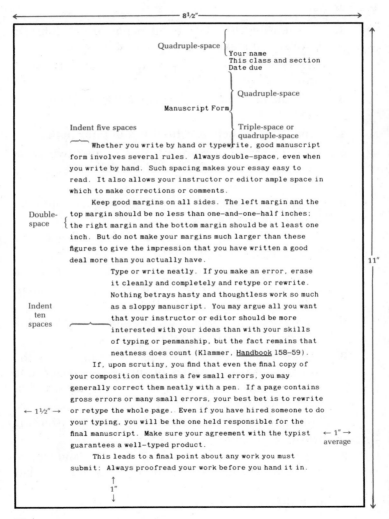

Figure 1.

13. Indent paragraphs five spaces.
14. Keep your paper neat and proofread it carefully.
15. Follow your instructor's directions for folding your paper and entering your name and other information on it.

14b Underlining and Quotation Marks

Underlining in longhand or typing is equivalent to italics in print. Underlining and quotation marks are linked in certain ways.

14b1 Underlining

Rule 1 Underline titles of book-length literary works, newspapers, magazines, works of art, radio and television programs (not single episodes), musical compositions, and names of ships and aircraft.

> Gustave Flaubert's <u>Madame Bovary</u> [a book]
> Tennessee Williams' <u>The Glass Menagerie</u> [a play]
> Vergil's <u>Aeneid</u> [a long poem]
> <u>Time</u> [a magazine]
> <u>Wall Street Journal</u> [a newspaper]
> <u>Star Trek</u> [a television series]
> Handel's <u>Messiah</u> [a musical composition]
> Chagall's <u>I and My Village</u> [a painting]
> the <u>Titanic</u> [a ship]
> <u>Air Force One</u> [an individual aircraft]

Compare this rule with Rule 3 for titles of shorter works (section 13c).

Rule 2 Underline foreign words and phrases that have not been fully Anglicized.

Consult a dictionary if you are uncertain about any word.

> Was it Schopenhauer or Schodinger—or neither—who suffered from <u>Weltschmerz</u>?

> Jackson noted three characteristics of the <u>fin de siècle</u>: decadence, realism, and radical social aspirations.

Rule 3 Words or phrases used as words or phrases (and not for their meaning) may be underlined.

> The slang phrase <u>out of sight</u> originated in the nineteenth century.

> Professor Stone's inaccurate use of <u>epistemology</u> confused his students.

While words used as words may be underlined or enclosed in quotation marks, they are never *both* underlined *and* enclosed in quotation marks.

Rule 4 Words or phrases may be underlined for emphasis.

> I kept quiet precisely because I <u>didn't</u> want the defendant found not guilty.

> For human survival we <u>must</u> discontinue all arms manufacturing.

Single words or short phrases, such as *not*, may be capitalized, instead of underlined, for emphasis. (However, underlining or capitalization for emphasis should be used judiciously, for overuse will cause readers to lose faith in the need for emphasis.)

14b2 Quotation marks

The use of quotation marks for enclosing direct quotations is covered in Chapter 13. In this section, we discuss quotation marks only as they are related to underlining (italics) of words and titles.

Rule 5 Use quotation marks to enclose titles of short stories, short poems, one-act plays, single episodes of radio and television programs, essays, chapters, and other short literary works (less than book or three-act-play length).

Underlining identifies major works or separate publications. Quotation marks are reserved for lesser works or parts of major works. No title is ever both underlined and enclosed in quotation marks.

> Frost's poem "Birches"
>
> Faulkner's short story "That Evening Sun"
>
> Fred Jacobs's short play "Golden Land"
>
> Thoreau's essay "Civil Disobedience"
>
> Chapter 14 is entitled "The Campaign of '48."

Rule 6 Do not put a title used as a heading in quotation marks.

> TITLE AS HEADING:
> > Abroad with Two Yanks

Units within the title as heading may, however, be enclosed in quotation marks.

> TITLE AS HEADING:
> > The History of "Gab" as Slang

Rule 7 A word or phrase used as a word or phrase (and not for its meaning) may be enclosed in quotation marks.

> "Biddable" is one of the most euphonious words in English.
>
> The expression "rattle your cage" is a merging of two slang terms.

Again, words used as words may be underlined or enclosed in quotation marks, but they are never *both* underlined *and* enclosed in quotation marks.

Rule 8 Use quotation marks to enclose a word or phrase used in a special ironic sense.

> Bernie likes to think he is a member of the "literary" set. [The quotation marks mean that the writer does not think Bernie's set has real literary attributes.]

14c Abbreviations

Rules for using abbreviations vary considerably, as you will observe in your reading. The rules given here are an acceptable guide for the sort of writing done in English composition courses. They do not apply to such writing as addresses on envelopes, lists, technical data, and other special forms of composition. (See subsection 17a16 for capitalization of abbreviations.)

14c1 Acceptable abbreviations

<u>Rule 9</u> Use the following abbreviations designating individuals:

Mr.	Messrs. (plural of Mr.)
Mrs.	Mmes. (plural of Mrs.)
Miss	Misses (plural of Miss)
Ms.	Esq. (an attorney, male or female)
St. (Saint)	Jr. (son of a Senior)
Sr. (Senior)	III (son of a Junior)

Ms. is the courtesy title for a woman without regard for her marital status; it is also the correct title for a woman who keeps her own name after marriage. Thus, *Ann Brown* (married to *Bob Smith* but keeping her own name) may be correctly addressed as *Ms. Brown* or *Ms. Smith* or *Mrs. Bob Smith* (but not as *Ms. Bob Smith*).

<u>Rule 10</u> Use abbreviations to designate any earned or honorary degrees or special awards.

DEGREES:
> A.B. (bachelor of arts)
> B.A. (bachelor of arts)
> M.A. (master of arts)
> M.D. (medical doctor)
> Ph.D. (doctor of philosophy)
> Ed.D. (doctor of education)
> D.D.S. (doctor of dental science)

D.D. (doctor of divinity)
J.D. (doctor of jurisprudence)
D.V.M. (doctor of veterinary medicine)
D.Lit. *or* D.Litt. (doctor of literature)
LL.D. (doctor of laws)
D.H.L. (doctor of Hebrew literature)

SPECIAL AWARDS:

O.M. (Order of Merit: English)
D.S.C. (Distinguished Service Cross)
D.S.M. (Distinguished Service Medal)

Rule 11   Use the following abbreviations designating time:

1800 B.C. (before Christ)
A.D. 1462 (*anno Domini*, in the year of our Lord)
DST, PST (daylight saving time, Pacific standard time)
4:12 A.M. *or* 4:12 a.m. (*ante meridiem*, before noon)
3:30 P.M. *or* 3:30 p.m. (*post meridiem*, after noon)

Do not say *12 p.m. midnight* or *4:12 p.m. in the afternoon;*
say either *4:12 p.m.* or *4:12 in the afternoon.*

Rule 12   Use abbreviations to designate well-known
agencies, organizations, and unions, either governmental or
private.

UN	CIA	USA (or U.S.)
UNESCO	VA	USSR
WHO	VFW	
CARE	ILGWU	
CAB	UAW	

While such abbreviations usually appear with no periods,
you may use periods if you wish. The important thing is to be
consistent and to make sure your usage will be clear to the
reader. Good writers write out the title and follow it with the
abbreviation within parentheses at the first usage, so the
reader will recognize the abbreviation in all future references.

Rule 13   Frequently used technical terms may be abbreviated.

mpg (miles per gallon)   rpm (revolutions per minute)
mph (miles per hour)   Btu (British thermal unit)

Rule 14   The abbreviations **no.**, **nos.**, and **$** are acceptable when used with numerals.

The winner was no. 4238.

Please pay particular attention to nos. 2, 6, 9, and 13.

My plumbing bill was $1239.62.

Rule 15   The following abbreviations of standard foreign phrases may be used.

i.e. (that is)   viz. (namely)
e.g. (for example)   cf. (compare with)
c. or ca. (*circa:* about)   etc. (and so forth)
                           et al. (and others)

Use the English rather than the Latin as often as possible in your writing.

Rule 16   In purely technical writing, abbreviations of technical terms are acceptable.

cc. (cubic centimeter)   gm. (gram)
cm. (centimeter)   in. (inch)

The examples in the above eight rules are representative. Other abbreviations of the same sort are acceptable. Consult a dictionary for a list of abbreviations.

14c2   Abbreviations to be avoided in semiformal writing

Rule 17   Do not abbreviate titles of individuals (except as specified in subsection 14c1, Rule 9).

WRONG: The *Pres.* will hold a press conference today.

RIGHT: The **President** will hold a press conference today.

WRONG: The committee includes *Prof.* Dingbat and *Sen.* Jonas and *Rev.* Smith.

RIGHT: The committee includes **Professor** Dingbat and **Senator** Jonas and **the Reverend** Smith.

Rule 18 Do not abbreviate first names.

WRONG:		RIGHT:	
Benj.			Benjamin
Geo.			George
Jas.			James
Theo.			Theodore
Wm.			William

Rule 19 Do not abbreviate the names of states, provinces, and countries.

WRONG: The Holdens went to *N.Y.* for their vacation.

RIGHT: The Holdens went to **New York** for their vacation.

WRONG: Professor Ainsley spent her sabbatical in *Eng.*

RIGHT: Professor Ainsley spent her sabbatical in **England.**

Rule 20 Do not abbreviate the names of days, months, and seasons.

WRONG: The last day of *Feb.* falls on a *Thurs.* this year.

RIGHT: The last day of **February** falls on a **Thursday** this year.

Rule 21 Do not abbreviate names of streets, avenues, boulevards, and courts.

WRONG: Phil just bought a house on Baylor *St.*

RIGHT: Phil just boughs a house on Baylor **Street.**

Rule 22 Avoid abbreviating the word **company** and avoid using the ampersand (&), unless it is part of the name of a firm.

WRONG: the Johnsons *&* the Smollets

RIGHT: the Johnsons **and** the Smollets

WRONG: T. L. Floyd *& Co.* is an equal-opportunity employer.

RIGHT: T. L. Floyd **& Company** is an equal-opportunity employer.

Rule 23   Do not use the abbreviation **Xmas** for Christmas.

Rule 24   Do not abbreviate weights and measurements.

WRONG:		RIGHT:	
oz.			ounce *or* ounces
lbs.			pounds
ft.			foot *or* feet
yds.			yards

Rule 25   Do not abbreviate common words.

WRONG:		RIGHT:	
yrs.			years *or* yours
bldg.			building
sch.			school
Rom. C.			Roman Catholic
con't.			continued
gov't.			government

14d   Numerals

Although usage varies, the following rules for the use of numerals and spelled-out numbers are a satisfactory guide.

Rule 26   For random figures, spell out numbers that require no more than two words; use numerals for numbers that would require more than two words if spelled out.

WRONG: Over 3000 years ago Daedalus tried to fly, but man has succeeded in only the last 75.

RIGHT: Over **three thousand** years ago Daedalus tried to fly, but man has succeeded in only the last **seventy-five.**

WRONG: The companies expected sales of 7 million; their exact total amounted to 6,398,207.   [Apparently this refers to units sold, rather than dollars.]

RIGHT: The companies expected sales of **seven million;** their exact total amounted to **6,398,207.**   [Note the use of

commas without spaces in the large figure written in numerals.]

RIGHT: Each year there are **174** days between the Fourth of July and Christmas.

Rule 27   In a sentence or passage that contains a series of figures, use numerals for all of the series.

My unit sales for each of my first seven workdays were **9**, **22**, **8**, **101**, **61**, **3**, and **102**.   [Note that the word *seven* is written out, since it is not part of the series.]

Rule 28   Use numerals in dates, addresses, and time when accompanied by A.M. or P.M.

July **11, 1922** *or* **11** July **1922** (military and technical style)
242 Columbus Street, Apartment **3B**
Room **701**, Hotel Padre
8:22 A.M.

On checks and other notations, dates may be written to show month, day, and year in this way: 7-11-22 *or* 7/11/22.

Rule 29   Use numerals to state measurements, page numbers, and money used with $.

You'll find **4″ × 6″** cards more convenient than **3″ × 5″** cards for library notes.

The point of the gable was **13′6″** from the floor.

You'll find answers on pages **386** through **407**.

The net cost per unit was **$18.73**.

But when simple, nonfractional numbers are involved, they should be spelled out.

WRONG: Our rival's center is nearly 7′ tall.

RIGHT: Our rival's center is nearly **seven feet** tall.

WRONG: We expect $20 to be sufficient.

RIGHT: We expect **twenty dollars** to be sufficient.

Rule 30　When decimals or fractions are involved, use numerals.

Last year the rainfall was **4.11** inches above normal.

The prime rate exceeded **20¼** percent in 1980.

Rule 31　Use numerals for code numbers, such as Social Security numbers, air flight numbers, and telephone numbers.

We needed kit number **4307884** to rebuild the carburetor.

Call **963-2171,** extension **250,** to register.

Rule 32　To prevent misreading when two numbers appear consecutively, spell out the first one and use numerals for the other.

I caught **six 8-inch** trout.

Rule 33　Except in purely technical writing, do not open a sentence with numerals.

POOR STYLE:
>*1250* partisan voters attended the rally.

PREFERRED:
>**Twelve hundred and fifty** partisan voters attended the rally.

With a little thought, you can rearrange a sentence to avoid writing out cumbersome numbers.

REVISED:
>Over **1250** partisan voters attended the rally.

Rule 34　Except in legal and commercial writing, it is not good style to enter numerals in parentheses after a spelled-out number.

INAPPROPRIATE STYLE:
>I purchased *twenty-five (25)* paperback books at the College Bookstore's recent sale.

BETTER: I purchased **twenty-five** paperback books. . . .

14e   Contractions

Nowadays, contractions like *won't*, *doesn't*, and *shouldn't* appear in semiformal writing in such magazines as *Harper's*, *Consumer Reports*, and *Science News* and in many books of nonfiction. Opinion among English teachers, however, is divided as to whether contractions should be allowed in writing assigned in college composition courses. You should ascertain your instructor's preference and follow it.

PART THREE

SPELLING

15

Spelling Rules

English spelling is full of irregularities because our language has borrowed so many words from other languages. Certain frequent regularities do occur, however, and an understanding of such regularities can improve anyone's spelling. If you are ever in doubt about a particular spelling, do not hesitate to check the dictionary, which is a record of acceptable spellings and definitions. Good spellers are people who have developed three habits: they read a great deal, they write frequently, *and* they check their dictionaries often.

The following pages list some rules about common spelling problems. Rather than explaining the rules in great detail, we shall rely on the examples to illustrate them.

15a Adding Suffixes: Doubling the Final Consonant

This rule applies to words that accent the *last* syllable and to words of one syllable.

Rule 1　When adding a suffix that begins with a vowel to a word that ends in a single consonant preceded by a **single** vowel, double the final consonant.

brag + ing = bragging	adMIT + ed = admitted
fad + ism = faddism	beGIN + er = beginner
fog + y = foggy	conFER + ed = conferred
jog + ing = jogging	exPEL + ed = expelled
lag + ing = lagging	occur + ed = occurred
man + ish = mannish	oMIT + ed = omitted
red + est = reddest	reBEL + ing = rebelling
star + ing = starring	reGRET + ed = regretted
swim + ing = swimming	

If the last syllable of a word is not accented or if more than one vowel precedes the final consonant, then the final consonant is not doubled when a suffix beginning with a vowel is added.

aim + ed = aimed	aBANdon + ed = abandoned
reMAIN + ing = remaining	proHIBit + ing = prohibiting
lean + ed = leaned	BANter + ing = bantering
reVEAL + ing = revealing	BENefit + ed = benefited

Note: When a suffix is added to a word that ends with a silent -e, the consonant preceding the -e is never doubled.

come + ing = coming	shine + ing = shining
dine + ing = dining	write + ing = writing
interfere + ed = interfered	

These five words are frequently misspelled because the consonants preceding the silent e's are incorrectly doubled.

15b　Adding Suffixes: Dropping the Silent -e

Many words in English end with a silent -e. When suffixes are added to these words, sometimes the -e is dropped and sometimes it is retained. In this section we will consider the rule that calls for dropping the silent -e.

Rule 2 When adding a suffix that begins with a vowel to a word that ends with a silent -**e**, drop the silent **e**.

dine + ing = dining	create + ive = creative
write + ing = writing	shine + y = shiny
guide + ance = guidance	fame + ous = famous
mange + y = mangy	confuse + ing = confusing
condole + ence = condolence	come + ing = coming
bite + ing = biting	hypocrite + ical = hypocritical
shine + ing = shining	imagine + ative = imaginative
interfere + ed = interfered	pursue + ing = pursuing

15c   Adding Suffixes: Retaining the Silent -e

There are two rules for retaining silent -e's when suffixes are added. The first is an important exception to the basic rule in the previous section.

Rule 3 When adding the suffixes -**able**, -**ous**, or -**ance** to a word that ends in -**ce** or -**ge**, retain the silent -**e**.

Retaining the silent -e keeps the consonants -c and -g "soft" in pronunciation—compare the words *replaceable* (soft *c*) and *implacable* (hard *c*).

replace + able = replaceable	courage + ous = courageous
notice + able = noticeable	outrage + ous = outrageous
trace + able = traceable	advantage + ous = advantageous
splice + able = spliceable	stage + able = stageable
peace + able = peaceable	charge + able = chargeable
enbrace + able = embraceable	change + able = changeable

Note: You should also be aware of special cases where words end with the letter -c pronounced hard as a k sound. When adding the suffix -y or a suffix that begins with -e or -i to such a word that ends in a hard -c sound, add a k in order to preserve that hard -c sound.

panic + ed = panicked	picnic + ing = picnicking
panic + y = panicky	politic + ing = politicking
picnic + er = picnicker	traffic + ing = trafficking

Rule 4   When adding a suffix beginning with a consonant to a word ending in a silent **-e**, retain the silent **-e**.

The long-vowel, short-vowel principle makes this rule necessary. For example, the silent -e in *fate* makes the *a* sound "long." If the silent -e were dropped when the suffix *-ful* is added, the pronunciation would be *fat-ful* (*fat* has a "short" vowel). Here are other examples of the rule in action:

like + ness = likeness   hate + ful = hateful
late + ly = lately   safe + ty = safety
complete + ly = completely   care + less = careless

The -e must be retained to prevent such pronunciations as *lik-ness* and *lat-ly*.

Sometimes the final silent -e does not make the preceding vowel long, but the rule still holds.

immediate + ly = immediately
appropriate + ly = appropriately
approximate + ly = approximately
delicate + ly = delicately

Misspellings due to the dropping of the silent -e when adding *-ly* are quite common.

Note: There are a few exceptions to the above rule. Here are some examples of words in which the silent -e is dropped even though the suffix added begins with a consonant.

whole + ly = wholly   argue + ment = argument
true + ly = truly   judge + ment = judgment
awe + ful = awful

15d   Adding Suffixes: Changing the Final **-y** to **-i**

Rule 5   When adding a suffix to a word ending in **-y** preceded by a consonant, change the **-y** to **-i**.

When adding the suffix *-s* to make the plural of a noun that ends in *-y* preceded by a consonant or when adding the suffix -s to a verb that ends in -y preceded by a consonant, change the -y to -i and add -es.

    ally + s = allies   try + s = tries
    reply + s = replies   deny + s = denies
    harpy + s = harpies   defy + s = defies

The rule also operates with many other suffixes.

    comply + ance = compliance   cry + er = crier
    mercy + ful = merciful   dry + est = driest
    lonely + ness = loneliness   easy + ly = easily

15d1 Exceptions: -y + -**ing** and -y + -**ist**

Rule 5 does not apply when the suffix is -ing or -ist.

    study + ing = studying   worry + ing = worrying
    hurry + ing = hurrying   copy + ist = copyist

In these words the -y is *never* dropped; misspellings such as *studing* for *studying* are common.

There are a number of other exceptions to the rule, all of them involving one-syllable words. Here are the main exceptions:

    shyness   slyly   dryness
    shyly   wryness   dryly
    slyness   wryly   dryer (the machine)

A minor rule that reverses the y-to-i rule is this:

15d2 When adding -**ing** to a verb ending in -**ie**, change the -**ie** to -**y**.

    die + ing = dying   tie + ing = tying
    lie + ing = lying   vie + ing = vying

15d3   When adding a suffix to a word ending in **-y** preceded by a vowel, do not change the **-y** to **-i**.

This rule is the logical reverse of Rule 5.

annoy + s = annoys   valley + s = valleys
convey + ed = conveyed   alley + s = alleys
stay + ed = stayed   donkey + s = donkeys
coy + ly = coyly   boy + hood = boyhood

There are few common exceptions to this rule:

lay + ed = laid   day + ly = daily
pay + ed = paid   gay + ly = gaily
say + ed = said

In these words the -y is changed to -i even though the -y is preceded by a vowel.

15d4   Proper nouns

The y-to-i rule does not apply in spelling the plural of proper names or in spelling the possessive form of any noun ending in -y.

the Bradys   Betty's car
the Kennedys   one ally's advantage
several Sallys   the company's president

15e   Spelling **ie** and **ei** Words

The ie/ei rules do not cover many words, but they do cover common words that are frequently misspelled.

Rule 6   Place **i** before **e** when pronounced as **ee** except after **c**. (Place **e** before **i** after **c**.)

ie {
believe   thief   niece
chief   brief   tier
achieve   relieve   mien
priest   yield
}

ei {
receive	conceit
deceive	receipt
deceit	ceiling
conceive	perceive
}

Exceptions: There are a number of exceptions to this rule; five of the exceptions can be mastered by memorizing this nonsense sentence:

Neither sheik seized weird leisure.

All five of these exceptions have an *ei* combination pronounced as a long *e* but not preceded by a *c*. (In some dialects *neither* is pronounced with a long *i* sound and *leisure* with an *eh* sound.)

Other exceptions: Rule 6 does not apply to such words as *science* and *atheist*, in which the *i*'s and *e*'s are pronounced in separate syllables. Nor does it apply to such words as *foreign* and *friend*, in which the combination is not pronounced as a long *e*.

Rule 7 Place **e** before **i** when pronounced as a long **a**.

Of course there are various ways of spelling the long *a* sound, but if the word has either an *ie* or *ei* combination, then the writer can know that it is *ei* if the pronunciation is a long *a*.

Here are some common words covered by this rule:

freight	reins
weight	vein
neighbor	neigh
sleigh	reign
heinous	deign

The words *their* and *heir* may also be put in this group, though the vowel sound in them is not exactly a long *a* in many people's dialects.

16

Spelling Lists

16a Double-Consonant Words

The following words are often misspelled because one consonant of a double consonant is omitted. The double consonants are in boldface.

accidental	committee	immediately	parallel
accommodate	communist	immense	planned
accomplish	controlled	intelligence	possess
accurate	curriculum	intelligent	possession
aggressive	different	interrupt	possible
annual	disappear	irritable	preferred
apparatus	disappoint	manner	roommate
apparent	dissatisfied	misspelled	stubborn
applies	disservice	narrative	success
appreciate	drunkenness	necessary	summed
appropriate	embarrass	occurred	supposed
approximate	equipped	occurrence	suppress
attitude	exaggerate	opponent	surrounding
beginner	excellent	opportunity	swimming
beginning	generally	opposite	unnecessary
biggest			

16b   Single-Consonant Words

The following words are often misspelled because a single consonant is incorrectly doubled. The single consonant is in boldface.

abandoned	coming	later
academic	confused	necessary
across	define	occasion
already	definitely	omitted
among	definition	operate
amount	dining	opinion
analyze	disappear	parallel
another	disappoint	primitive
apartment	during	profession
apology	eliminate	professor
becoming	fulfill	quarrel
benefited	holiday	relative
biting	imagine	shining
calendar	inoculate	tomorrow
career	interfered	writing
column		

16c   Words with **de-** and **di-**

The following words are often misspelled because an *e* is substituted for an *i* or an *i* for an *e*. The *de*'s and *di*'s are in boldface.

de
- **de**scend
- **de**scribe
- **de**scription
- **de**spair
- **de**spise
- **de**spite
- **de**stroy
- **de**struction
- **de**vice
- **de**vise

di
- **di**gest
- **di**gress
- **di**lemma
- **di**lute
- **di**sastrous
- **di**sciple
- **di**sease
- **di**vide
- **di**vine
- **di**vorce

16d   Omitted Letters

The following words are often misspelled because of the omission of one or more letters. The letters that are often omitted are in boldface.

accident**a**lly
accompan**y**ing
ac**q**uire
advertis**e**ment
appropriat**e**ly
approxim**a**tely
as**p**irin
ath**e**ist
basic**a**lly
barg**a**in
befor**e**
bound**a**ry
car**e**less
carr**y**ing
chang**e**able
charac**t**eristics
cloth**e**s
(two) communist**s**
competi**t**ion
complet**e**ly
(it) consist**s**
criti**c**ism
crow**d**ed
de**a**lt
definit**e**ly
dis**c**ipline
envir**on**ment
every**t**hing
exper**i**ence
extrem**e**ly
fami**l**y
fascin**a**te
fou**r**th

gover**n**ment
hero**e**s
hope**l**ess
hypocrit**e**
imagin**e**
immedi**a**tely
inte**r**est
knowled**ge**
lab**o**ratory
like**l**y
lite**r**ature
lon**e**liness
lon**e**ly
lux**u**ry
maga**z**ine
math**e**matics
me**a**nt
med**i**cal
Negro**e**s
nin**e**ty
notic**e**able
now**a**days
nume**r**ous
parti**c**ular
(be) prejudic**e**d
prim**i**tive
privi**l**ege
prob**ab**ly
quan**t**ity
re**a**lize
rem**em**ber
r**h**ythm
saf**e**ty

(two) scientist**s**
shep**h**erd
sincer**e**ly
soph**o**more
stre**t**ch
stud**y**ing
suppos**ed** (to)
temper**a**ment
temper**a**ture
therefor**e**
th**o**rough
undoub**ted**ly
use**d** (to)
use**f**ul
valu**a**ble
vari**o**us
w**h**ere
w**h**ether
wh**o**se

16e   Added Letters

The following words are often misspelled because of the addition of a letter. The incorrect letters that are often added are shown in parentheses. (Also see section 16b.)

among (no u after o)
argument (no e after u)
athlete (no e after h)
attack (no t after k)
awful (no e after w)
chosen (no oo)
disastrous (no e after t)
drowned (no d after n)
equipment (no t after p)
exercise (no c after x)
existent (no h after x)
explanation (no i after la)
final (no i after n)
forty (no u after o)
forward (no e after r)
genius (no o after i)
grievous (no i after v)
height (no h after t)

Henry (no e after n)
hindrance (no e after d)
jewelry (no e after l)
judgment (no e after g)
laundry (no e after d)
led (no a after e)
lose (no oo)
mischievous (no i after v)
ninth (no e after in)
pamphlet (no e after h)
personal (no i after n)
privilege (no d after le)
procedure (no ee)
remembrance (no e after b)
similar (no i after l)
statistics (no s after a)
truly (no e after u)

16f   Words with **-ant/-ance** and **-ent/-ence**

ant
ance

abund**ant**
abund**ance**
acquaint**ance**
admitt**ance**
appear**ance**
assist**ant**
assist**ance**
attend**ant**
attend**ance**
brilli**ant**
brilli**ance**

const**ant**
domin**ant**
domin**ance**
guid**ance**
hindr**ance**
ignor**ant**
ignor**ance**
import**ant**
import**ance**
inhabit**ant**

pleas**ant**
predomin**ant**
redund**ant**
redund**ance**
relev**ant**
relev**ance**
resist**ant**
resist**ance**
serv**ant**
warr**ant**

	absent	different	occurrence
	absence	difference	opponent
	adolescent	excellent	permanent
	adolescence	excellence	permanence
	apparent	existent	persistent
	coherent	existence	persistence
	coherence	experience	present
ent	competent	independent	presence
ence	competence	independence	prominent
	confident	ingredient	prominence
	confidence	insistent	reverent
	consistent	insistence	reverence
	consistence	intelligent	sufficient
	convenient	intelligence	sufficience
	convenience	magnificent	superintendent
	dependent	magnificence	superintendence
	dependence		

16g   Homophones and Confused Words

Homophones are words that are pronounced alike but that have different spellings and meanings, such as *course* and *coarse*. The following list consists of homophones that cause frequent misspellings and other pairs of words which sound so much alike that the spelling of one is often confused with the spelling of the other. Information about the words is also included. The abbreviations have the following meanings:

n. = noun   pro. = pronoun   contr. = contraction
v. = verb   prep. = preposition   sing. = singular
adj. = adjective   conj. = conjunction   pl. = plural
adv. = adverb   poss. = possessive

***ac*cept:** (v.) to receive
***ex*cept:** (prep.) not included

***acc*ess:** (n.) a way of approach or entrance
***ass*ess:** (v.) to estimate the value of

ad*a*pt: (v.) to adjust to a situation
ad*o*pt: (v.) to take in or take a course of action

advi*c*e: (n.) counsel, information, or suggestions given
advi*s*e: (v.) to give advice or counsel

***a*ffect:** (v.) to influence or have an effect on
***e*ffect:** (n.) the result of an action
***e*ffect:** (v.) to accomplish or execute

***a*isle:** (n.) a corridor or passageway
***i*sle:** (n.) an island

***all* ready:** (n. + adj.) everyone is prepared
***al*ready:** (adv.) at or before this time; previously

***all* together:** (n. + adj.) all in one place
***al*together:** (adv.) completely; wholly

***al*lude:** (v.) to refer to
***e*lude:** (v.) to evade or escape

***a*llusion:** (n.) a reference
***i*llusion:** (n.) a false impression

aloud: (adv.) audibly or loudly
allowed: (v.) permitted

alt*a*r: (n.) an elevated place for religious services
alt*e*r: (v.) to change

***al*ways:** (adv.) constantly; all the time
***all* ways:** (determiner + n.) in every way

an*e*cdote: (n.) a little story
an*t*idote: (n.) something that counteracts a poison

ang*el*: (n.) a heavenly being
ang*le*: (n.) figure formed by the divergence of two
  straight lines from a common point

ar*c*: (n.) a part of a circle
ar*ch*: (n.) a curved part of a building

ascend: (v.) to rise or go up
ascent: (n.) a movement upward
assent: (v.) to agree
assent: (n.) an agreement

assistance: (n.) help given
assistants: (n. pl.) helpers

band: (n.) a group
banned: (v.) excluded or prohibited

beside: (prep.) by the side of
besides: (adv. *and* prep.) in addition to

boar: (n.) a male hog
bore: (n.) someone who tires you

boarder: (n.) one who pays for room and meals
border: (n.) a boundary

born: (v.) given birth to (always in the passive voice)
borne: (v.) given birth to (always in the active voice); carried

brake: (n.) a mechanism to stop a vehicle
break: (v.) to cause to fall into two or more pieces

breath: (n.) air inhaled and exhaled
breathe: (v.) to take in breaths and let them out

canvas: (n.) a kind of coarse cloth
canvass: (v.) to search or examine or solicit

capital: (n.) a city that is a seat of government
capitol: (n.) a building occupied by a legislature

censer: (n.) container for burning incense
censor: (v.) to prohibit publication
censor: (n.) one who prohibits publication
censure: (v.) to reprimand or disapprove of
censure: (n.) disapproval

choose: (v.) to select (present tense)
chose: (v.) selected (past tense)
chosen: (v.) selected (past participle)

cite: (v.) to quote; to charge with breaking a law
sight: (n.) something seen; the sense of seeing
sight: (v.) to look at or aim at
site: (n.) a location

coarse: (adj.) rough; unrefined
course: (n.) school subject; a way or path

complement: (n.) items which complete
compliment: (n.) a statement of praise

conscience: (n.) what tells you right from wrong
conscious: (adj.) awake; alert

council: (n.) a group that deliberates
counsel: (v.) to give advice
counsel: (n.) advice given

descent: (n.) a going down
dissent: (v.) to disagree
dissent: (n.) disagreement

desert: (n.) a geographical area
desert: (v.) to abandon
dessert: (n.) food

device: (n.) a contrivance
devise: (v.) to prepare a method or contrivance

do: (v.) to perform
due: (adj.) used with *to* to specify the cause of something;
  owing

dual: (adj.) twofold
duel: (n.) a fight between two people

eminent: (adj.) famous
imminent: (adj.) likely to occur soon

envelop: (v.) to cover or enclose
envelope: (n.) an enclosure used for mailing

extant: (adj.) still existing
extent: (n.) the degree of something

form*a*lly: (adv.) in a formal manner
form*e*rly: (adv.) at an earlier time

forth: (adv., prep.) forward; onward; out
fourth: (n.) the one after third

human: (adj.) pertaining to people
humane: (adj.) pertaining to compassion or kindness

its: (poss. pro.) belonging to it
it's: (contr.) it is *or* it has

later: (adj.) after a specified time
la*tt*er: (n.) the last one mentioned

lead: (v.; pronounced *leed*) to conduct
lead: (n.; pronounced *led*) the metal
led: (v.) past tense and past participle of the verb *lead*

loose: (adj.) not tight
lose: (v.) to misplace; to be defeated

mar*i*tal: (adj.) pertaining to marriage
mar*t*ial: (adj.) military

maybe: (adv.) perhaps
may be: (v.) possibly may occur

meant: (v.) past tense and past participle of the verb *mean*
ment: not a word

pas*sed*: (v.) past tense and past participle of the verb *pass*
pas*t*: (n.) an earlier time

patien*ce*: (sing. n.) calm endurance
patien*ts*: (pl. n.) those under medical care

p*ea*ce: (n.) not war
p*ie*ce: (n.) a part of

person*al*: (adj.) pertaining to oneself
person*nel*: (n.) the employees of a company or organization

principal: (n.) head of a school; money owned
principal: (adj.) chief; most important
principle: (n.) a rule or doctrine

prophecy: (n.) a prediction
prophesy: (v.) to make a prediction

quiet: (adj.) not noisy
quite: (adv.) completely or almost completely

sense: (n.) ability to think well; meaning
since: (prep *and* conj.) before this time; because

stationary: (adj.) in a fixed position
stationery: (n.) paper to write on

than: (conj.) used to compare things
then: (n. or adv.) indicating time

their: (poss. pro.) belonging to them
there: (adv.) a place; also used as an expletive to begin
   sentences
they're: (contr.) they are

to: (prep.) generally indicating direction
too: (adv.) excessively; overmuch
two: (n.) the number

trail: (n.) a rough path
trial: (n.) experimental action, or examination before a court

vice: (n.) immorality
vise: (n.) a device for holding

weather: (n.) the state of the atmosphere
whether: (conj.) expressing alternatives

whose: (poss. pro.) belonging to whom
who's: (contr.) who is *or* who has

your: (poss. pro.) belonging to you
you're: (contr.) you are

16h Other Troublesome Words

The following common words, not included in the preceding sections, are also often misspelled.

a lot	eighth	nickel	schedule
actually	endeavor	optimism	separate
against	familiar	ours	sergeant
amateur	favorite	paid	source
amount	February	peculiar	speech
article	foreign	perspiration	supersede
battalion	grammar	practical	surprise
beauty	guarantee	precede	technique
bulletin	hers	preparation	theirs
buried	hundred	prescription	themselves
category	inevitable	prestige	tragedy
children	interpretation	proceed	Tuesday
comparative	involve	psychology	until
condemn	January	pursue	Wednesday
counselor	library	repetition	(one) woman
courtesy	marriage	ridiculous	yours
doesn't	minute	sacrifice	

17

Capitalization

Although practices in capitalization do vary, the following specific rules are adhered to by almost all writers. The name commonly used for small letters is **lower case**.

17a   Rules of Capitalization

For convenience, we will not only use our number-letter system of classification but also will number the rules.

17a1   The basics

<u>Rule 1</u>   Capitalize the first word of each sentence, the pronoun **I**, and the interjection **O**, but not other interjections unless one opens a sentence. In using direct quotations, follow the capitalization of the original author exactly.

O, say, can you see how tall **I** am?

My, o my—what a fuzzy cat!

17a2 Titles of literary works

Rule 2 In a title or chapter heading, capitalize the first letter of the first word and all other words except articles, short prepositions, and coordinating conjunctions.

TITLE OF A BOOK:
> *A Dictionary of American Idioms*

TITLE OF A SHORT STORY:
> "A Woman on a Roof"

TITLE OF A POEM:
> "Soliloquy of the Spanish Cloister"

CHAPTER HEADING:
> Changing Meanings and Values of Words

17a3 Specific school courses

Rule 3 Capitalize the name of a specific school course but not the name of a general subject-matter area, unless it is a proper name.

> Kathy is taking Social Studies 101 and Introduction to Psychology. She says she would rather be taking courses in art and music.

17a4 Proper nouns and proper adjectives

Rule 4 Capitalize all proper nouns and adjectives formed from proper nouns, unless the proper adjective—such as **venetian red**—is commonly spelled with a lower-case letter.

Consult a dictionary if necessary. A proper noun is the name of a specific individual, animate or inanimate.

Alabama	Kol Nidre	Rhine
European	Mark Boehne	San Sebastian
Filipino	Owen Stanley Range	Statue of Liberty
Havana	Pasadena	Thailand
Indian	Quaalude	Yosemite

17a5   Religions and related topics

Rule 5   Capitalize references to the Deity or Deities in all recognized religions, the names of religions, religious sects, divine books, and adjectives formed from these.

Allah	Christ	our Lord
Baptist	Christian	Mormonism
the Bible	God	the New Testament
Biblical	Hinduism	Protestant
Catholic	Jewish	the Upanishads

17a6   Relatives

Rule 6   Capitalize the titles of relatives when used with the person's name or as a substitute for the name, but not when the term designating the relationship is used with a possessive pronoun, such as **my.**

Did Aunt Helen send her usual Christmas package?

I'll have to write my aunt Helen to thank her.

You should see how my mother plays tennis!

What did Mother say when you told her we'd be late?

Everybody knows that Grandfather Patton plays golf daily.

17a7   Officials

Rule 7   Capitalize the titles of important officials when used with their names. Capitalize a title used in place of a name to designate a particular individual. Do not capitalize a title that designates an office but not a particular individual.

Vice-President Forbes

Senator Javits

Colonel Wetzler

Reverend Puder

The Congressman will not be in today.   [A specific congressman is understood]

The **D**ean left instructions for preparing the memo.
[A specific dean is understood.]

A college **p**resident does not have an enviable job.
[No specific president is meant.]

The office of **m**ayor is vacant.

17a8   Days, months, and holidays

Rule 8   Capitalize the days of the week, the months of the year, and official holidays. Do not capitalize the names of the seasons.

Memorial **D**ay
Easter
October
Valentine's **D**ay
Thursday
summer

17a9   Specific geographic locations

Rule 9   Capitalize the names of nations, states, provinces, continents, oceans, lakes, rivers, mountains, cities, streets, parks, and specific geographic regions. Do not capitalize the names of directions.

Arizona	**J**efferson **P**ark	the **S**outh
British **C**olumbia	**L**apland	**T**welfth **A**venue
Australia	the **N**ear **E**ast	the **U**inta **M**ountains
Boston	the **P**acific **O**cean	go **s**outh one block
East **O**range	the **R**io **G**rande	the **W**est **C**oast

17a10   Buildings

Rule 10   Capitalize the names of specific buildings.

Badgley **S**cience **H**all
the **G**ranada **T**heater
the **T**aj **M**ahal
the **P**entagon

17a11 Private and governmental organizations

Rule 11 Capitalize the names of private and governmental organizations.

the **S**tudent **S**enate   the **N**ewman **C**lub
the **R**ed **C**ross   the **V**eterans **A**dministration
the **J**aycees   the **A**merican **M**edical **A**ssociation

17a12 Historical documents, events, and eras

Rule 12 Capitalize the names of historical documents, events, and eras.

the **A**tlantic **C**harter   the **M**iddle **A**ges
the **B**attle of **M**idway   **P**ublic **L**aw 16
the **B**ill of **R**ights   the **R**enaissance
the **D**iet of **W**orms   **W**orld **W**ar II

17a13 Brand names

Rule 13 Capitalize brand names—but not the name of the product.

Shell gasoline   a **F**ord car
Ivory soap   **G**leem toothpaste

17a14 Outline headings

Rule 14 Capitalize the first word of an outline heading.

I. **G**impel denies his foolishness in several ways.

  A. **H**e receives benefits from the community.

    1. **T**hey provide the dowry for his wedding.

    2. **H**e grows rich as their baker.

  B. **H**e resists temptation successfully.

    1. **H**e refuses to strike back.

    2. **B**y overcoming the Evil One he saves his soul.

17b

17a15   Celestial bodies

Rule 15   Capitalize the names of some celestial bodies and of geographic regions of the moon.

Do not capitalize the words *earth, world, universe, galaxy, moon, star,* and *sun.*

Arcturus (a star)	**P**hobos (a moon of **M**ars)
the **C**rab **N**ebula	the **S**ea of **R**ains (on the moon)
Halley's **C**omet	**V**enus
peace on **e**arth	

Exception: When named as a planet among other planets, *earth* is generally capitalized.

In the solar system, **E**arth is between **V**enus and **M**ars.

17a16   Abbreviations

Rule 16   Capitalize abbreviations when the whole word or phrase would be capitalized.

See section 14c for other aspects of the capitalization of abbreviations and also for punctuation in abbreviations.

b. 1926	the **NAACP**
CARE	**N**ov.
47 **gpm** (gallons per minute)	the **UN**
pop. (population)	**NBC**

17b   Mandatory Lower-Case Letters

17b1   Centuries

Rule 17   Do not capitalize the names of centuries unless a century is being mentioned as a specific historical era.

It was my destiny to be born in the **t**wentieth **c**entury.

The Age of the Enlightenment is sometimes called simply the **E**ighteenth **C**entury.

17b2 Common animate and inanimate objects

Rule 18 Do not capitalize the names of foods, games, chemical compounds, general geographical formations, animals, plants, or musical instruments unless they designate specific individuals or kinds.

Sometimes, however, a proper noun, which is capitalized, is a part of the name of a species.

a **B**altimore **o**riole	**n**ut
basketball	**o**arlock
the **C**heshire **c**at	**p**arcel
cards	**p**iano
decoy	**r**elish
ebony	**s**chist
a **g**ame of **S**crabble	**s**eal
golf	**s**ulfur **d**ioxide
Lady **B**altimore **c**ake	**t**rout
mixer	**T**hompson's **g**azelle

17b3 Occupations

Rule 19 Do not capitalize the names of occupations.

doctor
engineer
professor

17b4 Diseases

Rule 20 Do not capitalize the names of diseases.

Sometimes, however, a proper noun, which is capitalized, is part of the name of the disease.

measles	**p**neumonia
scarlet fever	**H**odgkin's disease

18

The Apostrophe

,

The apostrophe is a mark used in spelling, not a mark of punctuation. Marks of punctuation clarify sentence structure, whereas apostrophes clarify word form.

18a   Possessive Constructions

There are several ways of expressing possession in English (aside from simply saying *I own something*). A writer can say, "This house *belongs to* Mr. Chatham" or use one of the *of*-constructions: "This is the home *of Mr. Chatham*." A third and more common way is to name the owner first, placing the noun or pronoun in the possessive case: "This is *Mr. Chatham's* home." Such possessive nouns use apostrophes.

18a1   Nouns

Use an apostrophe with a common or a proper noun in a possessive construction.

Spoken English simply adds an *s*-like sound to a noun that shows some idea of possession. Written English is not quite that simple; in addition to the *s*, it requires placing an apostrophe correctly (either before or after the *s*, never directly above it).

a. **Singular nouns always add the apostrophe first and then the letter s to form the possessive case.**

> Michael's backpack = backpack belonging to Michael
> Robyn's eyes = eyes belonging to Robyn
> Ben Johnson's plays = plays that Ben Jonson wrote
> the counter's surface = the surface of the counter

Even when the base form of the noun already ends in -*s*, add both the apostrophe as well as another *s* to form the possessive (though some writers add only the apostrophe).

> a waitress's tips   OR   a waitress' tips
> James's new job   OR   James' new job

b. **Plural nouns that end in -s**   Most nouns form their plurals by adding -*s* or -*es*; a few do not (man, men; woman, women; child, children; fish, fish; sheep, sheep; goose, geese; mouse, mice). When a plural noun shows possession, **always form the plural first and then add the mark of possession.** If the plural of a noun ends in -*s*, add only the apostrophe.

> the members' votes = votes of all the members
> the dogs' collars = collars of several dogs
> the shoes' prices = prices of all the shoes

c. **Plural nouns that do not end in -s**   If the plural of a noun does not end in -*s*, add both the apostrophe and an -*s*—in that order.

> men's habits = habits of many men
> women's interests = interests of many women
> children's programs = programs for several children
> oxen's hooves = hooves of more than one ox

In writing, do not confuse the simple plural with the possessive plural—though in speech they may sound alike. For example, if the parents of children of a family named Goss were to come to your house, you would write the following:

> The Gosses came.   [no apostrophe]

But if their car stalled on the way, you would use an apostrophe, as follows:

> The Gosses' car stalled.

Such a construction would indicate both the plural (by the -*es*) and possession (by the apostrophe).

Sometimes a possessive noun ends a sentence, and the thing possessed is understood though not named. Such a possessive noun takes an apostrophe.

> Carol's baby weighs more than Jane's (baby).

> My stereo cost more than Betty's (stereo).

18a2   Personal pronouns

Do not use an apostrophe with a personal pronoun in a possessive construction.

Personal pronouns (see subsection 1b6) may have two possessive forms. Use the first form when a noun follows.

> This is **my** lunch box.

> Did you buy **your** hat at The Bon?

> Dottie knitted **her** cap and gloves.

Use the second form when the following noun is understood. Note, however, that **the possessives of personal pronouns never take an apostrophe.**

> Their new car is blue, but **ours** is maroon.   [no apostrophe]

> We had our lunch in the main dining room. Where did you have **yours?**   [no apostrophe]

JoAnn bought her blouse at a boutique, but Stella made
hers.   [no apostrophe]

Distinguish between *its* (belonging to *it*) and *it's* (contraction of *it is*).

It's (= it is) too hot to work today.

My car runs fine but **its** muffler (= belonging to it) is shot.

18a3   Indefinite pronouns

Use an apostrophe with an indefinite pronoun in a possessive construction.

A group of words called **indefinite pronouns** (subsection 1b6) function as nouns and may be called noun substitutes. The chief ones that can be made possessive are *one, no one, someone, anyone, everyone, somebody, anybody, everybody, nobody, other, another, one another,* and *each other.* Also the *one* and *body* words are often used with *else,* as in *somebody else.* When one of these words is in a possessive construction, it requires an apostrophe and an *s.* Since none of these words ends in *s,* the apostrophe will always come before the *-s.*

Somebody**'s** scarf was left in the foyer.

We borrowed somebody else**'s** pickup.

Everybody**'s** excuses were interesting but invalid.

Have you seen each other**'s** photo albums?

18a4   Nouns that name periods of time and sums of money

Use an apostrophe to show a possessive construction with a period of time or a sum of money.

Words that name periods of time are frequently used in possessive construction in English. You will notice that such words take apostrophes just as any other nouns do.

I keep all of my New Year's resolutions—in my desk drawer.

Today's efforts produce tomorrow's results.

This month's snow storms were worse than last year's at this time.

An hour's parking cost us three dollars.

Words that name sums of money are also used in the possessive construction in English and require apostrophes just as other nouns do.

A dollar's worth of gas might take you ten miles.

Let me add my two cents' worth to the discussion.

Twelve-year-old Emily must have poured at least a quarter's worth of cologne on her hanky.

There wasn't a nickel's difference between their opinions.

18b Contractions

Use an apostrophe in a contraction.

In contractions, enter an apostrophe where one or more letters have been omitted.

don't	shouldn't (not should'nt)
doesn't (not does'nt)	o'clock
we've	I'm
you'll	Henry's here.
they're	Everybody's gone.

Caution: Do not confuse these pronoun contractions with their "sound-alike" personal possessive pronouns.

Pronoun Contractions	Possessive Pronouns
it's = it is or it has	its = belonging to it
who's = who is or who has	whose = belonging to whom
you're = you are	your = belonging to you
they're = they are	their = belonging to them

The possessive pronouns are already possessive, and so nothing else—not even an apostrophe—is needed to make them possessive.

Also, never put an apostrophe in one of these possessive pronouns:

yours   his   hers   ours   theirs

These words are already possessive, as *mine* is, and they do not take an apostrophe.

18c Plural Spellings

Use an apostrophe to indicate the plurals of figures, letters, and words referred to as words.

Use an **'s** to form the plural of words used as words (see section 14b, Rule 3 for underlining), of letters of the alphabet, of abbreviations, of numerals, and of symbols.

Don't put too many *if* **'s** in your proposal.

There are four *s*'**s** and four *i*'**s** in Mississippi.

Professor Smelly**'s** capital *C*'**s** look like his 9'**s**.

Joey is more concerned with rpm'**s** than with his girlfriend.

The 1700'**s** were good years for aristocrats.

You have too many +'**s** in your equation.

Caution: Never spell the ordinary nonpossessive plural of a noun with an apostrophe.

WRONG: Too many cook'**s** spoil the broth.

RIGHT: Too many cooks spoil the broth.

WRONG: Many cooks' are unsanitary.

RIGHT: Many cooks are unsanitary.

19

The Hyphen

■

Like the apostrophe, the hyphen is a mark used in spelling, not a mark of punctuation. It should not be confused with the dash (see section 11a), which is a mark of punctuation twice as long as the hyphen. In writing and typing, leave no space between the hyphen and neighboring letters.

19a Word Division at the End of a Line

Rule 1 When dividing a word at the end of a line, use a hyphen and divide only between syllables.

Never divide a one-syllable word, such as *tw-elve* and *len-gth*. Do not divide a word so that a single letter is left at the end of one line or the beginning of another, such as *a-muse* and *shin-y*. When necessary, consult a dictionary for proper syllabication.

19b Compound Numbers and Fractions

Rule 2 Hyphenate spelled-out compound numbers (twenty-one through ninety-nine) and spelled-out fractions (See section 14d).

If a fraction is unambiguously used with the indefinite article *a* or *an*, do not hyphenate it.

twenty-seven wins	three-fourths of the pie
thirty-nine losses	one-sixth of the total
her sixty-third birthday	a fourth of the profits

Caution: Do *not* hyphenate noncompound numbers.

WRONG: one-hundred, six-thousand

RIGHT: one hundred, six thousand

Note that *twenty-four* really means twenty plus four but that *one hundred* does not mean one plus a hundred. It simply tells how many hundreds are involved.

19c Compound Nouns

Rule 3 Hyphenate compound nouns when hyphenation contributes to clarity.

A compound noun is composed of two or more words that function as one noun. A few compound nouns—such as *son-in-law* and *self-control*—are always hyphenated, and some—such as *the White House* and *cooking apples*—never are. When necessary, consult a dictionary. Here are a few of the hyphenated compound nouns that appeared in one issue of a national magazine:

job-hunting	shadow-boxing
self-interest	kilowatt-hours
dry-goods	globe-trotters
well-being	by-product
Europe-firsters	passers-by

19d Prefixes and Suffixes

Rule 4 Use a hyphen to separate the following prefixes and suffix from their root words: **self-, all-, ex-,** (meaning former), and **-elect.**

a self-addressed envelope
an all-purpose detergent
the ex-president from Central America
the mayor-elect of Houston

Use a good dictionary to guide you in the use of such prefixes as *anti-, co-, non-, pro-, pseudo-, quasi-,* and *ultra-.*

Rule 5 Use a hyphen to separate a prefix when its last letter and the first letter of the root word are the same.

anti-industrialism   de-escalate
re-edit   pro-Oriental

Some common words, such as *cooperate,* do not now follow that rule. When necessary, consult a dictionary.

Rule 6 Use a hyphen to separate a prefix when nonhyphenation might be ambiguous.

a co-op and a coop
to re-sign a contract and to resign from office
to re-cover a sofa and recover from illness
two-bit players (not very good actors) and two bit-players (they played small parts)

Rule 7 Use a hyphen to separate a prefix when the root word is capitalized.

non-Christian   mid-August
un-American   anti-Kennedy

19e Compound Adjectivals

__Rule 8__ Hyphenate two or more words that serve as a single adjectival in front of a noun.

An adjectival is a modifier of a noun, and all kinds of English words can be combined to function as single adjectivals. Failure to hyphenate such adjectivals will often make a reader stumble momentarily or perhaps waste time figuring out word relationships. For example, this phrase appeared in a national advertisement:

> The new embedded in plastic printed wiring circuit

Probably most readers had to pause to think out the word relationships, whereas if the writer had followed the above rule (plus the rule for separating coordinate adjectives) the meaning would have been immediately clear:

> the new embedded-in-plastic, printed-wiring circuit

Rule 8 above is especially important for maintaining clarity in writing.

Here are some examples of Rule 8 taken from one issue of a national magazine:

cradle-to-grave needs	law-school faculty
two-fisted gesture	civil-rights battle
double-parked car	a soft-spoken type
all-too-human attributes	cigar-making firm
long-term outlay	an eight-year-old girl
state-supported schools	high-pressure steam

Long compound adjectivals should be hyphenated rather than enclosed in quotation marks.

> He took an I-won't-budge-an-inch-if-I-die attitude.

Note: Such adjectivals may correctly either precede or follow the nouns they modify. When they follow the noun, they are not normally hyphenated.

the law-school faculty	the faculty of a law school
all-too-human attributes	attributes that are all too human
an eight-year-old girl	a girl eight years old
a civil-rights battle	a battle for civil rights

Rule 9   When a conjunction is entered into a compound adjectival so that two or more adjectivals are intended, leave a space before and after the conjunction but put a hyphen after the word or words that precede the conjunction.

all third- and fourth-grade pupils

all first-, second-, and third-ranked candidates

PART FOUR

DICTION

20

Appropriate Word Choice

From Chapter 1 through Chapter 19 this brief handbook has dealt with the **correctness** of writing. The next six chapters concentrate on the **clarity** of writing. The two go hand in hand. You cannot have clear style if you do not write correctly. On the other hand, you may write technically correct English, but it may be stylistically poor—perhaps even incomprehensible.

Matthew Arnold (1822–1888) stated: "Have something to say, and say it as clearly as you can. That is the only secret of style." More than a century earlier, Jonathan Swift wrote to a young clergyman: "Proper words in proper places make the true definition of style."

A simple list of words makes up a vocabulary; the accurate and careful use of those words in speech and writing makes good diction (C. Hugh Holman). That means that you must choose the right words for the right audience (Swift's "proper words in proper places"). You might use a great deal of slang in a letter to a hometown friend, but such expressions would be inappropriate in a letter of application to a personnel officer.

The audience for your college writing is people like you: members of your English class; fellow students on campus who read your article in the school newspaper; even your instructors. In all such writing you use general purpose words. These include all the structure words (such as *no, some, about, such,* and *however*) as well as the common content words (like *house, dress, sentence, hungry, good,* and *common*).

Semiformal words are those that you do not ordinarily use in casual conversation and may not use often in your writing either. Some examples are *disburse* (for *pay out*), *tortuous* (for *winding* or *twisting*), *subsequent* (for *coming after*), *rectitude* (for *proper moral behavior*), *rectify* (for *make right*), and *altruistic* (for *selfless* or *charitable*). Occasionally such words may appear in your writing—but only if they express your meaning more exactly than do the less formal expressions. The following sections give advice about appropriate word choice.

20a Slang

Avoid using slang expressions.

Slang is the kind of vocabulary that people (usually young people) create to state an idea vividly and freshly. It seems to sprout from nowhere, and it just as often disappears as quickly as it came. Perhaps a good way to define slang is to list examples, but even such examples may seem out-of-date as soon as they are written down.

a swell guy	kick the bucket
a cool chick	get your act together
a real jerk	flat out exhausted
catch some rays	to be "into" something
crash at my pad	the gang hangs out
a fun thing to do	laid back

You should note the following points about slang:

1. Slang is not "bad" language in itself; it may fit a certain audience well—but is not appropriate in an essay for a college course.

2. Traditional four-letter obscenities and constructions such as *ain't got no* are not slang—they are non-standard expressions.

3. A word is not slang unless it has a higher level counterpart in the language. *Boogie-woogie*, for example, is not slang; it names a particular kind of music and there is no other word for it.

4. Some terms, such as *hang-up* and *burn artist* are effective coinages; others, such as *lousy* and *peachy-keen* are so limp and colorless as to be offensive to anyone who loves language.

5. Many standard words of today were once considered slang: *Freshman*, *tidy* (for orderly, neat), *club*, *tantrum*, and *mob*.

6. Many slang terms, such as *gab* (idle talk) and *guts* (courage), linger on as slang for centuries.

Since most of your writing for college classes (and later for the general public) is expository and argumentative, the general advice is to avoid slang. Such advice is not absolute, however. If you consciously think that a pungent slang term will make your sentence more effective, use it without apology (but do not enclose it in quotation marks). These examples show the slang terms and their corrections in italics:

POOR STYLE:

Though Harris had suggested we go to the concert, we just *goofed off* until it was too late.

BETTER:

Though Harris had suggested we go to the concert, we just *fooled around* until it was too late.

POOR STYLE:
> Mrs. Ward wouldn't let me explain, and that's what really *ticked me off*.

BETTER:
> Mrs. Ward wouldn't let me explain, and that's what really *made me angry*.

POOR STYLE:
> Hank *got real uptight* when Beth called him a *party pooper*.

BETTER:
> Hank *became irritated* when Beth *complained that he was spoiling everybody's fun*.

If such expressions already seem obsolete to you, that merely underscores the fact that slang is a poor way to express your meaning. Perhaps a greater flaw is the shift in the level of diction, particularly in the first two examples above. Both sentences begin with general purpose words; abruptly and inappropriately they shift to slang expressions. Such a shift may destroy your credibility.

20b Colloquialisms

Use colloquial diction sparingly.

The word *colloquial* comes from a Latin word meaning "conversation." Originally, colloquial diction was considered suitable for informal conversation but not for writing. The distinction between colloquial and slang and semiformal is difficult to make.

Colloquial diction stretches from almost-slang to almost-semiformal. *To butter up* (to flatter) is barely above the level of slang and normally would be inappropriate in semiformal writing. *To needle* (to goad or provoke) is close enough to the general-purpose category to pass without question in an article in a serious journal. As you mature educationally, you will become more and more able to judge the levels of diction.

To define the term is perhaps as difficult as it is to define *slang*. Here are some examples (with the colloquialisms in italics) that show the difference between colloquial and semiformal diction.

COLLOQUIAL:

In algebra I was able to *catch on* without *beating my brains out*, and that made me *feel a lot better* about *trying to go on* in college.

SEMIFORMAL:

I was able to understand algebra quite easily, and that encouraged me to continue my college studies.

COLLOQUIAL:

When I thought she was *giving me the eye*, I *got carried away* and *made a fool of myself* by *trying some shenanigans* in the pool with her.

SEMIFORMAL:

When I thought she was showing some interest in me, I overreacted and must have seemed foolish when I tried to get too friendly with her in the pool.

COLLOQUIAL:

The boys thought they could *get away with* it by claiming over and over that *they had told everything*, but they couldn't *bring it off*.

SEMIFORMAL:

The boys believed they could avoid their responsibility by claiming to be innocent, but they didn't succeed.

The colloquial sentences in these examples are *not* incorrect or even bad writing. However, the person whose writing vocabulary is limited to such a colloquial level will not be able to compose business letters, memos, and reports of the quality demanded in well-paying jobs of importance. So, though colloquial phrasing may work well in some situations, do not let it dominate your writing.

We should make two more points about colloquial diction. First, much colloquial diction in English consists of phrases that have single-word equivalents above the colloquial level. Here are a few examples:

down in the mouth=glum	put up with=tolerate
make a go of it=succeed	catch up with=overtake
give in=acquiesce	get on with it=continue

If you will think about your word choice, you will often find that you can improve a sentence by substituting a single-word equivalent for a colloquial phrase.

Second, we often use qualifiers to modify adjectives and adverbs. The ones most commonly used in semiformal writing are these:

GOOD STYLE:

> **very** irritable
> **quite** incomprehensible
> **rather** staid
> **somewhat** embarrassed
> **fairly** expensive
> **wholly** incorrect
> **especially** convincing
> **a little** disturbed

Avoid the following colloquial qualifiers:

POOR STYLE:

real intelligent	*sort of* peculiar
sure pretty	*kind of* sad
plenty excited	*awfully* conceited
awful bad	*pretty* imaginative

20c Jargon

Avoid jargon in your writing.

In its technical sense, *jargon* is the special vocabulary of a particular profession or group, ranging from the language of lawyers to that of doctors and economists, chemists, physicists, musicians, and artists. An essay dealing with such subjects will, of course, have to have some technical terms in it. If written for the ordinary reader, such essays should define the terms by using synonyms from a more-common vocabulary.

An example of such definition by synonym occurs in John McPhee's explanation of how oranges get their color. In one place he tells how certain gasses help eliminate the chlorophyll in the flavedo, and immediately follows the word *flavedo* with its definition, "or outer skin." Shortly thereafter he speaks of *carotenoids* and defines both that word and *chlorophyll* by explaining that the carotenoids are the orange pigments in the skin while the chlorophylls are the green pigments. By using synonyms he defines his technical terms and makes it possible for the common reader to benefit from the article.

In a broader sense, jargon is any inflated or pretentious diction by which a writer tries to sound ornate or flowery. It is puffed up language designed more to impress the readers than to inform them. Much writing in government, business, the military, and higher education is marked by needless jargon. Here are some examples of jargon (with translations into less-pretentious common English):

monetary remuneration=pay
scribal methodologies=writing habits
augmentation of federal receipts=tax increases
commence=begin
sanitation engineer=janitor
domicile=house or home
culturally different students=minority students
determine your goals and objectives=decide what you want to do
facilitate=help

Here is an example of jargon from a textbook on language.

Discussions on the possibility of a universal base (as distinct from claims about universal constraints on the form of the base component) have mainly been concerned with whether the elements specified in the rules of a universal base—if there is one—are sequential or not.

Perhaps your teacher can give you an understandable revision of this passage. This writer on language doesn't know what that writer on language meant.

In much course work (for example, in chemistry, physics, and psychology) you must use technical terms because they are the only words that identify precisely what you mean. But in the rest of the sentence or paragraph use your ordinary college-level vocabulary so that your meaning is clear rather than obscure.

20d Clichés

Avoid clichés in your writing.

A *cliché* is an expression that, because of long and thoughtless use, is trite, stale, worn out, and lacking in originality. For example, many people who use the phrase "feed at the public trough" don't even know that, when pigpens were common, they contained troughs to hold food for the greedy pigs, and thus many users of the phrase are unaware of its origin. Clichés are very common and have long lives because most people are too lazy or unimaginative to try to form their thoughts in their own language rather than in hackneyed phrases that are used over and over.

Here are a few examples of clichés:

ice water in his veins	on a silver platter
the acid test	a tower of strength
add insult to injury	the crack of dawn
take the bull by the horns	sadder but wiser
hard as nails	a hasty retreat
straight from the shoulder	the calm before the storm
dyed in the wool	better late than never
a moving experience	tired but happy
a crying shame	green with envy

In his essay "Politics and the English Language," George Orwell lists as his first rule for beginning writers the following admonition: "Never use a metaphor, simile, or other figure of speech which you are used to seeing in print." It's good advice.

Here are more clichés to avoid:

as fat as a pig	as heavy as lead
as skinny as a rail	as sober as a judge
as strong as an ox	as stubborn as a mule
as wise as an owl	as light as a feather
as pretty as a picture	sell like hotcakes
as sharp as a tack	quick as a wink

21

Exact Word Choice

21a Precise Meaning

Choose words that express your meaning precisely rather than approximately.

The English vocabulary is probably larger than that of any other language, and consequently it has many synonyms (words that are similar in meaning) and very many near-synonyms. Good writers try to choose words that say precisely what they mean, whereas careless writers are content with any approximation. Some examples from student writing, with the inexact words italicized:

INEXACT:
As an *uninterested* third part, Jackson *agreed* to the *proposal* by not voting at all.

EXACT: As a **disinterested** third party, Jackson **acquiesced** in the **proposition** by not voting at all.

There is some overlapping of meaning between the words in each pair, but those in the inexact version lack precision.

Uninterested implies no interest at all, while *disinterested* suggests that, while he had no personal stake in the matter, Jackson may well have been curious about the argument. That he did not vote requires the word *acquiesce*, which means "to remain silent"; a person who *agrees* actively gives his assent by saying yes. The last pair is almost interchangeable, and the matter may seem a minor point; *proposition*, however, generally indicates a written or formal statement as opposed to a merely spoken idea.

> INEXACT:
>> His *fond* parents *forgave* his youthful *wiles* as long as they could; finally, however, they *ceased* his *caprices*.
>
> EXACT: His **doting** parents **condoned** his youthful **shenanigans** as long as they could; finally, however, they **put a stop to** his **mischief.**

Fond implies loving, while *doting* suggests foolish affection brought on by old age; *forgive* equals pardon, but *condone* means overlook; *wiles* has the connotation of clever or cute, but *shenanigans* includes treachery and deceit; and action *ceases*, but people *put a stop to*; finally, *caprices* suggests impulsive or whimsical behavior, but *mischief* involves harmful conduct. The second version more clearly states what the author intended.

Do not be afraid to use new words. It is better to make mistakes and learn from them than to timidly avoid using a college-level vocabulary. Consulting a good dictionary or a thesaurus of synonyms and antonyms is a great aid in learning to choose words with the exact meanings you want.

21b Specific and General Words

Use words as specific as your meaning calls for.

The more specific a word is, the fewer objects or concepts it applies to if it is a noun, the fewer actions or states of being it expresses if it is a verb, and the fewer qualities it signifies if it is an adjective or adverb. Of course a general word is just the opposite. For example, note how specificity increases as you pass from the very general first word to the other words in each of the following lists.

animal	talk	contented
quadruped	discuss	happy
mammal	disagree	cheerful
canine	argue	overjoyed
dog	dispute	ecstatic
mongrel	quarrel	euphoric

Animal can refer to thousands of species—millions, if insects are included—but *mongrel* refers to just one type of one species. *Talk* can apply to dozens of types of oral communication, but *quarrel* specifies a narrow range. *Contented* can apply to numerous mental states, but *euphoric* means only the ultimate in emotional happiness. General words are very important in our vocabulary; quite often a writer wants such a general word as *animal* and no other. But the more specific words you choose, the clearer your meaning and the better your style will be.

Note how the words in boldface produce a more specific statement in each of the succeeding sentences below.

The **creature** enjoyed the **activity.**

The **human** enjoyed the **recreation.**

The **adult** enjoyed the **sport.**

The **man** enjoyed **trout fishing in the stream.**

John enjoyed **dry fly fishing in Catherine Creek.**

A writer may at times deliberately choose a general expression with the intent of following it up with specifics. For example, the thesis statement of an essay or paragraph is usually quite general; the paragraphs in the body of the essay or the remaining sentences in a paragraph should use specific words that give the supporting details.

21c Concrete and Abstract Words

As much as possible, try to choose concrete words for your writing.

Technically, a concrete word is one that names an object that you can perceive with your senses, such as *book* or *kitten*. An abstract word is one that names a concept, such as *socialism* or *devotion*, or a quality apart from the object that can possess it, such as *beauty* or *gracefulness*. All concrete words can form images in the mind; that is, if you hear or read the word *horse* you have no trouble visualizing one in your mind's eye. An abstract word cannot directly form an image in your mind. For example, the word *communism* is not the name of a tangible object; it cannot form an image directly. Whatever images come into your mind when you read the word are due to the associations you have made with the word. In that sense, certain abstractions do form images in the readers' minds. For example, such words as *leer*, *smile*, *pretty*, *smooth*, *kind*, and *song* are abstractions when they are used apart from the person or thing that can wear a smile or be pretty. But they have much of the image-forming effect of such concrete words as *snake*, *houseboat*, *lake*, and *owl*. The advice for you in this section is to choose, as much as possible, concrete words or nonconcrete words that have strong image-forming qualities.

Here are some examples of sentences full of abstractions, with revisions for concrete diction:

ABSTRACT:

The modifications that were effected in the subject's orientation to societal mores transformed the approaches and tendencies of her existence.

CONCRETE:
> The changes brought about in the woman's behavior altered the color and direction of her life.

ABSTRACT:
> Cooper observed the large majority of all phenomena with conspicuous nonsuccess in apprehending the nature of reality.

CONCRETE:
> Cooper saw nearly all things as through a glass eye, darkly.

ABSTRACT:
> Let us render inoperable those invidious machinations that endeavor to legalize the destruction of our movement.

CONCRETE:
> Let's defeat the legislative bills that would outlaw our political party.

Abstractions, such as the words *modifications, mores, apprehending,* and *invidious* in the above example sentences, need not be avoided *per se.* Individually they are good words, and we must use abstractions like them. However, when a sentence is little more than an accumulation of abstractions, it is usually not good writing. Concrete and image-forming diction generally improves clarity and style.

21d Euphemisms

Avoid overuse of euphemisms in your writing.

A euphemism is a mild or roundabout word or expression used instead of a more direct word or expression to make one's language delicate and inoffensive even to a squeamish person. Probably the most frequently used euphemism is *passed away* for *died.* The areas that demand euphemisms change over the decades. The Victorians, for example, found it convenient to employ euphemisms for bodily functions and parts of the body that might suggest sex. Even later than 1900 a great many genteel people would not use the words *leg* and *arm* because of their sexual suggestibility and talked instead about a person's *limbs*. For one satirist, *toes* became *twigs*. In our time we seem to need euphemisms for the areas of social and economic standing and war. For example, the poor nowadays are usually referred to, at least in public documents, as the *disadvantaged* or *underprivileged*; the very dull student as *educationally handicapped*; the crazy person as *emotionally disturbed*; old people as *senior citizens*; the sacking of a village in war as *pacification*; retreat in war as *planned withdrawal*; and lies as *inoperative statements*.

More examples of euphemisms:

Euphemism	Meaning
adult entertainment =	pornographic film
pass away =	die
predecease =	die before someone else
pre-owned automobile =	used car
inner city =	slums
negative savings =	debts
poorly motivated =	lazy
strategic withdrawal =	retreat or defeat

Most euphemisms probably do little harm. They may, in fact, be useful to keep from upsetting sensitive people. Most of us, no doubt, would rather hear the phrase *nasal discharge* than *snot*, or *halitosis* than *bad breath*. They can at times, however, be harmful and deceptive. As a writer and reader, you should know what they are and what they mean. Use them cautiously and never with the intent to deceive.

EUPHEMISM:

Johnny tends to rely on the work of others.

MEANING:

Johnny cheats.

EUPHEMISM:
> Ray is somewhat assertive in social situations.

MEANING:
> Ray is a bully.

EUPHEMISM:
> Oscar went to the hair stylist yesterday.

MEANING:
> Oscar went to the barber yesterday.

EUPHEMISM:
> Hitler's Germany resorted to the final solution.

MEANING:
> Hitler's Germany murdered 6 million humans.

21e Wordiness

Avoid wordiness in your writing.

Write concisely as well as precisely; that is, do not ramble or use excess words. Decide clearly what you mean; then say it directly. A wordy example from student writing:

WORDY:
> Faulkner put the ditch in "That Evening Sun" so that when it is crossed, as it is several times, the reader can get the understanding that what is on one side of it is completely separated from what is on the other side. What is on one side is the world of the white people and what is on the other side is the world of the black people.

CONCISE:
> The ditch in Faulkner's "That Evening Sun," crossed several times by some of the characters, is a symbol of the immense gap between the white and black worlds.

When revising, remove unnecessarily long sentence parts.

WORDY: The rock group which was brought to play in the pasture of Mr. Hollis was half-stoned by the time they got there.

CONCISE:

The rock group brought to play in Mr. Hollis's pasture showed up half-stoned.

The clause beginning with *which was* is longer than the equally clear phrase *brought to play*; *Mr. Hollis's pasture* is less wordy than the *pasture of Mr. Hollis*; and *showed up* is much more concise than *by the time they got there.*

Other kinds of wordiness are known as **deadwood** or **redundancy,** which means saying the same thing twice, such as *audible to the ear. To the ear* adds no meaning and is redundant because the word *audible* means "capable of being heard by the ear" (some sounds can be heard by machines but not by ears; they are not audible). Here are some examples of student sentences with deadwood or redundancy:

WORDY: I liked the biographical information *about Hardy's life* better than his *fictitious* novels.

CONCISE:

I liked Hardy's biography better than his novels. [If it is "biographical information," it is "about Hardy's life"; novels are "fictitious."]

WORDY: The foreign language department has established a *new* innovation *the purpose of which is* to reduce the time we have to study written material *in the textbooks.*

CONCISE:

The foreign language department has established an innovation to reduce the time we have to study written material. ["Innovative" means "new"; what is in textbooks is, naturally, written material; *the purpose of which* is simply unnecessary.]

WORDY: A metaphor is one kind of figure of speech *that is not literal* because the two *different* parts of the comparison are completely dissimilar to each other.

CONCISE:

A metaphor is one kind of figure of speech because the two parts of the comparison are dissimilar.

Even the concise revisions in these examples could perhaps be written better, but their aim is to show that deadwood—needless words—can often just be omitted, with a consequent improvement in the quality of the writing.

22

Correct Word Choice

In Chapter 21 we discussed the value of choosing words for the exact meaning you want, rather than words that only approximately express your meaning. In this chapter we will deal with the choice of wrong words—words that, if taken literally, do not even approximately express your meaning. For example, if you ask someone for change for a dollar and receive nineteen nickels, your request will have been approximately met; but if instead you receive a handful of pebbles, your dollar's change is not even approximately right but wholly incorrect.

22a Malapropisms

Consult a dictionary, if necessary, to prevent use of malapropisms.

A malapropism, named after a character in an eighteenth century play who mangled the language in almost every speech, is an incorrect word that sounds like the correct word. Several of Mrs. Malaprop's examples illustrate the term: *Illiterate* (for *obliterate*) *him from your memory; I would by no means wish a daughter of mine to be a progeny* (for *prodigy*) *of learning; she might reprehend* (for *apprehend the true meaning; I hope you will present her as illegible* (for *eligible*); *and I have interceded* (for *intercepted*) *a letter from him.*

Checking a dictionary to determine the correct word will help you avoid such malapropisms as appear in the following student examples:

MALAPROPISM:
> The fans were now supporting our team *voraciously.*

RIGHT: The fans were now supporting our team **vociferously.**

MALAPROPISM:
> He was driving under the *affluence* of alcohol.

RIGHT: He was driving under the **influence** of alcohol.

MALAPROPISM:
> Harold's *alligator* shoes gave him added height.

RIGHT: Harold's **elevator** shoes gave him added height.

MALAPROPISM:
> *Designating* the flag is now a Federal offense.

RIGHT: **Desecrating** the flag is now a Federal offense.

MALAPROPISM:
> I have been absent for the last week because I am going to get married and have been to San Francisco to get my *torso* ready.

RIGHT: I have been absent for the last week because I am going to get married and have been to San Francisco to get my **trousseau** ready.

MALAPROPISM:
> Every Thursday you can exercise your *abominable* muscles in the weight lifting room.

RIGHT: Every Thursday you can exercise your **abdominal** muscles in the weight lifting room.

MALAPROPISM:
> The patient reported that her blood pressure was somewhat *erotic*, going up and down without apparent reason.

RIGHT: The patient reported that her blood pressure was somewhat **erratic,** going up and down without apparent reason.

When people recognize such misuses of language, they get a chuckle out of them. If you use them intentionally, no harm is done. But if they creep into your writing unintentionally, you lose your argument, either because your reader breaks up in laughter or labels you as slightly less than well-educated.

22b Confused Words

Do not confuse a word with one similar to it in sound or meaning or spelling.

A number of pairs or trios of words are frequently confused and cannot be labeled malapropisms (which are seldom repeated). Check both the list in section 16g (for spelling purposes) and this list to avoid producing incorrect rather than merely inappropriate word choice.

accept is a verb meaning "to receive."
except is a preposition meaning "not included."

all ready is an indefinite pronoun plus adjective meaning "everyone or everything is prepared."
already is an adverb meaning "at or before this time."

all together is an indefinite pronoun plus adjective meaning "everyone in unison."

altogether is an adverb meaning "completely."

allude is a verb meaning "to mention indirectly." *Allusion* is the noun.

refer is a verb meaning "to mention directly." *Reference* is the noun.

anyway is an adverb meaning "in any case."

any way is a noun phrase meaning "whatever way possible."

beside is a preposition meaning "at the side of."

besides is a preposition or adverb meaning "in addition to."

broadcast is a verb with the principal parts *broadcast, broadcast, broadcast. Broadcasted* is nonstandard.

burst is a verb with the principal parts *burst, burst, burst. Bust* and *busted* are nonstandard for *burst.* (*Busted* is also a slang word for *arrested.*)

cite is a verb meaning "to mention or refer to."

site is a noun meaning "a place."

sight is a noun meaning "something that is seen."

colloquialism is a noun meaning "a word or phrase suitable for informal use."

localism is a noun meaning "a word or expression used only in one locality or region."

complement is a noun (and verb) meaning "something that completes or makes a whole."

compliment is a noun (and verb) meaning "praise given."

conscience is a noun meaning "a sense of right and wrong."

conscious is an adjective meaning "awake or alert."

could of, would of are incorrect spellings of "could've (have)" and "would've (have)."

council is a noun meaning "an official, deliberative group."

counsel is a verb (and noun) meaning "to give advice" (or "one who gives advice.") *Counselor* comes from *counsel.*

credible is an adjective meaning "believable."
creditable is an adjective meaning "worthy of praise."
credulous is an adjective meaning "willing to believe readily or easily imposed upon."

delusion is a noun meaning "a false belief."
illusion is a noun meaning "a deceptive appearance or false impression."

discreet means "careful about what one does or says."
discrete means "separate and distinct" or "one by one."

disinterested is an adjective meaning "impartial or having no personal interest."
uninterested is an adjective meaning "not interested."

farther is an adverb pertaining to physical distance.
further is an adverb pertaining to degree of advancement in ideas, concepts, and so on.

forecast is a verb with the principal parts *forecast, forecast, forecast. Forecasted* is nonstandard.

hanged is the past tense and past participle of the verb *hang* when it means execution.
hung is the past tense and past participle of the verb *hang* for all other meanings.

imply is a verb meaning "to suggest or hint."
infer is a verb meaning "to draw a conclusion or inference about."

inside of is colloquial for *within*.

irregardless is nonstandard. Use *regardless*.

kind of, sort of are colloquial phrases for *rather* or *somewhat*.

later is an adverb or adjective meaning "at a time after a specified time."
latter is an adjective (and noun) meaning "nearest the end or the last mentioned."

liable is an adjective meaning "responsible or legally bound or likely to occur."

libel is a verb meaning "to slander in print" and a noun meaning "slanderous articles."

lie, lay See section 8d.

loose is an adjective meaning "not tight."
lose is a verb meaning "to mislay or be deprived of."

marital is an adjective meaning "pertaining to marriage."
martial is an adjective meaning "pertaining to military operations."

maybe is an adverb meaning "perhaps or possibly."
may be is a verb form indicating possibility.

moral is an adjective meaning "right or ethical."
morale is a noun meaning "a mental attitude or condition."

nohow is nonstandard for *anyway.*

oral means "spoken." It is preferable in that sense to *verbal,* which refers to both oral and written language.

passed is the past tense and past participle of the verb *to pass.*

past is a noun meaning "of a former time" and a preposition meaning "passing beside."

persecute is a verb meaning "to harass cruelly or annoy persistently."

prosecute is a verb meaning "to bring suit against."

principal is an adjective meaning "chief or most important" and a noun meaning "head of school" or "money used as capital."

principle is a noun meaning "a rule or doctrine."

quiet is an adjective meaning "not noisy."
quite is a qualifier meaning "entirely or almost entirely."

sensual is an adjective meaning "lewd or carnal."
sensuous is an adjective meaning "characterized by sense impressions."

set, sit   See section 8d.

than is a subordinating conjunction used in a comparison.
then is an adverb of time or a conjunctive adverb meaning "therefore."

For words not on this list, consult your dictionary. Form the habit of relying on your dictionary and not just guessing.

22c Incorrect Idioms

Avoid incorrect idioms in your writing.

Strictly defined, an idiom is a construction "peculiar" to a language, not understandable from the meanings of the individual words in it, and not literally translatable into another language. For example, in the expression *He kicked the bucket,* neither *kicked* nor *bucket* has its regular meaning. Rather, the whole construction is a slang expression for *He died* and is an English idiom which can hardly be translated into another language or culture.

Again, *They lived high on the hog* (for *They lived in great luxury*) would produce a hilarious construction if translated literally into another language.

Idiomatic English is English phrasing that is natural, normal, and clearly understandable to a native speaker of English. We normally think of English idioms as containing at least one preposition, or a word that looks like a preposition, and that is the way we will consider idioms in this chapter on correct word choice. Thus, if (as once happened) a student should write *this contradicts with my opinion,* we would say the idiom was faulty, for native speakers would write *this contradicts my opinion.*

Faulty idioms are far more common in writing than in coversation, possibly because the writers are striving hard to express their thoughts in writing and make errors *because* they are striving so hard. Here are some faulty idioms from student papers.

FAULTY IDIOM:
My little sister thought she was *capable to* drive the tractor.

RIGHT: My little sister thought she was **capable of** driving the tractor.

FAULTY IDIOM:
The city council pleaded with the citizens *to comply to* the new parking regulations.

RIGHT: The city council pleaded with the citizens **to comply with** the new parking regulations.

FAULTY IDIOM:
While in the United States, Madame Noyes wore costumes *different than* those she habitually wore at home.

RIGHT: While in the United States, Madame Noyes wore costumes **different from** those she habitually wore at home.

FAULTY IDIOM:
Prior than signing the agreement, you should always read it carefully.

RIGHT: **Prior to** signing the agreement, you should always read it carefully.

FAULTY IDIOM:
In accordance to the Constitution, no man is required to testify against himself.

RIGHT: **According to** the Constitution, no man is required to testify against himself.

FAULTY IDIOM:
>
> Modern calculators are not only cheaper, but they are *superior than* the early models.

RIGHT: Modern calculators are not only cheaper, but they are **superior to** the early models.

No rules can be given to keep you from writing a faulty idiom occasionally. The best advice is to listen carefully to those whose speech habits you admire, to think calmly and without panic as you write, and to proofread your work carefully.

22d Omitted Words

Do not carelessly omit a needed word.

Sometimes the speed at which you write may cause you to skip a necesary word. Careful proofreading will help you to avoid such careless omissions.

OMITTED WORD:
>
> Professor Jambura was telling us in economics class the tax dollars go.

RIGHT: Professor Jambura was telling us in economics class **where** the tax dollars go.

OMITTED WORD:
>
> Alice knows a woman had a full-length coat made out of vicuña.

RIGHT: Alice knows a woman **who** has a full-length coat made out of vicuña.

PART FIVE

EFFECTIVE SENTENCES

239

23

Faulty Sentence Structure

Good writing is a complex mixture of many components, but at its heart is the sentence. The great English statesman and writer Sir Winston Churchill called the English sentence "a noble thing," and it is a truism that anyone who can write really good sentences can write longer passages well too. Sentences, however, are so complex that many things can go wrong with them—and often do. There is no shame in writing faulty sentences. Probably everyone does in the first draft. Success in writing comes from the ability to repair such flaws, and anyone can learn to do so. Repairing faulty structure requires the ability to recognize structure problems, and that is the subject of this chapter on the main kinds of errors in sentence structure.

23a Mixed Sentence Structure

Do not inconsistently shift structure in mid-sentence.

Mixed sentence structure usually occurs when a writer begins a sentence with one kind of structure, forgets that structure somewhere along the way, and completes the sentence with a different, incompatible kind of structure. Here is an example from a student paper:

MIXED STRUCTURE:
> Financial aid has made it possible for me to continue my education and not finding a job right away.

The shift in structure comes after the conjunction *and,* which indicates that either a second independent clause will follow or a structure beginning with *to.* The writer might have maintained a unified structure in either of two ways:

RIGHT: Financial aid has made it possible for me to continue my education, and **I did not have to find a job right away.** (a compound sentence with two independent clauses)

RIGHT: Financial aid has made it possible for me to continue my education and **to postpone finding a job right away.** (a simple sentence with two infinitive phrases in the predicate)

Here are other examples from student writing of mixed sentence structure, with revisions:

MIXED STRUCTURE:
> A dry-fly artist who has cautiously approached a pool and cast his fly delicately to the tail end of a riffle gives him a sense of excitement when the trout rises to the bait.

RIGHT: A dry-fly artist who has cautiously approached a pool and cast his fly delicately to the tail end of a riffle experiences a sense of excitement when the trout rises to the bait.

Long and involved subjects sometimes lead to confusion. The writer apparently lost track of the single subject *artist* and thought *who has cautiously approached a pool and cast his fly delicately to the tail end of a riffle* required the verb *gives*. The revision provides a suitable predicate.

MIXED STRUCTURE:
> All of this boils down to that computers will play a major role in private life as well as in business.

RIGHT:
> All of this boils down to **the fact that computers will play a major role in private life as well as in business.**

RIGHT:
> All of this **means that computers will play a major role in private life as well as in business.**

In the mixed sentence the writer failed to compose a subject-verb combination that would take the noun clause *that . . . business* as a direct object. Both revisions provide suitable subject-verb-object structures.

MIXED STRUCTURE:
> Those writers that Poe predicted would never make it, we have never even heard their names in our time.

RIGHT:
> Those writers that Poe predicted would never make it have never been heard of in our time.

In the mixed sentence the student writer composed the long but satisfactory subject *Those . . . it* and then, instead of providing a predicate for the subject, inconsistently continued with a complete independent clause. The revision changes the independent clause into a predicate that fits the subject.

23b Faulty Predication

Be sure that your subject and predicate are compatible.

The grammatical term *predication* means the fitting of a predicate to a subject to make an independent clause (or sentence), such as this grammatically correct sentence:

> The mayor of our town / is also the chief of police.

The slash (/) separates the subject from the predicate.

When a subject and predicate are not compatible, the error known as faulty predication occurs. For example,

Courageously / is a time of happiness

is obviously a nonsentence because its predication is faulty; the adverb *courageously* cannot serve as the subject of the predicate *is a time of happiness*—or, for that matter, as the subject of any predicate. Equally a nonsentence is this student's creation:

FAULTY PREDICATION:
> Through God's creation alone / is the only concept of God that man has.

The prepositional phrase *through God's creation alone* will not function as the subject of the predicate that follows. The student may have meant to say something like this:

RIGHT: The only concept of God that man can have / lies in God's creation of the universe.

However, as is often the case in sentences with faulty predication, what the writer meant to say is not entirely clear.

Here are some other examples of faulty predication, with revisions:

FAULTY PREDICATION:
> In our literature class the discussion / consisted of the professor and a few students.

RIGHT: Only a few students and the professor / carry on the discussion in our literature class.

RIGHT: In our literature class the discussion / is carried on by only a few students and the professor.

The faulty sentence incorrectly claims that the discussion is students and the professor. The revised sentences, one active and one passive, provide the appropriate verbs *carry on* and *is carried on*. Of the two, you should recognize that the active sentence is the better.

FAULTY PREDICATION:

>   First, the attitude of the father / may be disappointment toward the child's clumsy attempts.

RIGHT: First, the attitude of the father / may be one of disappointment toward the child's clumsy attempts.

The basic elements of the faulty sentence say that *the attitude . . . may be . . . disappointment*. The predicate does not fit the subject. In the revision, the pronoun *one* stands for *attitude* and produces a consistent structure, for the linking verb *be* must be followed by a predicate noun that renames the subject or a predicate adjective that describes it.

Here are some additional examples. These are examples of the faulty **is when, is where, is why, is because** kinds of sentences. Avoid these expressions. They reflect poor style as well as faulty predication. Usually a noun or noun substitute or an adjective must follow the verb *is*. Sometimes such sentences must be recast completely to provide proper predication.

FAULTY PREDICATION:

>   Another misconception / is when we try to visualize God.

RIGHT: Another misconception / is that human beings can actually visualize God.

FAULTY PREDICATION:

>   Characterization / is where I think Faulkner succeeded best.

RIGHT: Characterization / is the best aspect of Faulkner's fiction.

FAULTY PREDICATION

>   Because my alarm clock didn't go off is why I was late for work.

RIGHT: I / was late for work because my alarm clock didn't go off.

FAULTY PREDICATION:

> The reason he drove through the intersection is because the stop sign was hidden by a tree.

RIGHT: He / drove through the intersection because a tree hid the stop sign.

23c Faulty Parallelism

Make sure that the words, phrases, or clauses in any series in your sentences are parallel in structure.

In sentence structure, parallelism means the use of two or more similar constructions in a series, usually with a coordinating connective between the last two constructions. For example:

RIGHT: **Having no money** and **wanting to attend the festival**, I considered selling my typewriter.

The two boldface phrases are parallel in structure; they are similar in form (both begin with -*ing* words) and in function (both modify the subject of the main clause).

When two or more *dissimilar* constructions are in a series, faulty parallelism results. An example from student writing, with the structures in faulty parallelism italicized:

FAULTY PARALLELISM:

> Martha told the officer *that she had pulled out to pass a slow car* and *of her driving record.*

Here a dependent clause and a phrase are joined by *and.* The two structures must be the same to avoid faulty parallelism, like this:

RIGHT: Martha told the officer **that she had pulled out to pass a slow car** and **that she had a perfect driving record.**

Now the two direct objects are both noun clauses and thus parallel constructions.

Other examples from student work:

FAULTY PARALLELISM:
> Lincoln was a man *of great natural ability* and *who wanted to be a lawyer.*

A phrase and a clause modify the noun *man*. Changing the phrase to a relative clause makes the structures parallel.

RIGHT: Lincoln was a man **who had great natural ability** and **who wanted to be a lawyer.**

A different revision, using an appositive (in boldface) eliminates the problem of faulty parallelism.

RIGHT: Lincoln, **a man of great natural ability,** wanted to be a lawyer.

FAULTY PARALLELISM:
> Local color was flourishing, *with Harte writing about California* and *Cable wrote about Louisiana.*

RIGHT: Local color was flourishing, with **Harte writing about California** and **Cable writing about Louisiana.**

The incorrect sentence has a prepositional phrase and an independent clause in faulty parallelism. The correct sentence has two objects of the preposition *with* in proper parallel structure.

23d Dangling Modifiers

Do not let an introductory or terminal word, phrase, or clause dangle with no word or word group to modify.

Usually when a sentence opens with an introductory word, phrase, or clause that is not the subject, it modifies the subject that follows.

RIGHT: Having seen the menu, I gave my order immediately.

In such structures the subject of the main clause does whatever is mentioned in the introductory expression. Who saw the menu? I did. The sentence meaning is clear. But suppose the sentence were written like this:

DANGLING MODIFIER:
Having seen the menu, my order was given immediately.

Now the sentence says that my order saw the menu—obviously untrue. The introductory expression dangles; it has no word to modify.

Here is another example of a dangling modifier, with the dangler italicized:

DANGLING MODIFIER:
By bringing children up together in schools of equal opportunity, they will become friendly.

One way to avoid or correct such flaws is to think of the two parts as coming from separate sentences, both of which have the same subject: *We bring up the children* and *we allow them to become friendly* (the subject is *we* in both sentences). Then change the first to a modifier; it cannot dangle.

RIGHT: By bringing children up together in schools of equal opportunity, we allow them to become friendly.

Use the same method on the following sentence to correct it. Ask: Who or What provides security, and Who or What gives pleasure? The answer: Personal advice columns. The subject must be the same for both.

DANGLING MODIFIER:
Besides providing security for active people, shut-ins and hospital patients get pleasure from personal-advice columns.

RIGHT: Besides providing security for active people, personal-advice columns give pleasure to shut-ins and hospital patients.

You may correct an otherwise dangling modifier by providing it with its own subject and a finite verb (one that shows tense or time of action), thus changing it into a clause.

> DANGLING MODIFIER:
>> The church is a good place to go, *when unsettled in mind.*

The sentence seems to say that the church is unsettled in mind, and thus the terminal constituent dangles. Here is a revision:

> RIGHT: The church is a good place to go when you are unsettled in mind.

In this revision the dangler has been altered in structure so that it no longer dangles but delivers clear meaning.

23e   Misplaced Modifiers

Always place a modifier in a sentence so that the word or word group it modifies is immediately clear.

Most sentences in good writing have a number of modifiers, and most modifiers come as close to the word they modify as possible. The good writer must give thought to the placement of modifiers if the meaning is to be immediately clear. For example, consider this sentence from a news report:

> MISPLACED MODIFIER:
>> Collins was told that his services would no longer be needed *by the personnel officer.*

When the sentence is considered in isolation, it seems clear that the personnel officer will no longer need Collins's services (though others in the company may). But the whole report made it clear that the personnel officer was firing

Collins. Thus the writer misplaced the modifier *by the per-sonnel officer* and no doubt momentarily confused thousands of readers. The italicized phrase should have been placed after *told*.

Here are some other examples of misplaced modifiers, with the modifiers italicized:

MISPLACED MODIFIER:
> Dad chopped the wood we had gathered *with a small hatchet.*

The sentence seems to say we had gathered the wood with a small hatchet. In reality, *Dad chopped . . . with a small hatchet.* The modifier must clearly refer to the verb.

RIGHT: With a small hatchet Dad chopped the wood we had gathered.

RIGHT: Dad used a small hatchet to chop the wood we had gathered.

MISPLACED MODIFIER:
> Elka confessed to Gimpel how she had deceived him and slept with many men *on her deathbed.*

RIGHT: On her deathbed Elka confessed to Gimpel how she deceived him and slept with many men.

MISPLACED MODIFIER:
> Newspapers reported that Griggs had been accused of embezzlement *all over the country.*

RIGHT: Newspapers all over the country reported that Griggs had been accused of embezzlement.

MISPLACED MODIFIER:
> At the picnic they served the food to the children *on paper plates.*

RIGHT: At the picnic they served the food on paper plates to the children.

Words like *only* and *almost* are easily misplaced. The general rule holds true: place such modifiers so that they clearly say what you intend. None of the examples below is incorrect, but note how the meaning changes.

Only Art kissed Betty yesterday. [He was the only one who kissed her.]

Art only kissed Betty yesterday. [He did nothing else.]

Art kissed only Betty yesterday. [He kissed no one else.]

Art kissed Betty only yesterday. [That was the most recent time he kissed her.]

Art kissed Betty yesterday only. [Never at any other time.]

If a modifier can refer to more than one idea, it is unclear and misplaced. Sometimes these are called **squinting modifiers**.

UNCLEAR MODIFIER:
      Gloria and Curt announced at 5:00 o'clock they would leave.

CLEAR: At 5:00 o'clock Gloria and Curt announced they would leave.

CLEAR: Gloria and Curt announced they would leave at 5:00 o'clock.

24

Pronoun Reference

A pronoun gets its meaning through reference to some other word or word group, which is known as the pronoun's **antecedent.** Since the pronoun does not have meaning of its own, its reference—or antecedent—must be unmistakably clear if the sentence is to deliver clear meaning. Furthermore, even when its meaning is clear, a pronoun must be properly used if the sentence is to be effective and stylistically acceptable. Sentence effectiveness is easily diminished by faulty pronoun reference. (For the forms of pronouns see subsection 1b5).

24a   Reference to Titles

Do not use a pronoun in the opening sentence of a paper to refer to the title or a noun in the title.

Though themes, essays, and term papers should have suitable titles, such titles are not part of the composition itself; they are added only *after* the body of the paper has been written. Almost always a paper should be opened as though the title were not stated. Here, from a student's work, is an illustration of how *not* to use pronoun reference to a title:

TOPIC: Describe the placement of lights in portrait photography.

TITLE: Effective Techniques with Floodlights

IMPROPER REFERENCE IN OPENING SENTENCE:
     Several basic principles in using *them* give the successful photographer an advantage over the rank beginner.

The *them* in the opening sentence, referring to *floodlights* in the title (or does it refer to *techniques*?), produces a particularly ineffective sentence as a theme introduction.

Sometimes a careless student will even choose a topic from several written on a blackboard or handout sheet, not compose a title at all, and then begin the paper with a reference to the topic, while the teacher does not know which topic has been picked. For example, after being handed a list of seven topics to choose from, one student once opened a titleless paper with this sentence:

IMPROPER REFERENCE IN OPENING SENTENCE:
     First, I think *it* should be discussed more before *they* make a decision.

The *it* and *they* in the opening sentence ruined the theme at the outset.

24b   Ambiguous Reference

Do not use a pronoun so that it can meaningfully refer to either of two nouns or word groups.

Ambiguity means having two possible meanings, and pronoun reference is ambiguous when there is more than one clearly possible antecedent for the pronoun. Example from a student paper:

> AMBIGUOUS REFERENCE:
>> Jennifer wrote to Maureen every day when *she* was in France.
>
> CLEAR: When **Jennifer** was in France, **she** wrote to Maureen every day.
>
> CLEAR: When **Maureen** was in France, Jennifer wrote to **her** every day.

The ambiguous reference in the poorly worded sentence can mean either of two clear statements. Another example:

> AMBIGUOUS REFERENCE:
>> When my father took Uncle Ed into business with him, *he* did not know that *he* had already gone bankrupt once.

Who had already had one business failure? The second *he* is ambiguous (and one can argue that the first *he* is equally unclear). A revision makes it plain.

> CLEAR: When my father took Uncle Ed into business with him, he did not know that **my uncle** had already gone bankrupt once.

Sometimes ambiguous reference occurs when a pronoun is only understood and not stated. Example from an advertisement, with the understood pronoun in brackets:

> AMBIGUOUS REFERENCE:
>> The trunk on a Dart is actually bigger than the one on many full-sized cars. And a family of five fits inside [it] nicely.

The ad writer intended the understood *it* to refer to *Dart* but it seems to refer to *trunk*. The writer should have put *the car* after *inside*. Also note the inconsistency of specifying *one* trunk for *many* full-sized cars.

24c   Faulty Broad Reference

Avoid using **this, that, which,** and **it** with vague, indefinite, or ambiguous reference.

Broad reference means that a pronoun does not refer to an individual noun but to a whole idea expressed in an independent clause or word group. Broad reference is completely acceptable when it is clear, and, indeed, it is very common.

CLEAR BROAD REFERENCE:
Joyce's "Araby" depicts the disillusionment of a young boy's first puppy love, **which** is a relatively common theme in modern literature.

CLEAR BROAD REFERENCE:
The issue was between guns and butter. **This** became evident in the Congressional hearings.

CLEAR BROAD REFERENCE:
Had I studied harder, **it** still would have made no difference.

The *which, this,* and *it* clearly refer to whole ideas, not individual nouns, and the broad reference is acceptable, or even desirable.

Often, however, broad reference is vague, indefinite, or ambiguous, and then it destroys sentence effectiveness. First, here is an example from a nationally circulated advertisement:

FAULTY BROAD REFERENCE:
Any food you buy that you do not like or use reduces the amount of your savings, *which* after all is the main purpose of our plan.

The *which* seems to refer to the idea of *reducing the amount of your savings,* whereas obviously the writer had in mind *increasing the amount of your savings.* The common remark "You know what I mean" is no excuse for such bad writing.

The pronouns *this* and *that* are often misused in student writing.

FAULTY BROAD REFERENCE:

You've seen the ad on TV where four out of five doctors recommend the ingredients of a painreliever. How do we know *that* is true? But many people never give *this* a second thought.

The *that* could refer to the TV ad, the number of doctors, or the claim that they make a recommendation; the word *this* is hopelessly indefinite. A revision:

CLEAR MEANING:

You've seen the ad on TV which claims that four out of five doctors recommend the ingredients of a pain reliever. How do we know how many doctors—and which doctors—were included in the test? Or whether they referred to the painreliever or merely the ingredients? However, many people never give much thought to the truthfulness of TV ads.

The same kind of ambiguity often accompanies the pronoun *it*. Here, taken from a magazine, is an example of faulty broad reference:

FAULTY BROAD REFERENCE:

The odds are that such youngsters will drop out of school eight or ten years later with little to show for *it* but the experience of failure.

The *it* cannot logically refer to the idea of *dropping out of school*. Perhaps the writer meant to say "with little to show for their time but the experience of failure."

Another example:

FAULTY BROAD REFERENCE:
> My roommate told me last night he had been in jail once. *This* surprised me.

What surprised the writer? That his roommate told him? Or that he had been in jail once? The writer probably meant the following:

CLEAR MEANING:
> It surprised me that my roommate had been in jail once—as he told me last night.

One more example:

FAULTY BROAD REFERENCE:
> When someone mentions voter apathy, most people think of minority groups. *This* is not true.

The *this* is so indefinitely used that the reader must supply a sentence or two of his own to see that the writer means that voter apathy is not limited to minority groups.

So, take great care with your use of the broad reference *this* and also with the broad references *that, which,* and *it.*

24d   Remote Reference

Avoid using a pronoun so far removed from its antecedent that the reader has to pause to determine its meaning.

Here is an example from student writing:

REMOTE REFERENCE:
> The Wapiti League's regional play-offs forced us to find another location for our scrimmage, *which* is an annual event sponsored by the State High School Activities Board.

The *which* is so far removed from its antecedent *play-offs* that the reader momentarily stumbles and must re-read to be sure of the meaning.

And here is an example from a cookbook:

REMOTE REFERENCE:
> To enhance the flavor of roast chicken, spill a glass of white wine and sprinkle parsley over *it* while roasting.

Aside from the fact that the sentence seems to imply that the wine may be spilled on the floor and that the cook is roasting, the *it* is too far removed from its antecedent, *roast chicken*, for clear reference.

24e Implied Antecedents

Do not use a pronoun with an implied antecedent.

Pronouns may refer to whole ideas, but they should not refer to adjectives or to antecedents implied and not stated.

IMPLIED ANTECEDENT:
> Professor Stansbury is humorous and *it* makes her classes popular.

Though the meaning of the sentence is not obscured, *it* refers to the adjective *humorous*, a stylistically undesirable technique in English. The reader is forced to supply the noun *humor* for *it* to have an antecedent. A revision:

BETTER STYLE:
> Professor Stansbury's humor makes her classes popular.

Another example:

IMPLIED ANTECEDENT:
> My folks enjoyed their trip to Germany because they found *them* to be so helpful with the language problems.

Them has no antecedent. Instead of the pronoun, the writer should use *the natives* or *the citizens* to make the sentence clear. Two further examples:

IMPLIED ANTECEDENT:
> The house had plywood floors. *This* is cheaper than oak.

BETTER STYLE:
> The house had plywood floors, for plywood is cheaper than oak.

IMPLIED ANTECEDENT:
> Alex bought a bright yellow Yamaha motorcycle, *which* is his favorite color.

BETTER STYLE:
> Alex bought a bright yellow Yamaha motorcycle because yellow is his favorite color.

In both faulty sentences the pronouns incorrectly refer to adjectives (to *plywood* in the first and to *yellow* in the second). The revisions correctly supply the missing nouns.

Remember: a pronoun can stand for only a noun or a noun substitute.

24f   Relative Pronouns **who** or **that**, not **what**

Do not use **what** as a substitute for the pronouns **who** and **that**.

WRONG: The guy *what* sold me that car was a crook.

RIGHT: The guy **who** sold me that car was a crook.

25

Faulty Comparisons

Comparisons, which must consist of at least two expressions even if one is understood, occur frequently in our language, and three kinds of errors are commonly made in their use. (See section 5d for pronoun forms used in comparative constructions.) These errors diminish sentence effectiveness considerably.

25a Incomplete Comparisons

Avoid incomplete comparisons that in effect make nonsensical sentences.

Aside from the conjunctions *than*, *as*, and *like* and the prepositions *like* and *from* used to form comparisons, two other words—*other* and *else*—frequently help form comparisons. These comparative words should not be omitted.

Advertising copy often omits the *than* part of a comparison, perhaps intentionally.

INCOMPLETE COMPARISON:
Squeezo tastes better.

The ad writer wants the reader to understand *than other kinds of orange juice*, but such incomplete comparisons should be avoided in college writing. For example, don't write such a sentence as

INCOMPLETE COMPARISON:
> Living in the dorm is more convenient.

without specifying what it is more convenient than. Finish the comparison.

COMPLETE COMPARISON:
> Living in the dorm is more convenient than living in an apartment.

A second kind of incomplete comparison is perhaps even less acceptable because it forms a nonsensical (even though understandable) sentence. This is the kind of comparison that says that one thing is longer or kinder or more extensive than itself. Example from student writing:

INCOMPLETE COMPARISON:
> John Paul II has made more foreign trips than any pope.

Since John Paul II is himself a pope, the term *any pope* also includes him. The sentence literally says that John Paul II has made more foreign trips than even he himself did. If we apply logic, such a claim is nonsense. Complete the comparison by adding the word *other*, like this.

COMPLETE COMPARISON:
> John Paul II has made more foreign trips than any **other** pope.

Another example:

INCOMPLETE COMPARISON:
> My father has captured more mountain lions than anybody in our county.

The student's father presumably lives in "our county." Thus

the sentence says her father has captured more mountain lions than even her father, which is logical nonsense. The comparison-completing word *else* makes the sentence much more effective:

COMPLETE COMPARISON:
> My father has captured more mountain lions than anybody **else** in our county.

Now the comparison is complete and the sentence much improved.

Remember not to omit the words *other* and *else* in comparisons that call for one or the other of them.

25b   False Comparisons

Do not compose sentences that express false comparisons.

A comparison says that one thing is similar to, greater or lesser than, or different from another. But when the two parts of the comparison are incompatible for comparative purposes, a false comparison occurs and produces a bad sentence.

FALSE COMPARISON:
> When little Marty was first beginning to walk, his waddle was like a duck.

This sentence literally compares an action (a way of walking) with an animal (a duck). Three corrections are possible: use the possessive (which implies the missing word); change the expression by adding *that of*; or rewrite the sentence.

TRUE COMPARISON:
> When little Marty was first beginning to walk, his waddle was like a **duck's**.

TRUE COMPARISON:

> When little Marty was first beginning to walk, his waddle was like **that of** a duck.

TRUE COMPARISON:

> When little Marty was first beginning to walk, **he waddled like a duck.**

Here are other examples:

FALSE COMPARISON:

> We wanted to find some more romances to read like Virginia Holt.

FALSE COMPARISON:

> At that time they still didn't have automobiles but travelled instead like the nineteenth century.

FALSE COMPARISON:

> Despite the so-called sexual revolution, the moral standards of many young people today are similar to their parents.

Is Virginia Holt a romance? Does the nineteenth century travel? Are moral standards a parent? No. You must compare like things with like things.

TRUE COMPARISON:

> We wanted to find some more romances to read like **those by** Virginia Holt.   [*Those* refers to romances.]

TRUE COMPARISON:

> At that time they still didn't have automobiles but travelled instead **as people did in** the nineteenth century.   [Adding a subject and verb to the second element makes the comparison clear.]

TRUE COMPARISON:

> Despite the so-called sexual revolution, the moral standards of many young people today are similar to their parent**s'**.   (The possessive implies *their parents' moral standards*.)

25c   Omitted Comparative Words

In a double comparison, do not omit a needed comparative word, such as **than** or **as**.

Sometimes a double comparison calls for two different comparative words, and careless writers often omit one of the two. An example from a student paper:

OMITTED COMPARATIVE WORD:
>This coffee is as tasty if not tastier than what we used to drink.

COMPLETE COMPARISON:
>This coffee is **as** tasty **as** if not tastier than what we used to drink.

Mentally removing *if not tastier than* from the sentence shows that both parts of the *as . . . as* construction must be present. Use the same test in the following examples (that is, remove *or at least as difficult as*) to note that *than* must be used to complete the comparison.

OMITTED COMPARATIVE WORD:
>Running as anchorman in the 800-meter relay is more difficult, or at least as difficult as running a straight 200-meter race.

COMPLETE DOUBLE COMPARISON:
>Running as anchorman in the 800-meter relay is **more** difficult **than,** or at least as difficult as, running a straight 200-meter race.

26

Mature and Well-Formed Sentences

Merely avoiding errors may indeed produce *correct* writing, but it may not necessarily be *good* writing. Your prose must also show certain positive qualities. A comparison may make this point clear. Simply avoiding quarrels, fights, and other conflicts does not necessarily guarantee a happy marriage. Rather, the partners need to show affection for each other—must love, must share, and must be delighted with each other's company. Both the positive and the negative are important, not only in human relationships but also in writing. This chapter will discuss various positive attributes that will help you write effectively.

26a Sentence Expansion and Combining

Strive to achieve maturity of sentence structure; avoid excessive use of short, simple sentences.

Short, simple sentences have their place. Writers often need them to achieve a desired effect. However, most sentences in good writing consist of more than one simple independent clause. Various kinds of sentence expansions (large phrases and clauses) allow us to express two or more full ideas in one well-composed sentence.

Little children speak or write mostly in run-on simple sentences strung together by *and*. For example, a child might tell a story in this fashion:

> Grandpa came to our house and he took just me to lunch and we went to a restaurant and the lady came and she gave us water and we ordered and I got a giant hamburger and Grandpa got a cheese sandwich and I put ketchup on it and I tried to bite it and the ketchup squooshed out and I got my blouse all dirty and. . . .

Replacing each *and* with a period produces a series of simple sentences that can be arranged in a list, as follows:

> Grandpa came to our house.
>
> He took just me to lunch.
>
> We went to a restaurant.
>
> The lady came.
>
> She gave us water.
>
> We ordered.
>
> I got a giant hamburger.
>
> Grandpa got a cheese sandwich.
>
> I put ketchup on it.
>
> I tried to bite it.
>
> The ketchup squooshed out.
>
> I got my blouse all dirty.

Each sentence contains the basic information, but few writers would tell a story in that fashion. A mature writer *composes* sentences, using various sentence expansions.

When Grandpa came to our house, he took just me to lunch at a restaurant. After the lady came to give us water, we ordered—a cheese sandwich for Grandpa and a giant hamburger for me. I put ketchup on it, but when I tried to bite it, the ketchup squooshed out and I got my blouse all dirty.

The foregoing is an extremely simple illustration, but it expresses an important point. All your information comes to you first as bits and pieces that you can list as simple sentences; as a mature writer, you will want to *compose* sentences to produce an effective style. You need not know all the names to *use* them, but in section 26a we label such sentence expansions in order to talk about them.

26a1 Compound structures

In addition to joining two independent clauses into a compound sentence (see section 1d3), remember that you can also compound smaller parts of sentences: single words, subjects, predicates, whole phrases, and even dependent clauses.

SIMPLE SENTENCES:

> The fish inspected the bait. The fish decided not to take it. The fish was experienced. The fisherman was experienced. The fisherman cast his lure to the right. The fisherman cast his lure to the left. That day he caught only an old boot. That day he caught only a piece of driftwood.

Though the following does not necessarily constitute a good paragraph, it illustrates a variety of compound structures you can use.

COMPOUND SENTENCE:

> **The fish inspected the bait,** but **he decided not to take it.**

COMPOUND PREDICATE:

> **The fish inspected the bait** but **decided not to take it.**
> (No new subject)

COMPOUND SUBJECT:
>   **The fish** and **the fisherman** were both experienced.

COMPOUND PHRASES:
>   The fisherman cast his lure **to the right** and **to the left.**

COMPOUND OBJECT:
>   That day he caught only **an old boot** and **a piece of driftwood.**

26a2   Appositives

An appositive (section 1g) is essentially a noun-repeater; it defines or explains a noun that it is said to be in apposition to.

SIMPLE SENTENCES:
>   Our new car carried us across the country in comfort. It is a Volvo.

APPOSITIVE:
>   Our new car, **a Volvo,** carried us across the country in comfort.

26a3   Adjective clauses

An adjective clause (subsection 1c4) is introduced by one of the relative pronouns (*who, whom, whose, which,* and *that*), which usually has a noun antecedent in another part of the full sentence. Since it contains a subject and predicate, the adjective clause expresses a full idea, but one that is subordinated to an independent clause or a part of the main sentence. Like all the constituents we are illustrating in section 26a, the adjective clause allows us to *expand* a simple sentence and thus achieve more mature sentence structure.

SIMPLE SENTENCES:
>   The lab assistant worked for Dr. Ward. She brought out the equipment. We were to use the equipment in the day's experiment.

ADJECTIVE CLAUSES:

> The lab assistant **who worked for Dr. Ward** brought out the equipment **that we were to use in the day's experiment.**

26a4 Adjectives and adjective phrases

Almost all modifying adjectives (subsections 1a3 and 1d2) begin as predicate adjectives after the linking verb *be*, as in *that tree is tall*, or *our refrigerator is ancient*. A simple transformation puts such predicate adjectives next to the nouns they modify and improves a writer's style: *that tall tree* and *our ancient refrigerator*.

SIMPLE SENTENCES:

> Our refrigerator is *ancient*. It makes noises in the night. Those noises are *strange* and *disturbing*.

MODIFYING ADJECTIVES:

> Our **ancient** refrigerator makes **strange, disturbing** noises in the night.

Transforming the predicate adjectives into modifiers reduces sixteen words in three sentences to ten words in one sentence. Similarly, an adjective phrase in the appositive position can improve style by reducing wordiness.

An adjective phrase consists of an adjective as a headword, with modifiers clustering around it. As a phrase, it does not have a subject and a predicate. As a sentence expansion, however, it expresses a full idea.

SIMPLE SENTENCES:

> Art Hempel was tall for his age. He played varsity basketball in his freshman year.

ADJECTIVE PHRASE:

> Art Hempel, **tall for his age,** played varsity basketball in his freshman year.

The adjective phrase draws its meaning from *Art Hempel was* and thus expresses a full idea.

26a5 Adverb clauses

An adverb clause (subsection 1c4) is introduced by one of the subordinating conjunctions—*because, since, unless, if, though,* and many others. These subordinating conjunctions express such relationships as cause-and-result, contrast, condition, and time between the idea in the adverb clause and the independent clause or a part of the main sentence.

SIMPLE SENTENCES:

> We stopped at a convenience store. Mom bought some breakfast food. She had forgotten to buy it at the supermarket.

ADVERB CLAUSES:

> **When we stopped at the convenience store,** Mom bought some breakfast food **because she had forgotten to do so at the supermarket.**

Since the adverb clauses have a subject and a predicate, they contain full ideas. The subordinating conjunctions *when* and *because* express the proper relationships among the ideas.

26a6 Noun clauses

Noun clauses (subsection 1c4) usually do not function as sentence expansions but as subjects or direct objects in independent clauses. However, as appositives they can, and often do, function as expansions.

SIMPLE SENTENCES:

> A London-based group believes that the earth is flat. This is a ridiculous belief. It flies in the face of all the evidence.

NOUN CLAUSE:

> The ridiculous belief of a London-based group—**that the earth is flat**—flies in the face of all the evidence.

In the first of the simple sentences the noun clause functions as a predicate noun and is not a sentence expansion. Using *that the earth is flat* as an appositive in the revision produces superior sentence structure.

26a7 Prepositional phrases

Often a prepositional phrase (subsection 1b2) with a complex structure functions as a sentence modifier. As such it expresses a full idea and is a sentence expansion.

SIMPLE SENTENCES:
> The committee considered the impact of the proposal on the total tax structure. It tried to consider its significance for the individual taxpayer.

PREPOSITIONAL PHRASE:
> **Apart from the impact of the proposal on the total tax structure,** the committee tried to consider its significance for each individual.

Note that the relationship between the ideas in the simple sentences is not expressed, whereas the sentence with the prepositional phrase does express that relationship.

26a8 Verbal phrases

Various kinds of verbal phrases (the technical names of which you don't need to know, but see subsection 1b3) serve as sentence expansions.

SIMPLE SENTENCES:
> Professor Hermens went through all the steps himself. He directed us to repeat the experiment at our own lab tables.

VERBAL PHRASE:
> **Having gone through all the steps himself,** Professor Hermens directed us to repeat the experiment at our own lab tables.

Two points are to be noted here. First, the verbal phrase draws meaning from the other part of the sentence and thus expresses a full idea. Second, though it does not have a connective word to express it, the verbal phrase does express the relationship between the two full ideas.

SIMPLE SENTENCES:
> Peter wanted to finish the garage in three weeks. He had to work evenings as well as days.

VERBAL PHRASE:
> **To finish the garage in three weeks,** Peter had to work evenings as well as days.

Note again that even without a connective word (such as *because*), the verb phrase expresses a cause-and-result relationship between the two full ideas.

26a9   Absolute phrases

An absolute phrase is a construction that has a subject with a nonfinite verb form (that is, a verb form that cannot serve as a sentence verb). Naturally such a phrase contains a full idea.

SIMPLE SENTENCES:
> The deer ate all the buds off our rhododendron. Mother decided to plant roses instead.

ABSOLUTE PHRASE:
> **The deer having eaten all the buds off our rhododendron,** Mother decided to plant roses instead.

As in all our illustrations in section 26a, the *maturity* of the structure of the single sentence, as opposed to the simple sentences, should be clear to you.

26a10   Complex sentences in general
(see also subsection 1e3)

Few writers think about grammatical labels as they write, but good writers do think about composing mature sentences. Many of their sentences may well begin as short and simple constructions. When they revise and edit their earlier drafts, however, good writers generally work for better style, for better variety, and for greater clarity by using such sentence expansions as we have illustrated. These combine in any number of ways to produce an indefinite number of different but well-formed English sentences. An example from an issue of a leading magazine:

COMPLEX SENTENCE:

> When, like today, something moves me to get on the Fifth Avenue bus, my eyes invariably fall on one woman who seems, at least to me, the quintessential East Side woman, and her Martian differences quicken in me a sense of myself, a pang of self-recognition.

Though this complex sentence cannot really be called a typical sentence, it is by no means unusual; any page from a magazine of good quality will contain many sentences of as much complexity. Good readers expect such sentences in their good reading material. In addition to two independent clauses, the sentence also contains one adverb clause, one adjective clause, two prepositional-phrase sentence modifiers, and one appositive as sentence expansions.

26b Effective Subordination

Avoid weak coordination of independent clauses; achieve effective subordination.

Two full ideas of equal importance in one sentence deserve equal emphasis. In that case they are usually coordinated, as in the following examples:

PROPER COORDINATION:

> **At the beginning we thought the climb up Mt. Emily's face would be quite simple,** but **halfway to the top we realized its difficulty.**

PROPER COORDINATION:

> **Having tried various routes** and **having failed in each,** we reluctantly returned to our base camp.

In the first sentence, two independent clauses are coordinat-ed with the coordinating conjunction *but* joining them. In the second, two verbal phrases are coordinated. In each case the ideas, for effective sentence structure, deserve to be coordi-nated, or placed in equal rank.

Sometimes effective sentence structure demands that one idea be subordinated to another; coordination may make such a sentence sound childish.

WEAK COORDINATION:
> I had to carry all my books in my backpack every day, and it soon became quite heavy.

PROPER SUBORDINATION:
> **Since I had to carry all my books in my backpack every day,** it soon became quite heavy.

WEAK COORDINATION:
> The wound was quite deep, and it healed quickly.

PROPER SUBORDINATION:
> **Although the wound was quite deep,** it healed quick-ly.

The word *and* often produces weak coordination. Further-more, the two ideas in each of the examples are not of equal importance. In the sentences of proper subordination, the boldface adverb clauses carry important meaning, but their subordination to the main clauses makes the sentences sound right—makes them more effective.

26c   Emphasis

Compose sentences so that the most important ideas in them receive the most emphasis. Cultivate the active voice.

Choosing effective words (Chapters 20 to 22) and subor-dinating properly (sections 1h and 26b) are two ways to achieve emphasis. A third method is to place the most prom-inent idea at the end of the sentence. Note this example from student writing.

UNEMPHATIC:

> Teenagers often have disagreements with their parents and the main reason is that the parents are afraid that their children will behave as *they* did when young and they therefore unreasonably restrict their children's behavior.

This sentence has an interesting idea but its parts are strung out in such a way that no peak of emphasis emerges. A revision:

EMPHATIC:

> Since many parents are afraid that their teenage children will behave as *they* did in their teens, they unreasonably restrict their children's behavior, thereby causing disagreements.

Now all three ideas still appear, but "causing disagreements" (even though it is not the independent clause) receives the most prominence because of its position at the end of the sentence.

Another example:

UNEMPHATIC:

> Though on the surface he appears respectable, Willie Stark turns out to be the worst sinner of all: He murders, he corrupts the legislature, he has affairs with women, he lies, he drinks, and he uses bad language.

Most readers would find the last-named items less offensive than the earlier ones. Proper emphasis calls for a revision.

EMPHATIC:

> Though on the surface he appears respectable, Willie Stark turns out to be the worst sinner of all; aside from his bad language and his drinking, he lies, he has affairs with women, he corrupts the legislature, and he murders.

Now the use of subordination and the placement of the main

idea at the end of the sentence combine to produce proper emphasis.

The passive voice (subsection 1a2) is a proper grammatical construction, but the active voice produces a more effective style. Do not use the passive if there is no special reason to do so.

UNEMPHATIC:

> The Mahler symphony was concluded by the orchestra, and the musicians were given a standing ovation by the audience.

EMPHATIC:

> After the orchestra concluded the Mahler symphony, the audience gave the musicians a standing ovation.

The passive voice weakens the first sentence, but the active voice in the revision produces proper emphasis.

26d   Clarity

Above all, be sure that what you have written will be clear to the reader.

In many sections of this book we have discussed writing problems that diminish clarity, and we will not discuss those writing problems a second time. However, it is just such problems—from inappropriate word choice to faulty sentence structure—that lead to confusion. Here is yet another example of lack of clarity, taken from a nationally circulated magazine:

LACK OF CLARITY:

> Every animal has its place and role in nature's grand design, including the predator. Ecological balance is one of nature's laws. Occasional loss of livestock must be weighed against the good *these animals* [italics supplied] do.

Most readers would be at least momentarily confused when

they reached *these animals*. At first a reader may think the phrase refers to *livestock*, but that makes no sense. Eventually, it becomes clear that the phrase refers to *the predator*, but the damage of unclear writing has already been done. Besides, *predator* is singular and *these animals* plural, an inconsistency that contributes to the lack of clarity.

26e Variety

Vary the length and structure of your sentences as you compose paragraphs.

A series of sentences similar in structure and length produces monotonous writing. Two strategies can help you detect such monotony: (1) Draw a bold slash at the end of each sentence, and (2) underline each subject. If your slashes appear at regular intervals, and if your subjects are similar, revise your sentences by changing the length, by using various sentence expansions (section 26a), by using pronouns for some subjects, by beginning with elements other than the subject, and by occasionally using inverted word order.

MONOTONOUS SENTENCE STRUCTURE:

My father was most disturbed by my brief period of experimenting with drugs. / *He thinks* all drugs are bad. / *He doesn't* understand why young people want to experiment. / He doesn't remember his own experiences. / *He must have* gotten high occasionally. / *He took* me to our doctor. / *He discussed* the problem with him. / *He* (the doctor) *came* to the conclusion that I had no problem now. / *He finally accepted* the doctor's conclusion.

VARIETY IN SENTENCE STRUCTURE:

Though I gave him concern about various of my activities, my father was most disturbed by my experimenting with drugs, especially since he thinks all drugs are bad. He is old enough now not to understand why young people want to experiment, and he evidently has forgotten the pleasure (which I am sure he experienced) of getting high once in a while. Because of his concern about my brief use of drugs, he went with me to discuss the problem with our family doctor. The doctor, having a much better knowledge of young people than my father, quickly explained that I now had no problem that should worry my father. Upon hearing this, my father breathed a sigh of relief and showed his old trust in me.

The monotony of the original is eliminated by the variety of sentence structure in the revision.

26f Transitions and Coherence

Use connectives effectively both within and between sentences.

Essentially, writing consists of strings of ideas, and relationships exist between these ideas. Often no separate word between sentences or parts of sentences expresses a relationship; it is clear simply because of the nature of the writing.

Growing weary with his team's many mistakes, the coach called off the practice session.

The cause-and-result relationship between the two sentence parts is fully clear even though the sentence has no specific word to express the relationship: the growing weary is the cause and the calling off is the result.

In addition to the natural coherence expressed by the sentence structure itself, our language has many connective words (coordinating and subordinating conjunctions and conjunctive adverbs appear in Chapter 1) and transitional phrases (*for example, in addition, on the other hand,* and so on). These help to make clear the relationship between parts of sentences and between sentences themselves.

Good writers use such connectives wisely. They provide transition between ideas, which in turn helps to produce **coherence**—that all the parts in a passage stick together to make the writing clear, intelligible, and smooth.

Some examples from student writing:

POOR TRANSITION:
> The world has much good in it. If I were given the ability to make it better, I would take three steps.

CLEAR TRANSITION:
> The world has much good in it, **but** if I were given the ability to make it better, I would take three steps.

CLEAR TRANSITION:
> **Though** the world has much good in it, it could be better. **Consequently,** if I were given the ability to improve it, I would take three steps.

POOR TRANSITION:
> Today's world is moving at a tremendous pace. That pace produces many pressures in everyday living. There are many ways to relieve them.

CLEAR TRANSITION:
> **Though** today's world produces tensions **because** it is moving at a tremendous pace, there are many ways to relieve the pressures of everyday living.

POOR TRANSITION:
> For a change of pace, a person can read the sports page. The rest of the paper should not be ignored.

CLEAR TRANSITION:
> For a change of pace, a person can read the sports page, **but** one should not ignore the rest of the paper.

CLEAR TRANSITION:
> **Though** reading the sports page can give a person a change of pace, one should not ignore the rest of the paper.

The boldface connective words in the sentences labeled *clear transition* express the relationships between ideas, relationships that are not expressed in the sentences labeled *poor transition*.

Achieving clear transition through proper use of connectives is especially important in larger units of thought such as paragraphs and whole essays. In describing a process or in telling a story, for example, you can lead your reader through the steps you took or the events that occurred by writing: "**First,** we . . ." (and adding the details); continue with "**After** we had . . ." (and finishing that paragraph. Follow it by "**The next thing** . . ." (again, giving the information). You could perhaps conclude with "**The final step**. . . ."

Good writers make their writing coherent, which means that the parts of sentences, the sentences themselves, and the paragraphs in whole essays flow smoothly one after the other.

26g Logical Thinking

Avoid sweeping generalizations; strive for logical thinking.

People are entitled to their own opinions (at least as long as they do not let them harm others), and composition teachers certainly should not grade a paper down because they disagree with the ideas in it. However, human beings often fall into illogical thinking. When you have written an illogical sentence or passage, your teacher should mark the faulty logic.

The most common kind of illogical statement that appears in themes is the **sweeping generalization,** a gross overstatement of the truth of whatever idea is under discussion.

SWEEPING GENERALIZATION:

All students everywhere today are again giving serious attentions to their studies and avoiding political activism.

That might seem to be an innocent-enough sentence to appear in a theme, but its logic is faulty because the statement is too broad. It includes all students everywhere, and surely there are many students who are not giving serious attention to their studies and surely there are still many students who are politically active. Omitting the words *all* and *everywhere* would already modify the generalization somewhat by implying that the statement is true of only some. But even such a revision may imply more than is reasonable.

MODIFIED STATEMENT:

> Students today are again giving serious attention to their studies and avoiding political activism.

Such sweeping generalizations need qualifications, which means the addition of words so as not to overstate the case or include everybody when not everybody should be included.

QUALIFIED GENERALIZATION:

> **A great many** students today in **most parts of the country** are again giving serious attention to their studies and avoiding political activism.

Now the qualifying words *a great many* and *most* take the statement out of the sweeping generalization category. Generalizations are not out of place in college writing. They appear each time you write a topic sentence for a paragraph or for a whole essay and thus assert the point you wish to make. But you cannot use a generalization—certainly not a sweeping generalization!—to support your argument. For that, you need either specific facts or clear logic or both.

A good course in logic will help you develop habits of clear thinking. As it does so, it will point out additional fallacies to avoid. In the meantime, try to use sound reasoning in all your writing, avoiding such illogic as in the following sentence:

ILLOGICAL:
> The press should not have treated the Republicans so harshly, because the Democrats were up to just as many dirty tricks.

Even if the seond part of the sentence were true, the whole is still illogical because one group's wrongdoing does not justify another group's wrongdoing. If the Democrats were guilty of crimes during the period the student referred to, they too should have been prosecuted and punished for their wrongdoing. The student would have been much more logical had she written her sentence in this way:

LOGICAL:
> Though the wrongdoings of the Republicans cannot be condoned, there is evidence of Democratic wrongdoing at the same time, and the Democrats certainly should have been castigated for their crimes too. It is not right for the press to turn all its attention to the crimes of just one party.

Human beings are prone to illogical thinking, but you can write sound and reasonable papers if you give thought to the logic of the statements you make.

PART SIX

THE
RESEARCH
PAPER

Nature of the Paper
Selecting a Topic
Research Materials
Working Bibliography
Outlining
Note-Taking
Writing the Paper
Documentation
Sample Pages

27

Organizing
and Writing
a Research Paper

27a The Nature of the Research Paper

Much of what you do in your first college course in writing is designed to achieve two goals in particular. The first goal is to help you improve your ability to organize and write such whole essays as you may be called on to submit in other college classes. Often you will use a rhetoric and a reader and model your essays on the organizational patterns you observe in the writings of professionals.

The second goal is to help you develop an effective and correct style of writing as you review and improve your knowledge of the structure and use of the English language. Your study of *A Brief Handbook of English* will help you do just that, as will the comments of your instructors and classmates as they respond to what you have written.

A third and very necessary skill is essential to success in college and in later life. That is the ability to find information that you do not yet know, to evaluate it, and to present it—

with documentation—so that others may learn from your efforts. The final product of such an assignment is often called a **term paper,** or a **library research paper.**

In preparing a research paper, you will do practical research in a library, not original research, for you will be expected to seek out recorded knowledge, not to establish new knowledge. Yet in a sense your paper will be original; in it you will put together pieces of information from various sources in order to present a new view of the topic.

The work of preparing a research paper ordinarily follows certain steps. These steps are listed first in summary form and then are treated in detail in the remainder of this section.

1. Select a limited research-paper topic.
2. Become generally acquainted with the topic.
3. If possible, construct a tentative broad outline.
4. Build a working bibliography.
5. Read and take notes.
6. Construct a full outline.
7. Write the first draft, incorporating citations.
8. Revise and edit as necessary.
9. Prepare the final manuscript.
10. Proofread and submit on time.

It will be helpful to read Chapter 27 entirely before you begin actual work on your paper.

27b Selecting a Limited Topic

A freshman research paper normally runs between 2000 and 3000 words; its topic must be rather narrowly limited, for a broad or general topic cannot be well developed in so few words. Students who try to write papers on such topics as "Scandals in the Nixon Administration," "The Vietnam War," and "Shakespeare's Tragedies" are hopelessly lost at the beginning. After you decide on the general subject you want to write about, you must go through a process of reducing and reducing that subject until you reach a properly limited topic. The five notions of time, place, aspect, purpose, and attitude will help you do just that.

Suppose, for example, that you have chosen one of the topics just mentioned: the Vietnam war (which by now may already seem to you to be ancient history). So much has been written about it that you cannot possibly treat the whole subject. You can, however, limit your topic by **time.** "The Beginnings of American Involvement," "The Middle Years," "The Last Days of Saigon," or "The Vietnam Experience: Ten Years After" may suggest themselves as topics.

While the war was fought primarily in southeast Asia, its effects were felt elsewhere. You may wish to pinpoint certain locations, and thus you can narrow your topic by **place:** "Attitudes toward Vietnam in the American Midwest," "British Responses to the War," or "Hawks and Doves in the American Congress." Time and place can combine to produce a limited topic like this: "Early Responses in Congress to American Involvement."

One particular feature of the war may attract your attention, and treating only one **aspect** can help to narrow your topic. You could, for example, limit your search to the new weapons used, the combat strategies of jungle warfare, the role of the Air Force (or the Navy), the effects on the local economy, or the long-term medical problems of veterans. This last can be divided still further into the physical, the social, or the emotional effects.

A fourth method of limiting your topic, **purpose,** depends on which of two kinds of paper you choose to write: informative or argumentative. Most beginning research efforts are informative. They respond to a statement such as this: "I simply want to find out as much as I can about my subject and present it in an interesting fashion."

You may, however, want to argue a pet idea you already hold. If that is true, a word of caution is in order. You should approach your topic as if you knew nothing about it. That's what the word "research" implies—a careful, systematic, patient investigation to discover or establish facts or principles. As you become acquainted with your subject in your early reading, however, you may begin to develop an **attitude** that compels you to take sides and put your own conclusions into your paper after you have studied all the evidence on both sides of the question. True, your conclusions are opinions, but much of your paper will consist of the facts on which you base those opinions. Choosing to write an argumentative or controversial paper again limits your topic. You may, for example, decide on a topic like this: "Adverse Effects of the Vietnam War Ten Years After" (in which the word "adverse" reveals your attitude).

Rarely will you apply all of these five ideas mechanically to arrive at a limited topic. Instead, as you read to become generally acquainted with your subject (the second step in the series of activities), you will find that the limiting devices apply themselves. Such general reading will also suggest a number of questions you will want to answer. For example: What medical problems have developed among veterans since the war? What kinds of mental or emotional problems have evolved? How have various support groups helped the veterans cope with such problems? How has the government addressed these problems? and the like. With questions like these in mind (they can become the main headings in a tentative outline), you have a great advantage in beginning and pursuing your research.

27c   Research Materials in the Library

Your next step is to compile a working bibliography, a list of sources (books, magazine articles, news reports, and so on) that you hope will provide the information you will need to write your paper. To do that, you must know what source materials are available and how to use them. In the following sections we will classify the chief library research materials. If you need assistance in finding and using these materials, do not hesitate to call on the reference librarian for help.

27c1 General and special encyclopedias and reference books

General and specialized reference works are kept on open shelves in the library's reference room. Since these reference works are themselves the product of research, they alone cannot supply you with all the information you need for a good research paper. Remember, especially when contemplating the use of a general encyclopedia, that when one source supplies you with all the information you need for your research paper, you do not have a suitable topic. Nevertheless, the various reference works often supply researchers with useful bits of information, and you should consult them as necessary.

The two most important general encyclopedias are the *Encyclopedia Americana* and the *Encyclopaedia Britannica.* (An article in these works is sometimes followed by a bibliography, which may list useful sources.) Listed below, by subject, are the most widely used specialized reference works. Your library will probably have most of these, in addition to many lesser known reference books that there is not space to list here.

Agriculture

Encyclopedia of American Agriculture, 4 vols.

Art and Architecture

Cyclopedia of Painters and Paintings, 4 vols.
Encyclopedia of World Art
A History of Architecture

Biography

American Men and Women of Science, 11 vols.
Contemporary Authors, 52 vols.
Current Biography, 34 vols.
Dictionary of American Biography, 20 vols. and supplements
Dictionary of National Biography (British), 22 vols. and supplements
Who's Who (British)
Who's Who in America

Business

Economic Almanac, 34 vols.
Encyclopedia of Banking and Finance

Education

Cyclopedia of Education, 5 vols.
Education Index, monthly, with annual cumulations
Encyclopedia of Educational Research

History

Cambridge Ancient History,12 vols.
Cambridge Modern History, 13 vols.
Dictionary of American History, 6 vols.
An Encyclopedia of World History
Shorter Cambridge Medieval History, 2 vols.

Literature

Cambridge History of American Literature, 4 vols.
Cambridge History of English Literature, 15 vols.
Cassell's Encyclopedia of World Literature, 2 vols.
Encyclopedia of Classical Mythology
Granger's Index to Poetry
Mythology of All Races, 13 vols.
Oxford Companion to American Literature
Oxford Companion to Classical Literature
Oxford Companion to English Literature

Music

Grove's Dictionary of Music and Musicians, 9 vols. and supplement
Musician's Guide, 3 vols.

Political Science

Cyclopedia of American Government, 3 vols.
Dictionary of Political Science
Palgrave's Dictionary of Political Economy, 3 vols.

Religion

Encyclopedia of Religion and Ethics, 13 vols.
Encyclopedia of the Jewish Religion
Interpreter's Dictionary of the Bible, 4 vols.
New Catholic Encyclopedia, 14 vols.

Science

The Harper Encyclopedia of Science
Hutchinson's Technical and Scientific Encyclopedia, 4 vols.
McGraw-Hill Encyclopedia of Science and Technology, 15 vols.

Social Science

Dictionary of Philosophy and Psychology, 3 vols.
Encyclopedia of Psychology
Encyclopedia of the Social Sciences, 15 vols.

Yearbooks

The Americana Annual
The Britannica Book of the Year
Statesman's Yearbook
United Nations Yearbook
World Almanac

Don't hesitate to use any of these or other reference works to obtain useful bits of information and to verify facts, but *do not* expect to write a research paper using only reference works of this sort.

27c2 The card catalog

A library's card catalog lists, alphabetically, all the books and pamphlets in the library's holdings. To facilitate research, each book is listed at least three times:

1. under the author's name
2. under its title
3. under one or more subject headings.

Occasionally a college researcher will know the name of an author who has written on the researcher's topic but will not remember any of the author's titles. And occasionally the researcher may remember a title but not its author. Thus the listings by author and title can be useful. But most research-

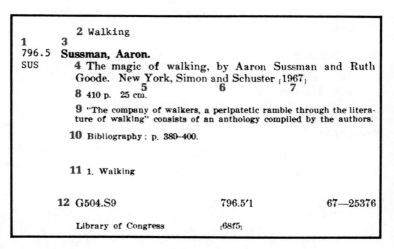

Figure 1.

ers rely mainly on subject headings to guide them to useful books and pamphlets. Figure 1 is a reproduction of a card entered in the card catalog by subject heading.

The numbers in color do not appear on the card in its file. They correspond to the following explanations:

1. Library call number	7. Date of publication
2. Subject heading	8. Length and size of book
3. Author	9. Statement by author or publisher
4. Title	10. 12-page bibliography in book
5. Place of publication	11. Subject heading
6. Publisher	12. Information for librarians

The above book, with the same information about it, is also entered in the card catalog under "Sussman, Aaron," under "Goode, Ruth," and under "The Magic of Walking," this last being alphabetized under the M's.

27c3 Cross-references

Even after you understand how books are entered three times in the card catalog, you may still feel insecure in doing research. You may not know any authors or titles that will provide you with useful information, and you may not know what subject heading to look under. Suppose, for example, you had seen the recent headline "Why 26,000,000 Johnnies Can't Read" and had become curious as to why so many Americans are functionally illiterate. You might eventually decide on the topic "Some Controversial Methods of Teaching First-Graders to Read." What subject heading would you look under? You might well feel baffled and frustrated. But the standardized techniques of library research come to your aid.

First you canvass your mind for subject headings that might possibly be in the card catalog and jot them down: "Reading," "Teaching Reading," "Teaching Methods" or "Methodology," "Phonics," "Look-Say Method," "Progressive Education," "Elementary Education," "Reading Readiness," and so on. Chances are high that at least one subject heading you thought of will be in the card catalog. Then cross-references will come to your rescue. Most subject headings have a cross-reference card that lists various related headings. These cross-reference cards come *after* all the cards listing books under a particular subject heading, and they begin with "See also." For example, in one card catalog, after a large number of books having the subject heading "Political Science," there are twelve cross-reference cards listing about one hundred subject headings, ranging from "Administrative Law" to "World Politics." Some subjects will have many cross-references; some may have very few. But learning to use cross-references is an essential part of learning to write research papers.

27c4   The periodical indexes

Periodical literature is that which is published at regular intervals: daily, weekly, biweekly, monthly, and so on. The hundreds and hundreds of reputable magazines and learned journals that have been published in the past or that are still being published are rich sources of information for writers of research papers. In fact, many topics—especially ones on contemporary issues or events—will send the researcher only to magazine articles, rather than to reference works and the card catalog. To facilitate a researcher's use of the various magazines, all good libraries purchase cumulative periodical indexes, which list articles that have appeared in all the periodicals that any one index chooses as its domain. Articles are listed twice: by author and by subject heading.

For the freshman composition student who is learning to prepare a research paper, the most useful periodical index, by far, is *The Reader's Guide to Periodical Literature,* which lists articles from about 200 widely circulated magazines.

The *Guide* begins at 1900 and covers many good magazines now defunct. About every ten to twelve weeks a small volume of the *Guide* appears, and the small volumes are then combined into large volumes that list articles for one or two years. All the volumes of the *Guide* are always kept on open shelves in a library's reference room.

Figure 2 is a sample of listings from *The Reader's Guide,* with an explanation of the first entry. The author's last name

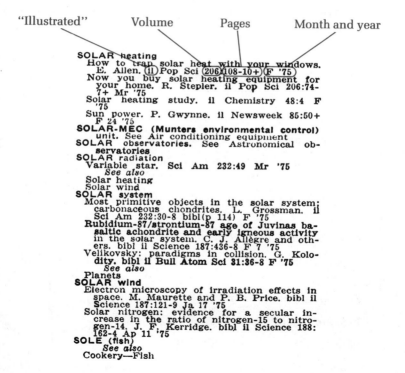

Figure 2.

and the subject headings are in boldface capitals. The title of each article is given in full. All abbreviations are clearly explained in the preface of each volume of the *Guide*. The first entry in the sample on page 295 refers to an illustrated article in *Popular Science*, volume 206, pages 108–10 and continued, February 1975.

Cross-references (such as that under "Sole") are as important in *The Reader's Guide* as they are in the card catalog. For example, there are twenty-six cross-references for the subject heading "Literature" in one volume of the *Guide*, ranging from "Authorship" to "Symbolism in Literature." Remember, cross-references are extremely important to researchers.

Other periodical indexes sometimes of use to beginning researchers are the following:

Art Index (from 1929)

Biography Index (from 1946)

Biological and Agricultural Index (includes books, pamphlets, and articles, from 1916)

Book Review Digest (lists book reviews by author, title, and subject, from 1905)

Dramatic Index (American and British, from 1909)

Education Index (includes books, pamphlets, and articles, from 1929)

Engineering Index (from 1884)

Index to Legal Periodicals (from 1926)

Industrial Arts Index (from 1913)

Poole's Index to Periodical Literature (covers American and British periodicals, most now defunct, from 1802 to 1906)

Public Affairs Information Service (covers books, periodicals, and pamphlets in economics, government, and public affairs, from 1915)

Quarterly Cumulative Index Medicus (covers medical literature, from 1927)

Social Science and Humanities Index (covers American and foreign periodicals, from 1907)

United States Government Publications (from 1895)

Most large libraries will have most of these indexes.

One other index that often is very useful is the *New York Times Index*, published monthly with annual volumes since 1913. It indexes all important news stories, editorials, and feature articles that appear in the *New York Times*, giving not only the location of the article but also a brief summary of it. Thus if your topic is one that at some time has been newsworthy—such as "The Entrapment of the Egyptian Third Army in the Yom Kippur War"—you can look in the *New York Times Index* for 1973 and find the location and brief summaries of news reports that will furnish useful information. Even if your library does not have copies of past issues of the *New York Times*, the *Index* is still helpful, for other daily newspapers would be likely to have had news stories similar to those in the *New York Times* that were published on the same day.

27c5 The periodical card file

The periodical indexes are useful to you, of course, only when your library has a copy of the magazine you want. So that researchers can quickly find out whether particular issues of particular magazines are available, most large libraries have a periodical card file, which is located in the reference room and which lists the issues of all magazines the library has in its holdings. Smaller libraries sometimes enter the periodical cards alphabetically in the card catalog, and some keep at the reference desk or checkout counter a typed list of all magazines in their holdings. Usually the magazines themselves are bound in volumes of six issues or more, with the inclusive dates printed on the spines, and are shelved alphabetically in the reference room. Libraries with large holdings often have old issues of magazines in storage and will make them available on request.

27d   Compiling a Working Bibliography

A bibliography is a list of books, articles, and perhaps other sources such as pamphlets or television tapes on a particular topic such as "Shakespeare" or "Shakespeare's Comedies" or "Shakespeare's *Twelfth Night*." The final bibliography you place at the end of your research paper will list all the sources you actually *used*. The working bibliography, however, is a preliminary list of sources that you *hope* will provide you with useful information. It is usually much larger than the final bibliography. You should not be surprised if many of the items in your preliminary or working bibliography later turn out to have little value.

Researchers compile as complete a working bibliography as possible before they begin to read seriously and to take notes. Four points are of especial importance here:

1. If you have been able to derive from your topic the few general questions you expect your paper to answer (see section 27b), you will be much less likely to enter useless sources in your working bibliography.

2. If a useful book listed in the card catalog contains a bibliography (see subsection 27c2), it is helpful to

check that book out at once and use its bibliography.

3. Be especially careful to make full use of cross-references in both the card catalog and *The Reader's Guide*.

4. After you have compiled a working bibliography and have begun reading and taking notes, watch for other sources that you can add to your working bibliography.

The working bibliography is fluid, not static; you will probably drop from it sources that turn out not to be useful, and you will probably add to it after you begin reading your source materials.

Use one 3″ × 5″ note card for each bibliographic entry. (Using note cards makes it easy to alphabetize your final bibliography later.) *Never* enter more than one source on one card. In the upper right-hand corners, number each card consecutively; having the cards numbered will let you identify the sources of your notes (see subsection 27f1) by number rather than by authors and titles. Be certain to enter on each bibliography card all essential information about the book or article; failure to enter complete information will cost you much wasted time in rechecking when you are ready to obtain materials from the library and when you write footnotes and prepare the formal bibliography for your paper. (If one or more bits of information are not available when you first make up the card for your working bibliography, be sure to add those items to the card when you begin to read in that source.)

Put on separate lines on each bibliography card all the following items of information that are applicable (some apply only to books; some only to magazine articles):

1. the library call number of a book or periodical

2. the full name of the author (last name first)

3. the exact title of the item (underlined or in quotation marks)

4. the place of publication, the publisher, and the date of publication

5. the exact name of a magazine

6. the date and volume number (if any) of a magazine and the pages on which the article appears

7. the name and volume number of any reference work, the title of the article, and the pages on which the article appears

8. a note as to whether the item has a bibliography of its own or some other feature, such as illustrations, that may be useful to you

All this information (except 7) can be obtained from the card catalog or *The Reader's Guide;* you need not check out materials from the library to compile a working bibliography. *The*

Library call number   Bibliographic information

> 403.8
> B43
>
> Brown, Roger
> Words and Things; an Introduction to Language
>
> New York
> The Free Press
> 1958
>   (Has bibliography)

Figure 3.

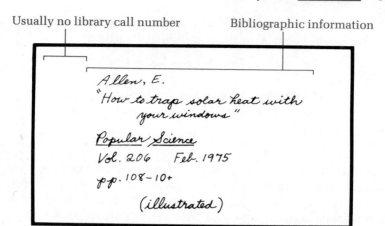

Usually no library call number   Bibliographic information

Figure 4.

value of following this standard procedure cannot be over-emphasized. Figure 3 is a sample bibliography card. And Figure 4 shows a card for a magazine article.

A bibliography card with complete information will allow you to write footnotes and to prepare the formal bibliography without consulting the card catalog or *The Reader's Guide* again. Also, numbering the bibliography cards (1, 2, 3, and so on) will let you indicate by number on your note cards where your information came from without having to write the title and author on the note card itself.

27e Outlining: Preliminary and Formal

27e1 Preliminary outlining

The next step after compiling a working bibliography is to make a preliminary scratch outline of the main points of your paper. These correspond to the questions you derived from your early reading. For example, if you select the topic

"Charles Dickens's Reactions to America and Americans," you might begin with this preliminary outline:

I. The number of and reasons for Dickens's trips to America.

II. His reactions to the social structure of America.

III. His reactions to the geography and climate of America.

IV. His contacts with and reactions to notable American writers.

Such an outline gives direction to your reading. You know what you are looking for, what information is useful, and what you can skip. You can also indicate by Roman numerals on each note card where the information will fit in your paper. This preliminary outline grows and changes as you continue your reading.

27e2 Formal outlining

The preliminary outline helps you find useful information as you read and take notes. A formal outline, which you construct only *after* you have done all your reading, helps you present your ideas in an orderly and logical manner. Your instructor may specify either a sentence outline or a topic outline (in which the headings are phrases).

T.S. Clark provides his story with variety of characters.

I. Some characters are admittedly types, whether the typicality is justified or not.

A. The slow-moving and supposedly ignorant old Negro appears as a philosopher of sorts.

B. The Protestant preacher is typically shown to be ineffective in a society to which he does not belong.

C. The one "female interest" in this Western story is a pretty, shallow-headed tart.

    D. Even Gil, the first character identified, is given the typical rambunctiousness of the youthful cowboy who acts more on instinct than on logic.

  II. Some characters show both good and bad traits that reveal them as individuals rather than as types.

    A. The moral Mr. Davies admits his own immorality through willful cowardice.

    B. Tetley, though ultimately despicable, reveals some admirable qualities.

The advantage of writing complete sentences already in your outline is twofold: it forces you to be precise, and it provides you with the opening statement of each of your paragraphs. Often, however, a topic outline is sufficient.

T.S. Varieties of characters in Clark's novel

    I. Types with one primary characteristic

      A. Males

        1. The old philosopher
        2. The ineffective preacher
        3. The rambunctious cowboy

      B. Females

        1. The shallow tart
        2. The rough-hewn pioneer woman

    II. Individuals with complex personalities

      A. Davies: moral yet cowardly
      B. Tetley: despicable, yet with some good in him

Your outline should observe the following principles:

1. State your thesis or main idea clearly in a simple sentence.
2. Use Roman numerals to identify the first major divisions or supports for your thesis.
3. Use capital letters to indicate subdivisions of the Roman numeral units.

4. Use Arabic numerals for further subdivisions.
5. Keep your outline balanced. It should not be a mere list; where a "I" occurs, you must have at least a "II", and an "A" must be paired with a "B."
6. Make your headings meaningful and parallel in content and structure.
7. Indent the various levels of the outline so that you can easily see the relationships among them.

An outline such as either of the examples above lets you check your logic, as follows:

1. Read only your thesis statement. Does it reflect exactly what you want to say, and does it state only one main idea in a simple or complex sentence?
2. Next, read all the Roman numeral headings together with your thesis statement. Are they appropriate divisions of your central idea?
3. Now read Roman numeral I with its A, B, and C. Again, are they clearly related? Continue with Roman numerals II and III and their subpoints until you have checked the logic and content of your complete outline.

Construct the formal outline only after you have read all your sources and are ready to write the first draft. In the following section we return to the matter of reading and gathering information.

27f Note-Taking and Some Related Problems

After you have compiled a working bibliography and have prepared as much of a preliminary outline as you can, your next step is to begin reading or scanning your sources to find information useful for your paper. Since you cannot remember all that you read, you must take notes, which should be written on 4″×6″ cards. Your reading may at first seem haphazard, but putting one idea on each card enables you later to arrange your information in a usable order.

As you take notes, do not simply copy word for word what an author has written; rather, digest and assimilate what you read, and then write the information in your own words in summary form. Copy direct quotations only when there is compelling reason to do so (subsection 27f2).

27f1   Techniques of note-taking

Not every item you have in your working bibliography will necessarily be useful to you. For that reason, you must learn to scan articles and chapters from books. The fuller your preliminary outline, the more effectively you can scan. When you see that a source has information important to your paper, stop scanning and read carefully to take useable notes.

A good format for a note card follows.

1. Use lined 4″ × 6″ cards.
2. Leave the top line blank for the time being; begin writing on the second line.
3. Immediately enter the page number(s) of your source, placing them in square brackets.
4. Write the note in your own words (or copy verbatim if it is appropriate to do so).
5. Examine what you have just written and, on the line at the top of the card, write a heading or title that identifies the content *of this card.* If your preliminary outline is fairly complete, you may also indicate by Roman numeral in which section of your paper this information belongs.
6. Identify the source of your information with the name of the author and at least an abbreviated title of the work you are reading.

> I   Reasons why Russia was willing to sell
> _____
> [21-22]   Quite clear why Russia wanted to sell
>   Russian America. The territory was a
>   burden. Produced no net income. Russian
>   American Company bankrupt, wanting
>   subsidies. Territory too far from seat of
>   Russia's government. On verge of war with
>   England and feared England might capture
>   the territory. Needed money and felt it
>   best to sell rather than risk total loss.
>   Chase. *Am. Hist. to 1850*

Figure 5.

Figure 5 is a sample note card, written for a paper entitled "The Purchase of Russian America."

The information, in summary form, came from pages 21–22 of the source (identified by author's last name and abbreviated title). Both the Roman numeral I and the heading written above the color line indicate that this information will support the first main point in the body of the paper.

27f2   Direct quotations

Direct quotations have four uses in research papers:

1. to give the exact words of an authority in order to lend weight to a point of view
2. to present original evidence as proof of a point
3. to emphasize a fact or opinion; and
4. to share a passage that is striking because of its excellent style, wit, or some other feature.

You should *not* use a direct quotation unless it clearly fulfills one of these purposes; do not aimlessly scatter quotations throughout your paper.

The presence of quotations marks on your note card is your signal to yourself that you have copied word for word. The absence of quotation marks tells you that you have condensed the information in your own words. If you omit anything from a direct quotation—either one word or a longer passage—use three spaced periods (. . .), called an ellipsis, to indicate the omission. If you add anything to the quotation, put your addition into square brackets like these: [ ].

When entering a direct quotation into your paper, lead smoothly into it with an introductory phrase or sentence that announces that a quotation is coming and indicates its purpose. For example, such a simple phrase as "According to the well-known cosmologist Fred Hoyle, . . ." can serve to introduce a quotation and tell the reader that an authority is being cited. Don't just use a direct quotation abruptly; announce it in some way.

In the paper itself, quotations that occupy five or fewer lines of type should be incorporated into your paragraph with quotation marks. Quotations of more than five lines are called insets. They are indented ten spaces, are double-spaced, and are *not* enclosed in quotation marks.

27f3 Paraphrasing and plagiarism

Since only a small part of your research paper will consist of direct quotations, most of your note-taking should not be verbatim but should be a condensed version of the information you expect to use. Thus as you take notes, use your own words as much as possible and compress the information so that you can re-expand it in your own words when you enter it into your paper. The process of using your own words instead of a direct quotation to incorporate source materials into your paper is known as **paraphrasing.** That is, you do not change the information but you do change the wording so that it is in your style and not the original author's. If you take condensed notes, paraphrasing will be much easier for you.

Failure to paraphrase is one of the deadly sins in research-paper writing, for it leads to **plagiarism,** which is literary theft, or pretending someone else's writing is yours. Many teachers fail research papers for plagiarism alone. Of course, since you are gathering your information from written sources, you must use some of the wording of the original, but you must not quote whole sentences and then, by not using quotation marks, pretend that you composed them. Even if you paraphrase, you can avoid the charge of plagiarism by giving credit to your source. A citation or a phrase like "Betts states that . . ." will protect you. Your research paper, for the most part, must be of your own composition. Technical terms, statistics, and some phrasing must be as they are in the original source; but the structure of the sentences and much of the vocabulary must be yours. As a rough guide, try never to have in one sentence more than five consecutive words exactly as they appear in the original source (except, of course, for direct quotations).

27g　Writing the Paper

The preliminary outline, the working bibliography, and the stack of note cards are the raw materials from which you fashion the finished essay. Several steps remain.

27g1　The full outline

The questions you asked yourself in your preliminary reading led to the tentative outline that guided you in reading and taking notes. You must now construct a full outline that incorporates the information you have gathered. Since you have acquired a sizeable amount of information, reflected in the stack of cards you have, your revised outline may differ considerably from the earlier tentative outline. Don't be alarmed at that. It is in reality a sign that you have done creditable research.

To construct the full outline, read all the headings or

titles you wrote on each of your note cards—and read *only* the headings at this point, not the content of each card. These headings (what you wrote above the color line) will enable you to separate the note cards into smaller stacks according to the divisions of your preliminary outline. You may find that you have more—or different—major parts than you started with. Each group of note cards represents one of the Roman numeral divisions of your outline.

Once you have clearly established the major ideas (represented now by the individual stacks of note cards), take each of these groups of cards and repeat the procedure, dividing them again into still smaller stacks. These become the subdivisions, the A's and B's and C's under the Roman numerals on your outline. Each of these in turn may be divided into the 1's and 2's and 3's as still smaller subdivisions of your capital letter units, should you so desire.

Do not try to write your first draft on the basis of a number of stacks of note cards. Rather, write out a full outline on sheets of paper as illustrated in subsection 27e2. On this outline list not only the ideas you will use but also the sources of those ideas (the author's name, the abbreviated title, and the page numbers you recorded on each note card).

After you have written a full outline on sheets of paper, it is good practice to lay it aside for a day or two. Such a rest period allows you to examine your outline with fresh eyes when you return to it. If the outline still reflects what you truly want to say, and if its logic satisfies you, use it. If, however, you see important revisions you should make in content or in organization, be sure to revise your outline before you go on to the next step.

27g2 The first draft

Now write the first draft on the basis of your outline. Begin at Roman numeral I, reserving the introduction for later. If you have written a sentence outline, you can simply copy that first sentence (the one for Roman numeral I) and add the details you have listed as the A, B, and C of your outline.

As you write, be sure to incorporate the sources from which you quote or summarize. Failure to add such information at this point will cause much unnecessary and wasted effort later on. Present-day practice calls for parenthetical citations within the text of your essay rather than cumbersome footnotes. This method of documentation is explained in section 27h and illustrated in the sample pages from a research paper in section 27i. It is the reason you identify the source on each note card you write.

Continue writing until you have treated all the divisions and subdivisions that appear on your outline. This forms the body of your essay. Your next step is to write the conclusion. In it you summarize the main points of your presentation and restate your thesis at or near the end of that paragraph.

One thing remains. You must write an introduction. It is not an easy task, but once you have completed the body of the essay and the conclusion, you have a clear picture of what it is you want to introduce. The opening sentence should in some way catch the interest of your reader. Several additional sentences—in some cases several paragraphs—lead logically to your thesis, and that thesis statement should appear as a simple or a complex sentence at or near the end of your introduction.

27g3   Revising, editing, and proofreading

The first draft is not the finished product. Lay it aside for one or two days. When you return to it again, you will certainly revise and edit, perhaps a number of times, before you are ready to make the final neat copy to hand in. Even then you must proofread and make minor corrections before you submit the paper. (See section 14a for manuscript form.)

27h Documentation

Documentation in a research paper is the acknowledgment of the sources used. It includes citations in the text (in parentheses) and the formal list of works cited, or the bibliography. In addition, some research papers use footnotes (at the bottom of the page) or endnotes (at the end of the text) to offer comments, explanations, or information that would interrupt the style and flow of the text itself. What follows conforms to the *MLA Handbook for Writers of Research Papers*, Second Edition (1984), a standard generally accepted by the academic community.

27h1 Uses of citations and footnotes (endnotes)

In research papers, citations in the text are used for two purposes only:

1. to acknowledge the sources of direct quotations
2. to acknowledge the sources of important paraphrased information that might be subject to question or that the reader might want to pursue further

Do not use parenthetical citations to document facts that fall into these four categories:

1. quotations (such as those from the Bible)
2. ordinary dictionary definitions unless one has some special purpose such as refuting widely accepted information
3. simple and easily ascertainable facts, such as birth and death dates of a famous person
4. paraphrased information that a critical reader will accept without question and that is not of considerable importance to the main point of your paper.

Footnotes or endnotes to enter explanatory comments that would be out of place in the text of the essay are rare in freshman research papers. Should you have need for them, it is more convenient to use endnotes (beginning a new page at the end of the text) rather than footnotes at the bottom of the page. Where you want to signal that additional information appears in an endnote, type or write a superior (or superscript) Arabic numeral above the line, like this,[1] without periods or parentheses or slashes. Such numbers follow all punctuation marks except dashes; they direct the reader to the end of the text where a corresponding Arabic numeral identifies the note itself.

27h2   Form, content, and location of citations

The *MLA Handbook* identifies citations within the text as "parenthetical documentation," and for good reason. Their **form** is straightforward. Simply enclose the reference within parentheses.

To identify clearly what is being cited, their **location** is important. Always place them *after* the information you are documenting. To avoid interrupting your own style, put the reference at the end of the material to which it refers but before any punctuation marks that may conclude a sentence, a clause, or a phrase containing the borrowed material. If you are using a direct quotation, the order is as follows: last word of the quotation, the closing quotation mark, the opening parenthesis, the citation, the closing parenthesis, and the final punctuation mark, like this: ". . . chiefly for the purposes of political indoctrination" (Skolny 4).

The content of each citation depends on what you have written or what you have omitted from your text. Adequate documentation requires that you list the source (by author's last name or by an abbreviated title if there is no author) and the page numbers. Such a short form directs your reader to the end of the paper where the list of works cited gives the full bibliographic information.

If in the text of your writing you have given only the information that supports your point but have omitted a reference to the author or the work, the parenthetical citation must include the name of the author (or title of the work if no author is listed) and the page numbers. However, if your own writing includes the name of the author (or work), list only the page numbers in parentheses.

INFORMATION ONLY:
> "The general principle of semantic interpretation ... is that deep structure defines meaning" (Chisholm 145). [Note that there is no comma between the author's last name and the page number.]

AUTHOR IDENTIFIED IN THE TEXT:
> Chisholm reasserts what others had stated that "deep structure defines meaning" (145).

Both citations refer to an item identified in the list of works cited as follows:

> Chisholm, William S., Jr. Elements of English
> Linguistics. New York: Longmans, 1981.

Remember that there is a direct relation between what you put into (or omit from) your own writing and what appears in the parenthetical citation. Remember also that such parenthetical documentation rests absolutely and only on the bibliography or list of works cited as described in the following section.

27h3 Bibliography, or works cited

At the end of your research paper you present a formal bibliography of the sources you have used or a list of works cited. Each bibliographic entry must contain as much of the following three elements as you can possibly provide: the name or names of the author(s), information about the work itself, and publication information. As you see in the following examples, each of these elements may contain a variety of data.

All bibliographic entries should be in one alphabetized list of authors' last names. You do not list only the pages you used but the entire work you consulted in each case. If a work is anonymous, alphabetize it by the title, but ignore *a*, *an*, and *the* as initial words. Authors' last names come first in bibliographic entries. If you list two or more entries by the same author, you may substitute a dash three hyphens long on the typewriter (---) for the name after its first use.

In bibliographic entries the first line is flush left; the next line is indented five spaces. Double-space each bibliographic entry, and double-space between entries. Do not number entries. Use the heading "Works Cited" or "Bibliography" centered two inches from the top of a new page, regardless of how much space is left on the preceding page. The following forms are modeled on those of the *MLA Handbook for Writers of Research Papers*, Second Edition (1984). Observe the punctuation of each entry closely.

A book: (**Note:** If there is more than one author, only the first author's name is inverted.)

> Foreman, Rachel, and Clive Sims. <u>Boswell's
> Politics</u>. New York: Harcourt Brace
> Jovanovich, 1971.

Two or more books by the same author: (**Note:** Works by the same author may be arranged chronologically or alphabetically by title.)

> Work, James. <u>Boswell's Youth</u>. New York: Vintage
> Press, 1972.
> --- <u>Boswell as Lawyer</u>. New York: Norton, 1975.

Edited books:

> <u>Essays on the Enlightenment</u>. Ed. Norman Thomas.
> Oxford: Clarendon Press, 1975.

or

> Thomas, Norman, ed. <u>Essays on the Enlightenment</u>.
>> Oxford: Clarendon Press, 1975.
>
> Boswell, James. <u>Journal of a Tour to the Hebrides</u>.
>> Ed. Thomas Parnell. Cambridge: Belknap
>> Press, 1969.

A work in several volumes:

> Parker, W. O. <u>Boswell: A Biography</u>. 2 vols. New
>> York: Holt, Rinehart and Winston, 1973.

A translated work:

> Brindle, Klaus. <u>Political Poetry</u>. Trans. H. T.
>> More. New York: Random House, 1952.

A later or revised edition:

> Tuttle, W. A. <u>Boswell in Holland</u>. 2nd ed. New
>> York: Viking Press, 1973.

A reference work:

> "Boswell, James." <u>The Dictionary of National
>> Biography</u>. London: Oxford Univ. Press, 1917.
>> II, 893–900.

An anonymous pamphlet:

> <u>English Political Morality</u>. London: The Society
>> of Friends, 1968.

An article in a learned journal:

> Hogg, Jonathan. "The Sources of <u>Rasselas</u>." <u>New
>> England Quarterly</u>, 27 (Summer 1954), 278–91.

An article in a monthly magazine:

> Puttle, Gary. "Boswell's Medical History."
>> <u>Harper's</u>, Oct. 1972, pp. 42–52.

An article in a weekly magazine:

> Uncles, Norman. "Mr. Boswell and Dr. Johnson."
> Saturday Review, 26 July 1969, pp. 20—25.

An unsigned article in a weekly magazine:

> "New Dirt on Boswell." Time, 4 July 1969,
> pp. 32—33.

Articles in newspapers:

> Kirsh, Robert. "New Material on Boswell." The
> Los Angeles Times, 9 Nov. 1974, Sec. 3, p. 26,
> cols. 2—4.
> "A New Boswell Scandal." The Spokesman Review
> (Spokane, Wash.), 8 Jan. 1975, p. 12, col. 3.

27i Sample Pages from a Research Paper

To help you set up your research paper, some sample pages are provided here to show you how your final pages should look. Remember to check section 14a for correct margin and spacing proportions.

- Outline page

- First page

- Inside page with name and page number

- New heading on page at end of paper

The Centrality of <u>Nada</u> in the Fiction
of Ernest Hemingway

Outline

Mark O. Stevens

Professor M. Ewing

English 120

May 18, 1985

The Centrality of <u>Nada</u> in the Fiction
of Ernest Hemingway

Almost every enthusiast of American literature
has more than a passing acquaintance with Ernest
Hemingway, and almost every serious critic has
added a statement to the burgeoning commentary on
his works. Even the briefest of his short stories
have been subjected to close scrutiny, to an
examination that belies the common belief that
Hemingway is a tough, matter-of-fact reporter of
the human scene and that gives way to a sense of
wonder at the depth of his perceptions. One writer
comments about the puzzle a widely-known tale
presents to the first-time reader:

> Here is a story, if ever there was one,
> with what are called "unsuspected
> depths." A reader might, in a tired
> moment, go through it casually,
> unaffected, or at any rate not much
> affected, and if asked afterwards what it
> was all about have some trouble in giving
> a meaningful answer (O'Faolain 112).

The critic could well have been writing about
the typical college freshman in an introductory
course in literature. A first reading of
Hemingway's "A Clean Well-Lighted Place" does leave
such a reader "unaffected, or at any rate not much
affected" until, with the help of an astute
instructor or classmate, the student begins perhaps

to see the horror inherent in the concept of nada—— or (if the student continues reading) the horror that permeates the entire universe Hemingway creates in his fiction.

Killinger surely is correct when he says that "the use of the term is not extraneous to the theme of the story, but is linked to the haunting oblivion which envelopes all that is outside the pale of the little clean, well-lighted place" (15). Neither the term nor the concept are limited to this short story alone. Rather, as Baker correctly states, "an arc of the nada-circle runs all the way through Hemingway's work" (132).

Killinger, too, concedes that, though the concept has "its most dramatic statement" in the little nada-story "A Clean, Well-Lighted Place," it pervades all of Hemingway's fiction. He notes particularly how it is apparent in "Big Two-Hearted River" (Nick Adams), in Death in the Afternoon (implied so strongly in the title), and in the thinking of such characters as Jake Barnes and Philip Rawlings (58).

That this story was written and first published in 1933 at almost the midpoint of Hemingway's life (and reprinted in Winner Take Nothing——note the translation of the term nada in the title of this collection) suggests that it serves as a summing-up of what had gone before and as the central concept of what was yet to come. "A Clean, Well-Lighted Place," then, may well be the touchstone, the open sesame, for the entire Hemingway corpus.

Works Cited

Baker, Carlos. Hemingway: The Writer as Artist.
    Princeton: Princeton University Press, 1952.

Brooks, Cleanth. The Hidden God. New Haven: Yale
    University Press, 1963.

Campbell, Harry M. "Comments on Mr. Stock's Nada
    in Hemingway's 'A Clean, Well-Lighted Place.'"
    Midcontinent American Studies Journal III
    (Spring 1962): 57-59.

Colburn, William E. "Confusion in 'A Clean,
    Well-Lighted Place.'" College English XX
    (February 1959): 241-242.

Gabriel, Joseph F. "The Logic of Confusion in
    Hemingway's 'A Clean, Well-Lighted Place.'"
    College English XXII (May 1961): 539-46.

Killinger, John. Hemingway and the Dead Gods: A
    Study in Existentialism. Lexington, Kentucky:
    University of Kentucky Press, 1960.

O'Faolain, Sean. "A Clean, Well-Lighted Place," in
    Short Stories: A Study in Pleasure, Ed. Sean
    O'Faolain. Boston: Little, Brown and
    Company, 1961 [Reprinted in Weeks, Robert P.
    Hemingway: A Collection of Critical Essays.
    Englewood Cliffs, N.J.: Prentice-Hall, 1962,
    pp. 112-113].

Stock, Ely. "Nada in Hemingway's 'A Clean,
    Well-Lighted Place.'" Midcontinent American
    Studies Journal III (Spring 1962), 53-57.

Warren, Robert Penn. Selected Essays. New York:
    Random House, 1951.

Weeks, Robert Percy, ed. Hemingway: A Collection
    of Critical Essays. Englewood Cliffs, N.J.:
    Prentice-Hall, 1962.

Index

Boldface numbers refer to chapter, section, or subsection rules; lightface numbers are pages.

C

CORRECTION CHART

ab	improper abbreviation (**14c**)
agr	faulty subject-verb agreement (**6a–f**)
apos	omitted or misused apostrophe (**18a–c**)
cap	capital letter needed (**17a**)
cl	lack of clarity (**26d**)
coh	lack of coherence (**26f**)
com	omitted or misused comma (**10a–c**)
comp	incomplete or false comparison (**25a–c**)
CS	comma splice or run-together sentence (**3a–c**)
D	faulty diction (**20a–d;21a–e; 22a–d**)
DM	dangling modifier (**23d**)
DN	double negative (**4c**)
frag	sentence fragment (**2a–d**)
glos	glossaries (**16g; 22b**)
hyph	omitted or misused hyphen (**19a–e**)
id	faulty idiom (**22c**)
ital	omitted or misused underlining (**14b**)
K	awkward construction
lc	lower-case letter needed (**17b**)
log	faulty logic (**28g**)
man	incorrect manuscript form (**14a**)
MM	misplaced modifier (**23e**)
mod	misused modifier (**4a–c**)